Socialist Economies in Transition:
Appraisals of the Market Mechanism

Socialist Economies in Transition: Appraisals of the Market Mechanism

Edited by

Mark Knell and Christine Rider

Edward Elgar

Published by
Edward Elgar Publishing Limited
Gower House
Croft Road
Aldershot
Hants GU11 3HR
England

Edward Elgar Publishing Company
Old Post Road
Brookfield
Vermont 05036
USA

A CIP catalogue record for this book is available from the British Library

A CIP catalogue record for this book is available from the US Library of Congress

ISBN 1 85278 438 5

Printed and bound in Great Britain by
Billing and Sons Ltd, Worcester

Contents

Preface   vii

Contributors   ix

1   Behind the Crisis in Centrally Planned Economies   1
    Christine Rider and Mark Knell

2   Justifying the Need for Reform:
    The Price-Theoretic Approach   21
    Christine Rider

3   Transitions from Centrally Planned to Market Economies   43
    Christian Gehrke and Mark Knell

4   Michal Kalecki and Early Attempts to Reform
    the Polish Economy   65
    Tadeusz Kowalik

5   The Failure of Demand Management in Socialism   83
    Edward Nell

6   From a Command Toward a Market Economy:
    The Polish Experience   117
    Kazimierz Laski

7   The Market Transformation of State Enterprises   140
    Branko Horvat

8   Failure of Monetary Restriction in Hungary and Yugoslavia:
    A Post Keynesian Interpretation   154
    Shirley J. Gedeon

9   State Monopolies and Marketization in Poland   170
    Helena Sinoracka

10 Whatever Happened to the East German Economy?   191
       Heinz D. Kurz

11 Lessons from China on a Strategy for the
     Socialist Economies in Transition   216
       Mark Knell and Wenyan Yang

12 Conclusion: Implications for Socialist Economies
     in Transition   236
       Mark Knell and Christine Rider

Index   244

Preface

The pace of change in Eastern Europe has been rapid in the last few years. These economies no longer fall into the official classification of *centrally planned economies*, rather they are now referred to as the *socialist economies in transition*. This transition includes the introduction or further spread of market mechanisms intended to improve the functioning of the economy. Although discussion of ways to improve these economies dates back many years, and has involved economists from both East and West, it seemed to us that something was missing. This was an appraisal of the reform process able to both show the need for change and how difficult that change would be.

Unfortunately, sometimes it seems that the difficulties and length of time this transition process will take have been glossed over. Partly this is due to the over-optimism of many Western advisers, and partly to the (legitimate) desire to move away from past failures as quickly as possible. It is in some sense a laboratory experiment, but more importantly we are dealing with real people in real societies, and a change will not be easy.

It is important to try to get things right, because mistakes in the economic sphere can have adverse spillover effects in other areas of life, and thus have highly costly results. So what we have done here is to present a new way of looking at the transition process, a way that is critical, rather than accepting without questioning what seems to be the new 'official line' in many of these post-communist societies.

We begin by presenting a historical background to the Soviet strategy of economic growth and crisis in the Eastern European economies (Rider/Knell). Then what may provide the theoretical justification for introducing market-oriented reforms, the model of Pareto-optimality, is criticized (Rider) followed by a broader, structuralist approach to the transition process based on the work of Adolf Lowe (Gehrke/Knell). We often forget that reform attempts date back many years: in Poland, these early attempts are associated with the Polish economist Michal Kalecki, whose influence on non-neoclassical theory and approaches to reform is extensive (Kowalik). The differences between the way capitalist and socialist economies operate make it difficult simply to introduce market institutions in the latter and expect them to resemble the former; this is the theme of the next paper (Nell).

Following are several papers showing the difficulties of the transition process and pointing out the problems as well as solutions which are either ignored or misinterpreted. the impact of the so-called 'shock therapy' programme in Poland has been heavy, and perhaps ultimately too costly (Laski). The rush to privatization and the introduction of capita markets have ignored alternative forms of enterprise ownership and control (Horvat). Monetary issues will take on greater significance in price signalling market economies, and the problems connected with the endogeneity of money have not so far been adequately thought through (Gedeon). Privatization and marketization will create tremendous problems of monopolization, again with an impact on efficiency (Sinoracka). The integration of a previously planned economy with a rich capitalist economy has resulted in problems larger than anticipated (Kurz). Finally, China has provided an alternative transition path which has integrated markets with planning (Knell/Yang). The volume will conclude with a discussion of some of the implications.

Acknowledgements

Many people have contributed directly or indirectly to this book. As editors, our major debt is to our contributors, who provided these papers and whose insights we know will help shed light on a difficult process. As always, the people at Edward Elgar were patient and helpful. Mark Knell thanks the faculty at Pace University, Pleasantville for a grant which enabled him to go to the Academy of Sciences in Poland and the University of Graz in Austria at an early stage of the preparation of the book. Special thanks also go to Steven Pressman. In particular, Mark Knell thanks Wenyan Yang, and Christine Rider thanks Gary Mongiovi, for their understanding during the book's gestation period.

Contributors

Shirley J. Gedeon is Associate Professor of Economics at The University of Vermont.

Christian Gehrke is an Assistant at The University of Graz, Austria.

Branko Horvat is Professor of Economics at The University of Zagreb and is at the Zagreb Institute of Economics, Croatia.

Mark Knell is Visiting Lecturer at The University of Michigan, Dearborn and Adjunct Lecturer at The Cooper Union for the Advancement of Science and Art, New York City.

Tadeusz Kowalik is Visiting Scholar at The Stockholm Institute of Soviet and East European Economies and is Professor of Economics at the Institute of History of Science, Education and Technology, Warsaw, Poland.

Heinz D. Kurz is Professor of Economics at the University of Graz, Austria.

Kazimierz Laski is Professor Emeritus of Economics at The Johann Kepler University of Linz, Austria and Acting Director of The Vienna Institute for Comparative Economic Studies.

Edward Nell is Professor of Economics at The New School for Social Research, Graduate Faculty, New York City.

Christine Rider is Associate Professor of Economics at St. Johns University, New York.

Helena Sinoracka is Assistant Professor of Economics at The Warsaw School of Economics (formally The Central School of Planning and Statistics (SGPiS)), Poland.

Wenyan Yang is Associate Economic Affairs Officer, Department of International Economic and Social Affairs of the United Nations Secretariat in New York.

1 Behind the Crisis in Centrally Planned Economies

Christine Rider and Mark Knell

1 Introduction

It is a commonly held belief that the crisis behind the collapse of the centrally planned socialist economies is inherent in the institutions of central planning and social ownership of the means of production. The general consensus of many economists is, therefore, that free markets and private property should be introduced in their place. Without concern for what these free market institutions imply, it is believed that a strategy for economic growth is best achieved through these institutions. However, there are many episodes in the history of economic development where central planning and social ownership of the means of production have achieved high rates of growth, including those in the Soviet Union, Eastern Europe and China. For example, before the 1917 revolution, 82 per cent of the Russian economy was rural. As a result of (planned) industrialization, the Soviet economy grew by a factor of ten up until its collapse in 1991—a growth rate faster than any of the world's industrial market economies.

Nevertheless, certain systemic problems do lie behind the crisis in centrally planned economies. There was a tendency to emphasize output growth, and sellers' markets predominated. These results were caused by overinvestment which in turn resulted in chronic excess demand. While chronic excess demand solved the unemployment problem plaguing capitalist economies, growth was often extensive rather than intensive, meaning that input use expands faster than output itself. In a sellers' market, there is little incentive for innovation to improve product quality or to reduce costs, and the resulting outcome tends to be characterized by inefficiency and product deterioration.

Because of these problems, systemic change within a centrally planned economy is inevitable, and many reforms were introduced in these economies during the period of communist domination. But the reform process has not been a smooth one. While economic reform has often brought rapid growth and improving living standards, growth-stagnation cycles also appeared. It is perhaps the inability to implement

1

'crucial reform' which will result in beneficial systemic change that lies behind the collapse of the centrally planned economies.

To better understand the crisis behind this collapse, this chapter will be organized so as to remove some misconceptions about planning and to provide a context for current developments. The difficulties which led to the creation of the Soviet-type economy are developed in section 2. Section 3 analyses the problem of growth and shortage in centrally planned economies and section 4 discusses these problems in the context of reforming the centrally planned economies of Eastern Europe. Finally, section 5 argues that this analysis in no way leads to the automatic conclusion that only the introduction of the market mechanism and private property is called for. In fact, as the papers in this volume demonstrate, such an introduction will create problems of its own, especially when done rapidly and without due concern for encouraging adaptive behaviour patterns, institutional change and re-education appropriate to a new environment.

2 The historical evolution of a Soviet strategy of economic growth

A review of the history of planning reveals that planning was first introduced shortly after the First World War, not as the result of ideological commitment to Marx, but rather in response to pragmatic economic problems. Indeed, while it can be said that the various socialist economic blueprints may have been inspired by Marx's claim of the superiority of socialism over capitalism, the lack of knowledge of how to run a country once in power was the biggest problem for the Bolsheviks. (Marx's writings contain an analysis and critique of a capitalist economic system; nowhere is there an equivalent detailing of how a socialist economy should be structured and operated, especially one just beginning a development effort.) At first the new Soviets searched for a feasible way to organize the economy and begin the process of economic development via industrial isolation; later they focused on accelerating growth. The need to come face-to-face with pragmatic realities also helps explain the almost continual adjustment, readjustment and reform of the planning mechanism.

Although central planning in the Soviet Union is often presented as if it was omnipotent and able to control every aspect of economic activity, this was not true even during times of extreme centralization. The essence of planning is that the horizontal relationships characteristic of market economies are replaced by vertical ones between central planning authority and economic actors. There is, however, no single blueprint to accomplish this, as can be seen by efforts to accommodate problems that have arisen over time. Indeed, the first blueprint, known as War Communism which lasted until 1920, was, as Gregory and Stuart (1990, p. 51) succinctly put it, 'an abortive attempt by the inexperienced Bolshevik leadership to attain full communism without going through any preparatory intermediate states: money was virtually eliminated, private trade was abolished, workers were militarized and paid equal wages in kind, and farm output was requisitioned'. It is debatable whether it was forced by circumstances precipitated by the Russian civil war or was a genuine attempt to build communism. But the result of this programme was a 23 per cent fall in industrial capacity from the 1917 peak by 1924, and industrial and agricultural output fell to 20 and 64 per cent of their respective levels in 1913 (ibid., p. 58). Rapid inflation and black markets also appeared, and opposition to War Communism intensified.

The second blueprint, known as the New Economic Policy or NEP, re-established a market economy through the reinstatement of peasant commercial autonomy, the introduction of a proportional agriculture tax to replace the system of requisitions, establishing peasants' right to own small plots and permitting private ownership of small enterprises with fewer than 20 employees. This allowed peasants to hire labour, lease land and sell any after-tax surplus in open markets or to the state at specified prices. At the same time the Supreme Council, created in 1917 to manage the economy, continued to coordinate enterprises producing basic goods. But it coordinated the remaining enterprises or 'trusts' only loosely as they were also given the right to enter into independent contracts (ibid., p. 60). What emerged was a mixture of markets and planning.

Although markets played an increasing role in the NEP, both the importance and feasibility of an overall plan was recognized. *Gosplan*, the State Planning Commission, was created in 1921, but did not develop a general plan until later in the decade because it had neither the time nor the resources required for the task. An electrification plan introduced in 1920 took the first step towards the creation of a national plan. This plan was an important experiment because it was the first to consider the problems of agriculture, industry and transportation together; it attempted to coordinate plans at both regional and industry levels; it set up targets in both physical and value terms; and it was a realistically long-term plan, 10-15 years. This was a breakthrough, as previously smaller scale plans had been prepared for shorter time periods. The entire concept of long range planning was not well understood at the time, although clearly for projects requiring investment, a one year time frame was insufficient. At this time, some other specific plans were also being made: there were four-year plans for metals, industry, transportation and agriculture. But most others were only for one year periods, and were often only extrapolations of past results.

The NEP was highly successful initially. By 1923, private trade accounted for 75 per cent of total sales, although concentrated more at the retail than at the wholesale level. Goals were achieved by 1926 when output in both industry and agriculture surpassed their levels prior to the revolution. The Soviet Union even established a convertible stable currency which was quoted on the currency exchanges for a while (ibid., p. 62). However, by 1927, increasing market disequilibrium and shortages resulted in an absolute decline in the activity of the nonagricultural private sector. Shortages of capital plagued the Soviet economy throughout the 1920s. A shortage of consumer goods became extensive after a 10 per cent reduction in official procurement prices for manufacturing goods because the new prices were often below the cost of production. This combined with the expectation that prices would rise again led to the 'grain collection crisis of 1927'. According to Nove (1990, p. 82) this may have been an attempt to limit the private 'second economy' through criticism of the private sector because it appeared that private enterprises were profiteering by holding back supply.

Whether or not the NEP was a conscious attempt to create a new blueprint or a temporary manoeuvre to prepare for the eventual adoption of more socialist policies, the collapse of the NEP in 1927 created a new economic crisis that required a new blueprint. Preceding the collapse, an intensive discussion of possible options took place among theorists. These discussions, known as 'the Soviet industrialization debate', centred on some of the same issues important to the transition process of the 1990s: sequencing and speed. A conservative group led by N. Bukharin argued that growth should be balanced and kept within certain limits. A more radical group led by E. A. Preobrazhensky argued for rapid and unbalanced growth. Both sides saw the need for the reconstruction of the economy and both sides agreed that an important goal was social ownership of capital. Although initially allied with the conservative group, Josef Stalin embraced the more radical proposal, perhaps in an attempt to consolidate his own power. With the grain collection crisis unresolved, the first five year plan (1928/29 - 1932/33) was adopted following the radical proposal of rapid industrialization.

The general aim of the first five year plan was the creation of a socialist society and its main focus was to promote industrialization. To accomplish this, a number of goals were to be attained: the creation and rapid expansion of heavy industry vital to the production of capital goods and national defence; the collectivization of agricultural resources in order to ensure that the necessary labour and raw materials for industrialization would be forthcoming; and stable growth rates. (An early question revolved around how long the high growth rates experienced during reconstruction could be sustained.) At the core of the plan, and of all subsequent plans, was a rapid industrialization strategy which promoted the production of capital goods to be used for the production of capital goods. Large construction projects were favoured over smaller ones, and heavy industry was favoured over light industry and agriculture.

This plan, however, was not comprehensive, and the government's ability to affect the entire economy was severely constrained. Only 44 industrial products were given quantitative targets; many targets were set even where government had only limited influence: this affected the areas of agriculture, retail trade and the remaining enterprises left in private hands. These areas could have been affected indirectly through manipulation of prices, wages and credit availability, but the preference instead for material targets via the allocation of investment within the state sector left them untouched. However, it was intended that all basic economic relationships would eventually be changed so that socialist ones would prevail. Other problems affecting the plan's credibility included statistical underestimation (for example, there were larger shortages of certain raw materials than expected, which made meeting targets difficult) and statistical accuracy in general.

Growth of labour productivity (chiefly by increasing the scale of operations), and an expansion of the socialist sector were central to the rapid industrialization strategy. As table 1.1 shows, there was a major shift in the percentage share of gross output of construction and small-scale industry to the socialist sector from 1928 and 1930. By setting up cooperatives in place of the 'trusts', the economy was centralized to gain control over the use of capacity and labour. To solve the grain collection crisis and increase labour productivity, the collectivization of agriculture began in autumn 1929. Table 1.1 reflects the initial collectivization effort, but it took until 1938 before 93.5 per cent of the peasant households were collectivized (Gregory and Stuart).[1] Labour productivity rose by 21.7 per cent in 1928, 15 per cent in 1929 and 12.7 per

cent in 1930 (Petrov 1985, p. 69); but, as data in table 1.2 indicate, there
was a decisive shift from intensive growth to extensive growth as the
contribution of the improvement in labour productivity to growth of industrial output fell from 95.5 per cent in 1928 to 55.8 per cent in 1930.
Nevertheless, by increasing the number of labour-hours rapidly, labour
unemployment was eliminated by 1931—a sharp contrast to the Great
Depression then experienced in the Western capitalist economies (UN
1965). Because capital shortages remained, the increase in employment
involved the use of a three shift day and a continuous work week in
many places; massive recruitment of new workers and an expansion of
technical training; the introduction of new incentives to offset high
turnover and low labour productivity (such as emphasizing collective
values through education and extra privileges such as extra food, housing and vacations for those workers internalizing these values) and limits on labour mobility.[2] In the end per capita consumption of workers
increased but by less than labour productivity because a large share of
national income had to be devoted to investment in the capital goods
industries for the industrialization strategy to work.

Table 1.1: Percentage share of socialist sector in the Soviet Union (gross output).

	1928	1929	1930
Census industry[a]	99.0	99.4	99.8
Construction	59.7	70.4	88.6
Small-scale industry	28.0	48.5	66.4
Agriculture	2.1	4.8	21.1

Source: Petrov 1985, p. 83.
[a]Census industry includes industrial units which used mechanical power and at least
16 workers or at least 30 workers without mechanical power.

The fact that the outcome of any plan depends on more than just getting the numbers and techniques right became clearer as the 1930s
progressed. Again, the overall goals were rapid industrialization along
socialist lines so as to catch up to the industrialized Western market
economies. (In 1931, Stalin wanted to close the gap, then estimated at
about 50 to 100 years, within 10 years.) The setting, however, was not
encouraging. Although lessening dependence on the outside was one
goal, the effects of the Great Depression and the embargo placed upon
the Soviet Union by the League of Nations did have an impact: the
terms of trade moved against the Soviet Union and exports fell below
their planned level. Politically, fear of external attack reemphasized the
priority given to defence-oriented industry; internally, the purge of party
members and technical personnel removed not only potential sources of

opposition but also those with needed skills; peasant resistance to collectivization imposed much higher costs (and for a longer period of time) than originally expected, while doing nothing to improve the labour productivity problem. In 1930, this was aggravated by poor weather (and climatic conditions overall in much of the grain growing region of the Soviet Union are not as favourable as in equivalent regions elsewhere). Furthermore, shortages of consumer goods led to dissatisfaction, queues, high prices and, in some cases, black markets. The large scale of the construction projects required more resources than originally estimated for completion, and even when plans were revised, heavy industry still fell short of its targets.

Table 1.2: The industrial transformation of 1928-1931.

	1928	1929	1930	1931
Percentage change in census industry				
Gross industrial output	22.4	24.3	25.8	...
Labour-hours	1.0	7.8	11.4	...
Per capita worker consumption	...	1.5	6.2	12.0
Accumulation fund	...	15.2	66.8	46.9
Share of national income				
Accumulation fund	19.4	19.6	25.7	30.3

Source: Petrov 1985, p. 69 and pp. 95-97.

Responses to these problems resulted in what has become known as the Soviet administrative planning model. Officially, the longer (usually five years) plan set out goals and targets—the vision of the future—while the one year plans were the operating ones. Alongside this duality based on time or function was another duality: an official over-optimistic plan for propaganda purposes, and a second plan which was subject to modification as conditions changed, based on a hierarchical system of goals. Such a ranking of priorities had begun during the War Communism period. It became even more necessary because of a basic flaw in a taut planning process using material balances rather than financial data, and where information is not perfect. That is, under the plan, allocations were based on balances of resources and needs. If these were accurately calculated and an allowance made for reserves, priorities would not need to be ranked because demands would be likely to be satisfied. But because increasingly permanent deficits were built into the plan, it became necessary to rank priorities (Zaleski 1971, p. 176). Essentially what happened was that shortage became institutionalized and the 'allocation' of shortage became politicized as government intervened to protect its essential activities.

This makes evaluating a plan's success difficult, especially for the first five year plans, because the plans themselves were continually changing. Some areas were overfulfilled, others underfulfilled. By 1932, national income was roughly 30 per cent below planned levels, and average real wages were below half of planned levels. These statistics imply an increase in investment, but already investment, although a priority area, reached only about half planned levels, and was beginning to show a characteristic pattern. Resources tended to be concentrated into 'core' production areas, with investment in auxiliary or supportive areas (e.g. transportation, communications, storage or infrastructure) either left for later or minimized. This gave rise to a situation of high investment rates, bottlenecks, shortages, lengthy construction periods and an ever-increasing demand for more investment to overcome the problems of previous unbalanced high investment.

As actually practiced, it is true to say that the Soviet experience involved higher costs, although theoretically, planning should reach the same goals at a lower cost than a market economy, *mutatis mutandis*—a conclusion based on extending Lange's (1936) theoretical justification for socialism. The best estimate is that the level of Soviet GNP in the mid 1970s was about two thirds that of the United States, far from meeting Stalin's goal of catching up. But throughout the centralization phase, the growth rate was consistently higher than that of the US or the OECD countries. However, as previously noted, a high growth rate is not the sole criterion by which success should be judged. The Soviet criteria were rather the construction of large-scale projects, social transformation and the refinement of the planning mechanism—not to mention the desire on the part of Soviet leadership to hold on to power.

3 Growth and shortage in the centrally planned economy

The Soviet-type strategy for economic growth was the main characteristic of socialist economies as practiced in the Soviet Union, Eastern Europe and China. Its main features were the rapid growth of industry; selective, unbalanced growth emphasizing the basic goods sectors or 'engines of growth' such as iron and steel and heavy engineering; and the maximization of the utilization of capital and labour (Brus and Laski 1989, pp. 24-25). By 1931, it was becoming clear that the initial successes could eventually lead to stagnation and crisis. In this regard, Lange (1949, p. 167) understood the functioning of the socialist economy well when he pointed out that:

The high investment program, which results from the fact that all these economic plans are connected with a political decision of industrialization at a rather speedy rate, produced everywhere an inflationary gap which is being solved in some countries by rationing, in different ways in other countries. ...This makes for a constant pressure of excess demand in all markets, which in turn, creates a situation that any increase in output, in whatever field, appears as a desirable thing.

Because a centrally planned economy tends to experience chronic excess demand, labour and capacity appear fully employed. This simply means that everyone able and willing to work can obtain a job and does not include unemployed workers and capacity when shortages of inputs appear. What is clear in Lange's statement is that rapid industrialization tends to generate chronic excess demand. What is missing from this story, however, is that chronic excess demand implies sellers' markets that skew the industrialization strategy towards extensive growth because of the lack of demand-induced incentives to innovate.

As pointed out by Brus and Laski (1989, pp. 28-30), while the overall growth rate was high since the industrialization strategy was implemented, the growth rate of the productivity of capital was 'negative over the entire half-century, with decline strongly pronounced in the last 25 years'. Ofer (1987) estimated that over the entire 1928-1985 period, GNP grew at an annual average rate of 4.2 per cent while capital grew at 6.9 per cent; over the same period combined input use grew at an annual average rate of 3.2 per cent and contributed 76 per cent of total GNP growth, while factor productivity grew at an annual average rate of only 1.1 per cent, contributing the remaining 24 per cent of growth. In the presence of chronic labour shortages, the growth of capital will thus determine the overall growth rate of output, given also the reality of declining productivity. Because the incremental capital-output ratio was rising throughout this period, ever-increasing share of investment in national income is required to maintain the growth rate.

To show the problems inherent in the Soviet industrialization strategy, Kalecki (1986) introduces a simple formula to show the relationship between national income, investment and the growth of capacity in the determination of the rate of growth. Using more contemporary notation, the rate of growth g can be expressed as:

$$g = \frac{I}{K} = \frac{s}{v}u$$

where $s = \frac{I}{Y}$ or the share of investment I in national income Y, and $\frac{v}{u}$ is the incremental capital-output ratio $\frac{K}{Y}$. Kalecki defined the incremental capital-output ratio in this way to separate technical elements v from organizational elements u where $v = \dfrac{K}{Y_c}$, $u = \dfrac{Y}{Y_c}$, and Y_c is potential output at a given price level. Thus, to sustain rapid growth, a high share of national income must be invested. But if this rapid growth rate is extensive growth, implying a rising incremental capital-output ratio, then the ability of the new potential capacity to produce output diminishes, reducing the growth rate. If depreciation is added to the picture, then investment demand becomes all the more important to maintain the growth rate.

Kalecki used this simple formula to illustrate the effect of chronic excess demand. As mentioned by Lange, when a large share of national income is committed to investment, there will be a constant pressure of excess demand. When there is constant pressure, then various resource constraints are encountered, creating chronic shortages and bottlenecks in particular industries. This will tend to lower the utilization of labour and capacity, and therefore the rate of growth of the economy as a whole. Moreover, because a large share of investment tends to lengthen the construction period, large amounts of capital are 'tied up in construction rather than contributing to a more rapid development of that industry' (Kalecki ibid., p. 88). Indeed, as table 1.3 suggests, even at the beginning of the Soviet industrialization programme, lengthening construction periods already appeared.

Table 1.3: Incomplete building as a percentage of expenditure in the Soviet Union.

	1928	1929	1930	1931
Socialist sector	25.0	33.0	47.3	56.2

Source: Petrov 1985, p. 77.

For Kalecki the institutional framework in which the Soviet strategy of economic growth is set explains the persistence of chronic excess demand. Because there is an insatiable desire for growth at all levels of the economy, enterprises try to produce at full capacity and increase productive capacity as fast as possible. The enterprise and the planning authority negotiate for credit, with the semi-autonomous enterprise attempting to obtain as much credit as possible. Because rapid industrialization is an objective of the planning authority, a large portion of national income is invested. Consequently, effective demand will continuously outstrip capacity and enterprises, fearing shortages, will stockpile raw materials, inputs, equipment and other supplies. These near universal shortages strengthen the inducement to invest, further intensifying the pressure of demand on capacity. The result is lower capacity utilization, longer construction periods and a lower growth rate.

Kornai (1992) suggested that there is a feedback mechanism between the institutional framework and the bias toward extensive growth. Indeed it could be argued that the goal of maximizing growth requires a certain institutional framework, so that this framework creates, of necessity, a rapid growth path. Chronic overinvestment is thus rooted in the motivations created by the institutional framework and the macroeconomic environment. At the same time, the creation of vertical dependence between enterprises and the state ensured the survival of the rapid industrialization strategy. This was done through the nationalization of industry and the collectivization of agriculture. Enterprises became financially dependent on the planning authorities which would no longer force them to be financially accountable. The result was an institutionalization of a sellers' market which encouraged extensive growth and discouraged industrial innovation.

Kalecki and Kornai were, in essence, arguing against an extensive growth strategy. Because shortages and bottlenecks are a result of technical and organizational constraints, innovation is necessary to overcome these constraints. In other words, growth must be based on innovation and not simply on using more resources. However, Nelson (1988, p. 314) pointed out that centrally planned economies do not have all the necessary institutions to support a national innovation system. Because industrial innovation is an evolutionary process, there needs to be 'multiple sources of initiative, and a competition among those who place their bets on different ideas'. From this perspective, the only solution to the problem is to change the underlying institutional framework.

The inability to create a dynamic relationship between productivity and output growth is perhaps the most important economic reason behind the crisis in centrally planned economies. The institutionalization of sellers' markets and the vertical dependence of enterprises creates little incentive to innovate. Even if research and development could be managed by the planning authorities, the lack of a profit motive and financial responsibility separates the R&D process from the enterprise and/or the consumer.[3] As Kaldor (1966) has argued, evidence from the Western industrialized countries shows that a dynamic relationship between total industrial output and labour productivity can be explained by a simple technical progress function embodying both supply and demand factors, i.e. there is cumulative causation between different factors. Evidence from the Soviet Union and Eastern Europe in the 1960s and 1970s suggests, however, that increasing returns do not play an important role in determining productivity growth and that these countries are still following a path of extensive growth (Bairam 1988). If this is the case, then it is impossible for the centrally planned economy to catch up to the industrial leaders.

The institutional setting underlying the socialist economies also generates investment and reform cycles. In a socialist economy, investment expenditures and shortage tend to move pro-cyclically because increases in effective demand create bottlenecks that limit, or possibly reduce, the growth rate when it becomes increasingly difficult to complete projects on schedule. Bauer (1978) argued that the cycle starts when there is an acceleration and expansion of the number of projects. As investment expenditures rise, bottlenecks and shortages spread, causing the ratio of unfinished to finished projects to rise. Then bottlenecks and shortages intensify, so an austerity programme is introduced, severely reducing the number of new projects. Once existing projects are completed, capacity rises and investment expenditures tend to fall, which reduces bottlenecks and shortages only to start the process over again with a renewal of investment.

Because credit is allocated through the central planning mechanism, these investment cycles are essentially political-economic cycles which are often observed in the West as reform cycles. Indeed, economic tensions can stimulate political change and economic reform. Similarly, political change can result in economic change. Thus, the interaction of political shifts and economic tensions can appear in many forms, as was the case among the different Eastern European economies.

4 Attempts to reform the centrally planned economy

After the Second World War, Eastern Europe adopted the Soviet centralized planning model and strategy for economic growth. Although all of these countries followed a general policy of placing priority on investment in heavy industry and full utilization of labour and capacity, they started from different levels of industrialization and had different opportunities. It could be expected that this alone would lead to differences in plan specifics and growth paths.

Nationalization and the introduction of central planning were an integral part of the reconstruction effort following the Second World War. There was an initial wave of nationalization in Eastern Europe: in Czechoslovakia all basic industries, the glass industry and all large enterprises were nationalized in 1945; in Poland almost all of the industrial sector including transport, banking, insurance and commercial enterprises was nationalized by decree in January 1946; and Hungary gradually nationalized a number of enterprises, including commercial banks, between 1945 and 1947. Central planning was introduced during the first phase of the reconstruction: Czechoslovakia followed a two year plan emphasizing the industrialization of Slovakia; Poland followed a three year plan placing high priority on coal mining, transport and communications; and Bulgaria followed a two year plan emphasizing agriculture.

As table 1.4 indicates, a second wave of nationalization occurred in 1948 when almost all remaining industrial enterprises were nationalized in Eastern Europe, except in East Germany which nationalized them later. However, in contrast to the Soviet Union, collectivization of agriculture did not occur until much later, and in some cases, as in Poland, only a small percentage occurred. Nevertheless, almost from the beginning, there were frequent attempts at decentralization, only to be followed by recentralization, as well as frequent changes in direction. The first major change came in 1950, when Yugoslavia, dissatisfied with the results of central planning, adopted instead a strategy of market socialism which included worker self-management and decentralized decision-making of enterprises. This meant that producers make decisions about how work will be organized and the profits distributed, with planning boards at regional and national levels primarily concerned with investment decisions which they are able to influence through credit accessibility.

Table 1.4: Percentage share of socialist sector in Eastern Europe (gross output).

		Industry		Agriculture
	1947	1948/49	1952	1952
Bulgaria	...	98	100	53
Czechoslovakia	80[a]	96	98	43
East Germany	...	69	77	7
Hungary	45[a]	81	97	27
Poland	80	...	99	15
Romania	11	95	97	16

Source: United Nations 1953, p. 28 and p. 37.
[a]Employment.

After 1953, cycles of decentralization plus some guarded moves towards introducing market forces followed by a period of recentralization appeared. As this happened, the periods of liberalization were widely publicized—but the swings back were not. The universal motive for these reforms was to improve the effectiveness of the planning model and to try new planning techniques. Differences between countries appeared in methods and results. The Soviet Union and East Germany, for example, introduced only limited reforms which were aimed at strengthening the functioning of centralized management. At the other extreme, Hungary, and until the late 1960s, Czechoslovakia, went further in decentralization. Their aim was to allow some market mechanisms to regulate enterprises within established limits—effectively allowing profits or losses to replace compulsory quantitative targets—shifting emphasis from micro-level decision-making to macro-level targets, policy and direction. Differences in results depended partly on internal conditions, especially how large and already industrialized the country was, and external factors. For example, intensification of the Cold War led to the signing of the Warsaw Pact in 1955, which increased military expenditures at the expense of consumption; increasingly large agricultural shortfalls, especially in the Soviet Union, led to increased trade with the West, although the planners were trying to minimize it; and the external inflationary pressures of the 1970s affected especially the more open Eastern European economies.

The reason for economic reform was to counter dissatisfaction with the inability to raise living standards. This was shown by the persistence of urban overcrowding due to lagging residential construction, food shortages and scarce supplies of other consumer goods. However, the policy reversal back to recentralization was inherent in the reforms themselves because increasing investment in a sellers' market exacerbated shortages and lengthened the construction period. For example, relieving urban overcrowding required more residential construction, but this could only be accomplished if materials were available. If they were not, then priorities had to be rearranged again to pump more resources into the producer goods industries.

Another area in which liberalization contained the seeds of its own destruction was allowing more imports of consumer goods. This became a quick fix that was ultimately unsuccessful because the growth of a trade deficit and hard currency indebtedness to the West put increasing pressure on the export industries. In those countries which exported manufactured goods, this implied fewer goods available for domestic consumption and increasing difficulty in maintaining export competitiveness because of lagging innovation. Even the Soviet Union with its huge reserves of natural resources was not immune from similar pressures resulting from changes in world prices, as it often sold commodities such as oil and natural gas to Western buyers.

These reform cycles are indicative of the generalized failure of the Soviet strategy for economic growth. Also, to the extent that the administrative planning model did produce rapid industrialization, it too contained the seeds of its own destruction. At the beginning of an industrialization process, central planning focused attention on the highest priority areas, the need to produce basic goods. As industrialization proceeded, however, the economy became more complex.[4] In this more complex environment, retention of the original mechanism is insufficient—gaps appear, and to the extent that attempts are made to close them, too much rigidity is introduced. Hence the various experiments introduced to improve some planning mechanisms either by giving some autonomy to enterprises or introducing new levels of supervision or new incentives.

All of the cycles involve three types of reform. First, there was an attempt to improve productivity and output levels in agriculture. Especially in the Soviet Union, this has been a chronic problem. From being an net exporter of farm products prior to centralization, it has frequently been a net importer of them since the 1960s. A second type of reform attempted to raise the output of consumer goods and improve living standards. The third type of reform focused on the optimal amount of investment (both absolutely and as a share of national income) that will sustain growth rates, provide a self-sustaining growth path and be allocated so as to have a positive impact on both the production of consumer goods and the trade balance. All this was also meant to meet other goals, i.e. catching up with the West, maintaining military preparedness, and the maintenance of political power.

In 1953, reforms to increase the output of consumption goods and revitalize agriculture were apparent, especially in East Germany, Hungary and the Soviet Union. In the Soviet Union, taxes on privately owned plots of land were reduced and the amount of livestock that could be privately owned increased. Elsewhere there was either a temporary halt in the process of collectivization or actual decollectivization such as in Czechoslovakia and Hungary.

Many of these reforms were reversed in 1956 and 1957, after uprisings in Hungary and Poland and increasing economic imbalances throughout Eastern Europe. The reversal came through recentralization in some areas, including renewed collectivization, increases in investment spending and a return to fixing ambitious targets (which partly avoided the need to answer questions about consumption). In the Soviet Union, although the general line was harder, farms gained more responsibility as part of the agriculture revitalization programme. They were to be responsible for financing and managing their own equipment, effectively transferring the burden from the state. But as measured by income levels, this decentralization was not a success. Incomes stagnated, and in 1961, the state resumed the responsibility for investment in agriculture.

While retaining the overall system of centralized management, Poland introduced profit-sharing and gave increased autonomy to enterprise managers. This was not very effective, because the prices that existed were not market prices, hence 'profits' were really meaningless and could not be taken as a measure of success. By 1959, enterprises had overestimated their investment plans while simultaneously granting wage increases. The result was inflation, both open and repressed, which combined with a growing trade deficit, shortages of capital and consumer goods and agricultural shortfalls, led to a restoration of central control over wages and investment. Similar attempts at decentralization in Hungary and Czechoslovakia met the same fate.

The basic problem with these attempts to reform the centrally planned economy was the failure of the price system, an inherited one, to reflect true opportunity costs in combination with the retention of a centralized allocation system. Because shortages persisted, it was impossible for enterprises to make their own decisions and be able to act on them. Therefore, although there was a recognition throughout the period that the extensive growth strategy was not effective, which led to continual restructuring, inherited problems did not go away, and continual failure to meet targets tended to lead to more intervention.

The question of balance between investment and consumption (or heavy and light industry) had not been satisfactorily solved. One aim of these reforms had been to improve living standards, but repeated problems resulted in the share of consumption in output to be lower in the mid 1960s than in the early 1950s. As growth slowed in the mid 1960s, a new series of reforms began. What was common was more enterprise access to resources, a changed incentive formula (with more emphasis on material incentives) and more autonomy in management decision-making. The aims were to improve efficiency, speed up technological development, switch to an intensive growth path, and, as a result, improve living standards. There was still political interference, especially with respect to overall targets and long-term choices.

Major changes were seen in the mechanisms used, however. The introduction of a tax on capital for the first time meant that finance capital was no longer free to the enterprise. However, increased enterprise autonomy did not lead to increased competition between enterprises. Instead, smaller enterprises were merged into larger ones and 'associations of enterprises' were created to replace the previous centralized management agencies, and they effectively prevented competition. Price reform was also introduced, but the problem of distorted prices remained. The aim was to reform prices so that they would reflect production costs. This required the elimination of centralized price controls, but in fact the price structure was so distorted that if prices were truly reformed, especially consumer goods' prices, they would rise so much as to risk social upheaval as they did in Poland and Russia after price liberalization. Consequently, prices remained administered, with an unrealistic pattern of subsidies holding down many retail prices unnecessarily.

In practice, reforms varied greatly, being most limited in East Germany and the Soviet Union, and most far-reaching in Hungary. In the Soviet Union, reforms were aimed at perfecting centralized control. Although on paper enterprises were to have more responsibilities, so long as centralized allocation of resources existed, this autonomy was limited. East Germany's reforms were called the New Economic System, and lasted until 1971-72. The aim was to loosen planning somewhat and encourage moderate growth by increasing the role of profits as enterprise incentives and regulators. Centralization was reduced, as new intermediate levels (associations of enterprises) took care of relationships between firms in the absence of market relationships and took over many everyday decisions. Before 1968, this worked, but ironically, success accelerated the structural transformation which led to more centralization.

At the other end of the reform spectrum, Hungary attempted in 1968 to improve the workings of central planning by introducing more market mechanisms. The idea was to use them to control enterprise activity within guidelines set by planners. Enterprises were no longer given compulsory targets, and profits were to determine the level of bonuses and wage increases paid. While the next three years did show an increase in national income and living standards, other goals of the reforms were not met. This was partly due to the problems associated with a small economy which was easily dominated by a few large enterprises, and partly due to continuing centralized financial regulation.

By the beginning of the 1980s, it became clear in these economies that neither a pure model of centralized planning nor various attempts to improve it were successful. More radical attempts at reform were attempted in the 1980s. But as table 1.5 shows, the growth path in Eastern Europe and the Soviet Union continued to follow an extensive growth path with little gains in labour productivity and negative growth in capital productivity. Moreover, unfinished construction as a share of construction investment rose in the Soviet Union from 112 per cent in 1970 to 169 per cent in 1985, indicating that chronic shortages remain prevalent (UN 1990). Similarly, investment cycles could also be observed in Eastern Europe. From this it becomes immediately apparent that it is the institutional framework which lies behind the crisis in centrally planned economies. But this does not mean that the institutional framework behind free markets and private property is the only alternative.

Table 1.5: Extensive growth in Eastern Europe and the Soviet Union during the 1980s (average annual percentage change).

	Labour productivity		Capital productivity	
	1981-85	1986-89	1981-85	1986-88
Bulgaria	3.5	4.0	-2.9	-2.2
Czechoslovakia	1.1	2.1	-3.6	-2.1
East Germany	4.3	3.5	0.2	-1.3
Hungary	2.1	2.9[a]	-2.2	-0.8[b]
Poland	-0.1	4.5	-3.4	1.2
Romania	4.2	4.5[a]	-4.2	-1.2[b]
Soviet Union	2.7	3.3	-3.1	-2.3

Source: United Nations, 1990, p. 93.
[a]1986-88. [b]1986-87.

5 Behind the collapse in centrally planned economies

It is the institutional framework of the centrally planned economy which lies behind the collapse of Eastern Europe and the Soviet Union. However, while nationalization and centralization are integral parts of this framework, they should not be viewed simply as *the only* cause of the crises and subsequent collapse. They may be *a probable* cause, but at the same time they may also be part of the solution. A certain amount of nationalization and centralization has been, and still is, necessary for growth and development. One only needs to look at the use of planning by the capitalist industrialized economies after the Second World War to see that such a mix could work in Eastern Europe and the Soviet Union.[5]

Overcentralization in the Soviet Union and Eastern Europe was perhaps the most important factor which led to the collapse of these countries. The problem of overcentralization does not imply, however, complete decentralization. As Nelson (1988, p. 314) pointed out, the job of institutional design is to get an appropriate balance of the private and public aspects of technology, enough private incentive to spur innovation, and enough publicness to facilitate wide use'. To accomplish this, Brus and Laski (1989) suggest the creation of a viable private sector to ensure *exit* and make state enterprises behave more entrepreneurially. Of course, *voice*, a mechanism through which consumers can influence producers, can still play an important role in the state sector so long as the economy does not experience chronic excess demand.[6]

The collapse of Eastern Europe and the Soviet Union has led to a larger crisis with characteristics of the capitalist market economies during the Great Depression. It has become apparent that the hoped-for results may not emerge, and that new problems are emerging, such as unemployment, homelessness, inflation and poverty. Only a careful analysis of the real causes of failure would have prepared the way for a thoughtful transition, using the best of insights, institutions and advice from both East and West. One hopes that the jumping on the ideological bandwagon that has occurred now will not prove to be as severe a mistake as the earlier adoption of the Stalinist planning model.

Notes

1. It should be noted that Stalin's industrialization policy often ignored Gosplan, as it implied faster construction of factories, creation of new branches of industry, opening up new areas of the country and a lessening of dependence on other countries. (Foreign trade was never too important for a large country like the Soviet Union, but this policy shift was dramatic. The share of exports in national income was estimated at 10.4 per cent in 1914, 3.1 per cent in 1929 and 0.5 per cent in 1937 (Holzman 1963, p. 290).)
2. The high demand for labour and the legal guarantee for equal pay led to an extremely high participation rate: 86.6 per cent of those aged 15 to 64 were in the labour force in the Soviet Union, the highest labour force participation rate in the world as of 1980. This high rate was also the result of a different social and economic structure: few part-time jobs or legal nonwork income sources are available as in Western economies, and all able bodied men are required to have a job.
3. Nevertheless, some innovation has occurred in those industries tied closely with the planning authority such as defence. But even in this case, these enterprises appear to be followers instead of leaders in the development of technology. However, trade barriers also limit technological diffusion from the West. Knowledge of this technology was often acquired in a costly, time-consuming way by reverse engineering. The overall effect on economic development has been to reinforce the trend of declining productivity. Without innovation, growth is forced into an extensive path and the contribution of incremental units of inputs becomes less.
4. One of the major issues is that as development progresses, the economy becomes more complex, and the information needed for effective planning becomes more difficult to obtain. There may indeed be a principal-agent problem because centralized planning cannot intrude into every economic decision, especially at the micro-level. Moreover, once the principal-agent problem is admitted, obtaining the necessary information becomes all the more difficult because there are incentives for misreporting information.
5. It should be added that Jan Tinbergen and Ragnar Frisch, the first Nobel Laureates,

emphasized the need for a mixed economy in order to maintain high economic growth and social justice.
6. The distinction between voice and exit is found in Hirschman (1970).

References

Adam, J. (1989). *Economic Reforms in the Soviet Union and Eastern Europe since the 1960s*, New York: St. Martin's.

Bairam, E. I. (1988). *Technical Progress and Industrial Growth in the USSR and Eastern Europe*, Aldershot: Avebury.

Bauer, T. (1978). 'Investment Cycles in Planned Economies', *Acta Oeconomica.*

Brus, W. and Laski, K. (1989). *From Marx to the Market*, New York: Oxford.

Dosi, G., Freeman, C., Nelson, R., Silverberg, G. and Soete, L. (eds,) (1988). *Technical Change and Economic Theory*, New York: Pinter Publishers.

Erlich, A. (1960). *The Soviet Industrialization Debate, 1924-1928*, Cambridge: Harvard.

Gregory, P. R. and Stuart, R. C. (1990). *Soviet Economic Structure and Performance*, Fourth edition, New York: Harper Collins.

Hirschman, A. O. (1970). *Exit, Voice, and Loyalty*, Cambridge: Harvard.

Holzman, F. (1963). 'Foreign Trade', in Bergson, A. and Kuznets, S., eds, *Economic Trends in the Soviet Union*, Cambridge: Harvard.

Kaldor, N. (1966). 'Causes of the Slow Rate of Growth in the United Kingdom' in *Further Essays on Economic Theory*, London: Duckworth [1978].

Kalecki, M. (1986). *Selected Essays on Economic Planning*, Cambridge: Cambridge University Press.

Kornai, J. (1992). *The Socialist System: The Political Economy of Communism*, Princeton: Princeton University Press.

Kowalik, T. (1989). 'On Crucial Reform of Real Socialism', in Hubert Gabrisch, ed., *Economic Reforms in Eastern Europe and the Soviet Union*, Boulder: Westview.

Lange, O. (1936).'The Economic Theory of Socialism', *Review of Economic Studies*, IV: 1 and 2.

Lange, O. (1949).'The Practice of Economic Planning and The Optimum Allocation of Resources', *Econometrica.*

Nelson, R. R. (1988). 'Institutions Supporting Technical Change in the United States' in Dosi, G. et al.,(1988).

Nove, A. (1990). *Studies in Economics and Russia*, New York: St. Martin's.

Ofer, G. (1987). 'Soviet Economic Growth: 1928-85', *Journal of Economic Literature*, XXV, December.

Petrov, A. (1985). 'General Results of the National Economic Balance for 1928, 1929 and 1930', in Wheatcroft and Davis (1985).

United Nations (1953). *Economic Survey of Europe Since the War*, Geneva.

United Nations (1965). *Economic Planning in Europe*, Geneva.

United Nations (1989). *Economic Reforms in the European Centrally Planned Economies*, Economic Studies No. 1, Geneva.

United Nations (1990). *Economic Survey of Europe in 1989-1990*, Geneva.

Wheatcroft, S. G. and Davis, R. W. (1985). *Materials for a Balance of the Soviet National Economy, 1928-1930*, Cambridge: Cambridge University Press.

Zaleski, E. (1971). *Planning for Economic Growth in the Soviet Union, 1918-1932*, Chapel Hill: University of North Carolina.

2 Justifying the Need for Reform: The Price-Theoretic Approach

*Christine Rider**

1 Introduction

The changes and proposed changes that have taken place in the socialist economies of Eastern Europe and the Sov'.t Union make it difficult to continue to refer to them as 'centrally planned' economies. Even the United Nations no longer uses the classification 'centrally planned economies,' preferring instead 'socialist economies in transition'. But what are they in transition to? Some observers, especially in Western countries, seem to believe that the end result will be a complete 180° turn to a capitalist market economy. A less radical version sees a continuing commitment to socialist principles combined with a much greater use of the market mechanism. This implies the introduction of some private property rights—the privatization aspect of the reforms—plus increased independence for enterprises and a decreased, but still visible, role for government.

In particular, and the focus of this paper, introducing market-oriented reforms into centrally planned economies is seen as a necessary step to improving their efficiency. Implicit is the belief that markets *are* more efficient than central planning, and therefore that certain desirable outcomes will emerge. These outcomes include higher output levels, more consumer goods and a faster rate of economic growth. While there have been previous attempts to improve economic efficiency dating back to the 1950s, it is the reforms of the 1980s that have attracted significantly more attention. This is due to the recognition that the early promise of central planning was not realized, hence the current problems of the planned economies called for a new approach (e.g. Bergson 1987; *Financial Times* 1990; Hewett 1988; Kornai 1986, 1990).

Another element that emerged with what may be called the Revolutions of 1989 is that for the first time, a willingness to consider new forms of ownership of productive resources was apparent. At its most extreme, this could be seen as a desire to embrace capitalism, but it is more likely that it represents a recognition that different types of ownership may be appropriate in different situations, which will involve some privatization of state-owned enterprises and a larger role for various cooperative and individually-owned enterprises. What may be the best outcome is a social market economy resembling that of the Scandinavian countries, although the discussion in many of the countries involved *appears* to focus on the perceived benefits of moving to a pure capitalist market form of economy with individual property ownership and enterprise. Political demands were also more important at the end of the decade, but are beyond the scope of this paper.

The primary focus of this paper, therefore, is on the question of whether these reforms will produce the results intended. A specifically microeconomic approach will be used to provide an answer. Because the reforms are giving a significantly greater role to price-oriented behaviour and profit-making by independent enterprises, a theoretical rationale based on a simplified version of neoclassical general equilibrium theory will be elaborated. The introduction of market-oriented mechanisms is apparently justified by the presumption that markets *are* more efficient than any alternative. Consequently, the reasons for making this choice should be validated by intellectual enquiry. This paper will not be concerned with macroeconomic issues (which are discussed elsewhere in this book), political considerations or socio-cultural concerns. It will try to abstract certain general themes and concepts that are more or less common to all the reforms, rather than concentrating on one specific country's experience, so it is at a fairly high level of abstraction.

After having done this, it will then attempt to evaluate the likelihood of their success, based on purely microeconomic grounds. While no overt justification for introducing these market-oriented changes has been explicitly given, the decision to make them must, if the decision-makers are rational, rest on some sound theoretical basis. Hence this paper is somewhat speculative, trying to read into practical policies and actions a theoretical justification that may not exist.

There is always a problem trying to understand the motives or rationale for behaviour when these are not specified, and it is possible that the motives ascribed to the reformers are not the correct ones. However, given the emphasis on the need to improve economic operations by introducing profit-oriented behaviour in a market setting, it is not irrelevant to assume that this can be intellectually justified by that version of equilibrium theory which shows the desirable results of such an introduction.

It should also be pointed out, however, that it is too easy to criticize the concept of Pareto-optimality associated with the attainment of that general equilibrium, because it is so highly restrictive, focusing as it does only on the allocative functions of markets and ignoring their many other functions. The reason for assuming that this version of equilibrium theory provides the justification for reform is that it presents a consistent justification for the price mechanism and markets that is comprehensible. The point is not to explore the analytics underlying reform proposals, but to look at the most commonly accepted view of how the market economy works. This vision of the pure laissez faire market economy, the self-regulating ideal, has always held a particular attraction, so it is not surprising that having become dissatisfied with its opposite, heavily centralized planning, the concept of a pure laissez faire optimizing market economy holds some appeal to the reformers.

The paper is structured as follows. The second section describes some of the problems that have encouraged a movement away from a highly centralized planning model to a more market-oriented, decentralized model. This will be followed in the third section by a discussion of the aims of the reforms and a description of their main elements. The fourth section will discuss some of the reasons why the reforms will not achieve their aims. Finally, the poverty of the pure price-theoretic, Pareto-optimizing approach in dealing with real life issues requires an alternative approach. Some of the issues that need to be explicitly introduced are summarized here; these are the issues that are discussed at greater length in the other papers.

2 Why reform?

In the comparative economic systems literature, a distinction is made between ownership patterns and economic mechanisms when classifying economies (e.g. Zimbalist *et al.* 1989). Private ownership of the means of production predominantly characterizes capitalist economies, while some form of social ownership predominates in socialist economies. The most common mechanisms for coordinating economic behaviour are the market mechanism and the planning mechanism, and planning in turn can be either centralized or decentralized. The question of which is the most effective decision-making *mechanism* is being raised by the reforms. Some moves to privatization (changes in ownership forms) have taken place or are being encouraged in many countries, inspired in many cases by the ideology of individualism and private property rights, and by the belief in the virtues of private ownership as an incentive for improved economic performance. However, it also seems that privatization is not intended to completely reverse these countries' commitment to socialist principles by introducing capitalist institutions and behaviour patterns. The most favourable interpretation is that a wider variety of ownership forms and a larger role for market-oriented behaviour will be compatible with socialist principles within a more diversified economy.

From a historical perspective, the process of development along capitalist market lines was time-consuming. The emergence of mature, capitalist industrial economies did not happen quickly. (It is difficult to put a time frame on this, because some economic behaviour has always been oriented to market gain. The question for the economic historian is to identify when market-oriented activity ceased to be merely an adjunct to economic life and became instead the dominating principle.) Theoretically, it can even be argued that a market economy does not generate growth if the economy is lacking the basic infrastructure associated with a modern industrial economy, because price signals reflect only what is in place, not what should be in place. It is often forgotten that industrialized capitalist economies did not rely only on market forces during their period of initial development. They preceded and accompanied their industrialization with mercantilist policies, which resulted in the necessary infrastructure to facilitate private activity being put into place. The moral of this historical digression is that individual activity alone cannot initiate change; the surrounding socio-cultural economic environment must also be favourable to change and supportive of it.

The problem of how to encourage development was a particularly crucial issue immediately after the 1917 revolution in the Soviet Union. At that time, the most pressing need was to speed up the industrialization and modernization of what was essentially still a semi-feudal economy with only a tiny industrial sector. This forced some conscious decisions to be made about the direction of the economy.

Any economic mechanism must perform two major functions. It must decide what to produce and for whom to produce. The determination of this depends on the distribution of purchasing power (wealth or initial endowments). If economic resources available are limited, this forces choices to be made about where they will be used. Furthermore, if economic actors are independent of each other, then actions will be coordinated through the operation of the price system. A pure market system essentially accomplishes this coordination after the fact. An equilibrium set of prices, quantities and production methods emerges after initial decisions are made, and act to influence further choices through variations in prices, quantities and so on. It is these variations in prices that give rise to pure economic profits or losses—the search for the former and the desire to avoid the latter is profit-motivated behaviour. Given certain restrictive conditions, these price and profit signals determine that the output mix will be the one most satisfying to consumers. (While there is a timing problem here, it can be minimized by assuming simultaneity.)

The second function is to determine how to produce, or, given the goals, how to attain them. This involves the issues of information, implementation and adjustment. In a market system, information is provided by the signals emerging from the operation of market determined prices. In a private enterprise economy, implementation is accomplished by independent enterprises acting on their own behalf. If the system is capitalist, motivation comes from the desire to maximize profits. Given this, adjustment occurs in response to changing price signals.

In contrast, a planned economy makes choices essentially prior to the start of activity. It must specify society's priorities (goals), which become apparent in decisions regarding the direction of development, the composition of output and the strategies to be used. Then the second function, how to produce, raises the technical questions of how these priorities are to be accomplished. Answers to these questions must take into account existing institutions and relationships between them as well as available resource supplies. It is also desirable that procedures for incorporating new or feedback information be in place so that targets and standards can be revised and adjusted as necessary.

Planning in general is characterized by politically-inspired decision-making and by direct control of investment. Depending on the degree of centralization, there is also ex ante price and wage setting, and in a socialist economy, greater emphasis on maintaining full employment and providing other aspects of economic security. Information is provided through a complex chain of authority moving between the individual enterprises (which are operating but not decision-making units) through industry branch or financial ministries to central planning authority. There are prices in planned economies, but they are not formed in the same way as in a market economy, and they perform different functions: they are accounting prices rather than allocative prices reflecting relative scarcity. Prices are determined at the central authority level, theoretically to reflect production costs (although in practice, often serving some political end), and preferably producing a rough balance between supply and demand.

Quantitative targets are more important to the functioning of a planned economy than prices. The idea behind giving operating units quantitative targets and providing them with input allocations was to replace the instability and inefficiencies of a market system based on adjustment to prices with a system designed to maximize efficiency. That is, if enterprises are freed from the need to react to price changes for outputs and inputs, they can focus exclusively on the technical question of how to achieve maximum output most efficiently. In addition, it was thought that emphasizing the *physical* allocation of resources would speed up industrialization by focusing on priority areas and rationing resources in short supply to the most urgent needs.

In practice in the Soviet Union in the 1920s, centralization of decision-making preceded planning, and both preceded the theoretical justification for a planned economy. Because modernizing the economy was felt to be the most important goal, this led to the practice of concentrating resources in a few key areas, which resulted in the building up of heavy industry taking place at the expense of the (large) agricultural sector. Initially, planning was undertaken on a fairly flexible, trial and error basis—necessary because good information on the economy was lacking (Ofer 1987).

Planning became heavily centralized in the Stalinist period of the 1930s and 1940s, and it was this centralized version that was imposed on the East European economies in the post-World War II period. These economies were at different levels of development, which helps explain some of the differences apparent today. In the late 1940s, Czechoslovakia and the German Democratic Republic were the most industrialized, while Bulgaria and Romania were almost entirely agricultural.

At this time, the priorities were the same as in the USSR in the 1920s: industrialization and the building up of heavy industry. But fairly soon, while impressive results were obtained in some areas, the overall results achieved by the planned economies were inferior to those of Western market economies. Growth rates, which were high in the 1950s and 1960s, began to slow. The priority given to heavy industry did not result later in the period in expanding overall productive capacity, and the output of consumer goods failed to rise. Depending on the country, living standards either stagnated or fell, and shortages of consumer goods remained common and often intensified. In addition, agriculture became a problem area, and agricultural modernization became necessary. However, those countries adopting collectivization measures ran into resistance, forcing at least some concessions to peasants in order to prevent further declines in output.

In general, several specific inefficiencies and distortions began to appear in the planned economies. These problems lowered overall efficiency and also affected the ability to adapt and adjust, which tended to institutionalize rigidity. Inevitably, this rigidity made reform attempts more difficult.

These problems appeared in the price structure, which became more distorted over time, bearing less resemblance to production costs. Prices were rarely changed, hence could play no role in reflecting either changing consumer demands or changing input prices and supplies. This undoubtedly contributed to the peculiar pattern of shortages of certain goods coexisting with surpluses of others. The pricing of new goods seemed arbitrary, having little regard for either production costs or consumer demand.

Because the original motive behind planning was to speed up industrialization, intermediate goods were systematically underpriced in order to encourage their wider use, which expanded the output of intermediate goods and enabled producers to tap economies of scale. But over time, this practice reduced the incentive to introduce new technologies or to economize on inputs. Innovation was also discouraged because physical input use was centrally determined, and anyway, enterprises had incentives *not* to overfulfill plan targets in case all output targets were revised upwards. Also energy inputs were underpriced, again to encourage rapid industrialization. Comparing planned with nonplanned economies showed the former with much higher coefficients of intermediate goods and energy inputs per unit of output, a wasteful pattern that still prevails.

To the extent that plan overfulfillment was rewarded and that enterprises had an incentive to overcome specific input shortages, certain other distortions appeared. For example, some found it advantageous to use 'expediters' to gain access to needed but scarce resources or to 'simplify' their tasks or shorten bureaucratic lines. These individuals were not part of the official planning mechanism, but the planning bureaucracy tended to ignore their existence because when successful, the results of their activity deflected attention from the real problems of planning. Another example of an enterprise-rational but socially costly adjustment was the widespread practice of hoarding skilled labour or material inputs. This is rational to the enterprise, because in a shortage economy, even when shortages may be only infrequent or shortlived, lack of some vital inputs creates problems for the entire production process, so enterprise hoarding ensured that such bottlenecks would be less likely. In consumer goods markets, evidence of official plan malfunctioning appeared in widespread black market activity. Again, it was expedient to ignore these because they siphoned off pressure from the plan and helped hide its imperfections.

3 The economic reform process

In the late 1980s, the socialist economies opted to move in the direction of giving a larger role to market forces and reducing the role of bureaucratic decision-making, instead of improving the planning process. As previously noted, justification for introducing market reforms seems to be provided by the development of a static general equilibrium model and the positing of a Pareto equilibrium position—a Walrasian general equilibrium that is both efficient and desirable, and that is obtained by the functioning of the market mechanism (Bergson 1948; Pareto 1971). This provides both a goal: maximum output and social utility at minimum cost; and a mechanism: the use of the equi-marginal principle within a market setting. Theoretically, static efficiency is improved because use of this principle results in resources being allocated to their best use. It is desirable because resources cannot be reallocated without lowering at least one agent's utility.

The achievement of Pareto-optimality depends on price flexibility. Prices will perform their desired role when certain restrictive conditions are met, conditions which can be adequately summarized by the concept of perfect competition. In this situation, prices measure two values. On the buyer's side of the market, the price measures the extra satisfaction to be obtained from the purchase of one more unit. On the supplier's side, the price measures the marginal resource cost (or opportunity cost) of the resources used to produce that last unit. At the market equilibrium price, buyers are maximizing satisfaction and cannot reallocate spending to do any better (although some may do worse). Similarly, resources are being allocated efficiently and any other output mix, given the initial allocation of endowments, purchasing power and preferences, will be worse. If price flexibility cannot be achieved because perfect competition is not present, then there is no guarantee that the market mechanism will produce a 'better' outcome than any other. In this case, the only reason for introducing market-oriented reforms is a normative preference for 'markets' as opposed to 'planning'.

What is also important about this model is the role of economic profit, which gives credence to its real life equivalent in the profit motive. At the equilibrium position, all resources are being paid their opportunity cost, no more, no less, so economic profit is zero, only normal profits occur, and all capital owners are receiving a rate of return on invested capital that is uniform and equal in all lines of production.

Any change in prices—due, for example, to shifts in consumer preferences or exogenous alterations in resource supplies—will lead to the appearance of economic profit or loss. In response, capital owners in areas where now below-normal rates of profit are being made will attempt to transfer capital to the areas where above-normal rates of profit are being made. Although this is a heavily oversimplified version, the movement of resources in response to the desire to make profits and avoid losses is considered to be the dynamic force of a capitalist economy driven by the profit motive. There is no doubt that this desire is powerful; whether it operates in exactly the way the textbooks describe is open to question.

What is also open to question is whether these behaviour patterns will be automatic once the market mechanism institutions have been introduced. In the capitalist countries the East European economies are now emulating, such behaviour patterns took centuries to become both common and acceptable. Moreover, it is expected that new institutions will engender the desired results, but is it sufficient to introduce the institutions and expect everything else to fall into place? It has been argued that the market economies in the West work well not just because they allocate resources efficiently (and in fact they are not that good at this task) but because they impose discipline by making economic agents accountable for their actions (Gintis 1986, 1991). This implies that the democratization of the post-communist societies is as important to the success of the economic reforms as the reforms themselves.

The market response to the problems of the planned economies also seems to imply a convergence theory of economics. That is, assume that the optimal position for any economy is the same, and that real economies can be ranked on a continuum ranging from a pure laissez faire market economy to a pure centrally planned economy. If the planned economy does not reach that optimal position, all that needs to be done is to introduce more market mechanisms and move along the continuum for improvement to appear.

Five key ideas characterize the reforms and express this belief in the benefits of a market system: (1) a significant amount of privatization will occur (several different forms of private ownership have been proposed or implemented); (2) the economy will be decentralized by reducing the duties of the planning bureaucracy. (How large a role it retains depends on the degree of decentralization.); (3) enterprises will become decision-making as well as operating units; (4) enterprises will become financially self sufficient, responsible for financing their own capital needs, i.e. investment decisions will no longer be made by the central authority and financed by the state but will be based on decisions on how much capacity to have, and how to finance it; and (5) price reform will remove much of the central bureaucracy's role in setting prices, and give it to the enterprises. The intention is to make it possible for enterprises to both generate and respond to signals and thus improve the working of the economy.

It is not likely that the role of the central authority will be completely eliminated, probably more for pragmatic reasons than as the result of an ideologically inspired rationale, although differences in different countries are likely to persist. Certain prices and decisions will probably still come under central authority, chiefly regarding the overall level of investment spending and the interest rate. This is intended to prevent a full-scale move to the complete 'anarchy of the market' with the short-term horizons typical of independent profit-seeking enterprises. In other words, the central authority is presumed to be able to take the long-term view and act in the social interest, which the individual enterprise cannot or will not do. This is because the authority has access to more and better information, can take account of externalities and can redistribute part of the national income in accordance with some socially-determined criterion. If this is indeed the case, it is this function in particular which is intended to make the reformed socialist economy preferable, assuming that it does not intend to transform itself completely into a laissez faire, private enterprise capitalist market economy. Adding the efficiency aspects of a market economy without at the same time adding the income inequalities, presumably could produce this more desirable result (Dobb 1969).

Given this possible qualification, it is obvious that a much greater role for the profit motive is envisaged in the reforms. The expansion of functions of enterprises essentially turns them into profit-oriented units. They will no longer respond to quantitative targets; now a normative system based on profits and losses will provide enterprise incentives. Enterprises become responsible for acquiring inputs, determining the level of output and product mix. If they are successful, they can retain part of their profits to finance investment and/or increase wages and/or indulge in any other type of spending, and presumably are free to choose any criterion for doing this that they wish. If they are not successful and losses result, they are faced with two options: reorganize or close down. This is intended to eliminate inefficiency by preventing state bailouts of failing firms.

Two very important implications derive from this. First, enterprise profits are the measure of social contribution, hence it is necessary that the prices to which the enterprise responds are the correct ones and truly reflect all opportunity costs. This is why it is so important that the underlying theoretical model justifying the introduction of market pricing be logically consistent and viable. Second, if enterprises are to be responsible for making *all* their production decisions, including those on input use, then they are no longer committed to offering full employment. This involves a serious departure from one of the most deepseated ethical principles of a socialist economy, the principle of economic security as shown in the commitment to full employment.

In summary, reforms replace centralized decision-making and give more independence to the enterprises; they replace centralized price setting with market-generated prices; they replace quantitative targets with financial ones in which the attempt to generate profits is intended to be the pivot of the incentive system. This has only briefly sketched the general principles underlying economic restructuring. It has ignored many other issues, such as taxation, foreign trade, the creation of an 'appropriate' financial structure (including revamping the banking system and the creation of institutions for handling credit and debt). However, if it has captured the main elements, it is sufficient for the purpose at hand.

4 Can reform work?

There are several ways to evaluate the prospects for reform. In this section, consideration is given to a purely price-theoretic evaluation, using neoclassical theory's own terms of reference to raise doubts about their success. What will not be done here is to question the reforms within a macroeconomic context; that will be done in the other papers in this book. What is basic to the neoclassical paradigm as expressed above is an abstract model of rational choice and behaviour which focuses on self-interested individuals attempting to maximize utility by making consistent (rational) choices between alternative options. This can be extended from economic to political choice (e.g. Dearlove 1989), and undoubtedly, the views of public choice theorists have influenced current reform efforts, especially because of their criticism of the role of government. Interestingly, while the idea of Pareto-optimality and maximum welfare achievable through the functioning of markets under certain conditions was subject to considerable criticism both by welfare theorists themselves and by later critics, and has been shown to be theoretically and practically inconsistent, it is still implicit in introductory economics textbooks (e.g. Samuelson and Nordhaus 1989, ch. 31). This means that while professional economists question its validity and understand its limitations, there are millions more individuals who have passed through introductory economics courses only, and who therefore have only a narrow view of how markets are supposed to work. This adds a difficulty, because no reform proposal explicitly states that the goal of introducing market reforms is to achieve some 'social welfare optimum'. Because the goals are implicit, it then become easier to criticize those who criticize. There are many other reasons for being pro-market as well as wanting to maximize social utility. However, certain problems emerging from the restructuring process do become much easier to see and understand if it is assumed that these other reasons are less important. This is why an unrealistic and oversimplified approach has been taken in this paper. That is, it is presumed that the reforms are not introduced purely and simply to produce a market economy, in which case the resulting structure, performance and results will be irrelevant. Instead, they have been introduced to improve the economy's functioning; and perhaps implicitly, to achieve economic efficiency and maximum social utility in the textbook sense (with the emphasis, as noted earlier, on this as an implied goal). Consequently, introducing market reforms will only be successful if the following four points hold true: (1) a unique optimum position for the economy can be identified which is characterized by Pareto-optimality as described above; (2) this optimum position is the same for both capitalist and socialist economies. (If they are different, then there is no point in introducing those market mechanisms associated with attaining a capitalist goal.); (3) this optimum position is attainable—there is no point in changing reality to try to reach an unreachable goal; and (4) this optimal position should be attained, i.e. it is socially desirable.

Those in favour of introducing market reforms must believe that all four points have validity. However, while markets perform many functions well, for example, they can transmit various types of information and can allocate consumer goods better than other mechanisms, there is reason to be less than wholeheartedly uncritical.

Criticism of general equilibrium theory and its welfare aspects originated at the same time that the theory itself was developed. The development of pure theory resulted in an increased rigour and more precise specification of the conditions necessary to achieve an equilibrium. Ironically, this rigour has made it less relevant for policy applications.

The general criticism focuses on the proof of the existence and attainability of a Pareto-optimum equilibrium. Such a criticism undercuts the rationale for the equi-marginal principle, and means that market pricing cannot result in a consistent set of rational prices that uniquely defines the optimum. The implication therefore is that there is no logical reason to prefer a 'pure' market pricing mechanism to any other on efficiency and optimization grounds alone.

Not only is it impossible to reach the kind of Pareto-optimum equilibrium position that provides justification for these reforms, there is also no way of demonstrating that such a unique position is preferable to any other. For example, Bergson (1948) discusses the different sets of conditions that are necessary to derive the equilibrium position. One problem pointed out is that if a position of maximum social utility is defined as the position where the sum of all marginal utility changes is zero, this in fact does not guarantee that there is no other position with greater welfare, only that there are no other positions in which the welfare of one person is greater without another's being less. Dobb (1969, p.7) concludes that while it is possible to specify a limited number of conditions necessary for maximizing economic welfare, there is no unique position unless *something is introduced from outside*. This, however, violates the implicit assumption that the free operation of markets produces preferable results because it opens up the possibility for non-market intervention. Even at the beginning of the welfare economics research programme, Wicksell (1934, pp. 82-83) pointed out that the maximum characterized by Pareto-optimality was only a relative maximum—relative to the starting point initial distribution of resources and the range of neighbouring positions—and does not necessarily produce the greatest social advantage. These considerations remove the intellectual justification for the reforms because market pricing will not result in a coherent set of rational prices that uniquely defines the optimum position. More important, if one moves away from the static resource allocation problem to a dynamic growth process where increasing returns exist, the problems with marginalist pricing mechanisms become even clearer.

Finally, and this is an important consideration if these economies wish to retain their commitment to socialist ideals, they do not even meet the criterion of desirability because the reforms imply a weakening of these principles. As noted before, decentralized decision-making is incompatible with full employment. It can also be shown that income inequality is likely to increase (although a continuing role of the state in income redistribution and taxation could offset this). In other words, what may happen is that an increase in inefficiency plus a failure to achieve some of the reform's goals plus an introduction of some unwanted side effects will be socially undesirable because it threatens social stability. (This effect could well be reinforced if political considerations are added, as the revolutions of 1989 in Eastern Europe and the pro-democracy demonstrations in China make clear. That is, if movements on the economic front encourage rising expectations which are not paralleled by accommodating political changes, the results may well be destabilizing.)

Criticisms of the neoclassical concept of general equilibrium challenge these reforms on several grounds. General equilibrium theory proves that all resources are fully used, that the market mechanism allocates all resources efficiently, that the output level and mix satisfies buyers' needs, and that the equilibrium set of prices is unique, stable and satisfies the conditions of Pareto-optimality. However, real economies do not tend to reach equilibrium positions; quantity adjustments are significant, especially in modern mass production economies, prices do not reflect scarcity values and factor prices are not measures of marginal productivity. Also, because of the existence of externalities, private markets cannot generate prices that cover all social costs or account for all social benefits: they can only equate private costs to private benefits. In general terms, these considerations undercut the uniqueness, comparability and attainability of an optimum position (Armstrong 1951; Bergson 1948; Kaldor 1966, 1972, 1975, 1979; Sraffa 1926; Young 1928). The problem revolves round the restrictiveness of the assumptions made to generate the theoretical result in a real, growing economy moving through time.

Perhaps the main problem, as Kaldor among others frequently pointed out, is that many of these assumptions are simply axioms and therefore incapable of being tested. If they are testable, then they have been found to be wrong. This puts in doubt the continuing use of a theory which is internally inconsistent. Hence developing policies to achieve ends that are automatic outcomes of that theory would seem to be foolhardy. Very early in the development of welfare theory, Kaldor (1934) pointed out that the assumptions made were simply those necessary to make the equilibrium determinate: a closed economy, perfect knowledge, perfect competition and direct exchange of goods. Given these, and the independent variables—utility and production functions—the equilibrium can be identified.

Kaldor also shows that even if an equilibrium can be identified, it may not be attainable. This may be the case because every step taken towards it alters the conditions of equilibrium, and it can only be reached if instantaneous reactions are assumed—i.e. those associated with a Walrasian process that prohibits non-equilibrium transactions or with Edgeworthian recontracting. A further requirement is that the equilibrium must be associated with converging tendencies—demand must be elastic relative to supply.

These problems were never addressed in subsequent developments of general equilibrium. As Kaldor (1972, p. 1240) noted almost forty years later:

> ...Equilibrium theory has reached the stage where the pure theorist has successfully (although perhaps inadvertently) demonstrated that the main implications of this theory cannot possibly hold in reality, but has not yet managed to pass his message down the line to the textbook writer and to the classroom.

This problem arises because the development of this version of theory has concentrated too much on the allocative functions of markets rather than on their strategic or financial functions. Perhaps this occurred because of the desire to demonstrate that economics could be as 'scientific' as the natural sciences, and this version of equilibrium analysis is highly congenial to mathematization. The result is a high degree of abstraction—but the quarrel is not that the assumptions are abstractions, but rather that they are contrary to experience (Kaldor 1972).

The list of assumptions required for universal perfect competition to exist--so that a unique optimum will be generated—is long. Perfect competition involves easy substitution between factors; linear, homogeneous production functions; no technical progress (unless it is Harrod neutral); no increasing returns; no learning effects; no oligopolistic competition; no uncertainty and no obsolescence (Kaldor 1966). Kaldor also criticizes the idea that markets operate so as to enforce the equality of factor prices to marginal productivities. This can only hold in a Walrasian world in which there is no debt-issuing government, no uncertainty and no increasing returns. But increasing returns do dominate, hence it is not possible to posit linear homogeneous 'well behaved' production functions (Kaldor 1972). They dominate because of the nature of technological change over time, which means that costs per unit of output change as plant capacity increases, as simplification and mechanization occur and as increased experience leads to new innovations.

Based on Young's (1928) path-breaking work the impact of assuming increasing returns to scale is far-reaching. Not only does it make economic change endogenous, it is also impossible to predict the actual state of the economy. This obviously contrasts with general equilibrium theory, which requires that the operation of economic forces is constrained by a given set of exogenous variables (production and utility functions) and that a convergence occurs. Convergence and equilibrium depend on the assumption of increasing marginal costs. If increasing returns are possible, any reorganization of productive activities creates the opportunity for yet more change which otherwise would not have been possible (Kaldor 1972). This makes the idea of an optimum allocation of resources, one in which no economic resource can be reallocated so as to make a greater contribution to output, meaningless.

The difficulties with a single equilibrium can be further compounded if it is recognized that capital/labour ratios are not equal in all industries, that some markets are competitive and some are imperfectly competitive, and that quantity adjustments are more significant in the latter than are price adjustments. In addition, the role of 'trader' or intermediary who keeps markets functioning in an orderly way by being willing to sell out of stocks, undercuts the idea of goods exchanging directly for goods, as does the reality of a money and banking system which can create credit.

A second flaw is seeing the market process as one in which the substitution principle predominates to achieve an efficient allocation of resources. Markets are not just allocative devices—they can also signal change which is important for an economy which evolves through the introduction of new products, processes and knowledge. Many markets do not have market clearing prices (the capital and labour markets, for example) and/or clear through quantity changes (the labour market or oligopolistic markets dominated by large enterprises with price-setting powers, for example). Another critique of the vision of the market as an allocation mechanism only is that real markets are not Walrasian markets. Most function in a stable way because there are market makers: wholesalers or dealers who are willing to hold inventories and whose actions are constrained by what is thought to be acceptable business practice. Real markets, in other words, are not impersonal and anonymous to their participants.

Another problem with the emphasis on substitution—which is required to make the equi-marginal principle result in Pareto-optimality—is that complementarity is forgotten. Complementarity is important in everyday life for both products and factors. This is especially clear when a growing economy is concerned. Static analysis sees capital and labour as being substitutes for each other, with marginal changes in their use taking place in response to relative price changes. However, in a growing economy where capital accumulation is taking place, this creates a demand for increased employment, meaning that capital and labour are not substitutes for each other, but complements. Furthermore, in a modern economy, industrial processes are not independent of each other, processing raw materials into a single product intended for final consumers. Instead, they are interdependent—the output of primary sectors is required for secondary processes—and they are rarely single-product producers. The reality of multiproduct/joint production oligopolies makes a pricing theory based on atomistic single product producers difficult to accept.

In addition, in the past, economies have been characterized by increasing returns, not constant returns. This is the legacy of the Industrial Revolution, and it leads to several related issues. Static theory is based on substitutability between given resources such that prices reflect scarcity values and marginal productivities. In real life, returns increase because of the nature of technical progress which usually results in plant costs per unit of output decreasing as plant size increases.

With increasing returns, prices can no longer reflect either scarcity values or marginal productivities; a unique set of equilibrium prices cannot be determined because prices depend on the scale of output, so it is impossible to identify a unique, unambiguous optimum position. As Adam Smith was the first to notice when he pointed out that the division of labour depended on the extent of the market, economic change is progressive, not static, convergent and allocative. An increase in productivity enlarges the market for, commodities which expands the possibility for a further division of labour and increase in productivity. Moreover, any reorganization of production can set off a chain of further changes which would not otherwise have existed. In this situation, there can be no such thing as an optimum allocation of resources because there are many alternative uses of a resource, and the prices existing at any given time cannot be the measure of marginal productivities and vice versa.

If prices reflect neither scarcity values nor marginal productivities, and are based only on private costs and benefits, then it is necessary to question whether profits truly measure efficiency. Profitability has become the new incentive for the restructured socialist economy, and the profit motive has become its rallying point. But profit can indicate improved efficiency in the sense of more output per unit of input only if prices are those associated with equilibrium values, an unlikely occurrence. In an economy just beginning to introduce market-determined pricing, profit differentials are less likely to measure differences in efficiency and more likely to indicate market power positions resulting from the inherited structure of prices. This is especially likely to be true in smaller economies or if significant competition does not exist. An additional problem arises if externalities exist, as at the beginning of a development process, so prices can not generate the correct signals for socially desired behaviour. Finally, if social considerations determine that a market-generated outcome is undesirable, then introducing a market process will not achieve social goals.

These considerations can be briefly summarized. While equilibrium analysis and the idea of Pareto-optimality have an undoubted appeal, they are not useful as a rationale for restructuring socialist economies because they are not useful for understanding how real life economies work. Hence, policies based on this are unlikely to achieve useful results. It is not enough to say that this does not matter how unrealistic or abstract the assumptions are so long as the theory's predictions are valid: to a certain extent, all theorizing has problems with abstraction. What is relevant is that this conception of equilibrium does not describe how real life prices are set or what truly motivates economic behaviour.

These flaws could be traced to four major failings of general equilibrium theory (Sawyer 1991). First, it assumes that relationships between people are only exchange relationships—but there are many other types of relationship between people that can have an effect on economic behaviour. Second, it fails to incorporate firms as institutions into the theory. This is important because the reforms are planning changes in the ownership of firms as part of the restructuring, but firms are not market institutions, although they must precede markets because they are responsible for producing the goods and services that will be exchanged in them. Third, the price mechanism has more than an allocative function. Prices can be set for strategic purposes (to win customers, or close out competitors, for example) and to finance growth, and the better they are at fulfilling these other functions, the less likely they are to fulfill their allocative functions effectively. Finally, there is no money and no monetary or financial institutions in equilibrium theory. Once this reality is admitted, then general equilibrium theory loses its viability.

Other issues also emerge. To assume that there is an either/or choice between markets and bureaucratic planning as coordinating devices is oversimplifying. Both exist to a greater or lesser degree in all economies, because each has a useful function to perform. In addition, if the *only* function of markets is thought to be their function in generating economically efficient prices, then the attempt to introduce reforms to obtain market prices is doomed. Prices observed in real markets are not generated in the way equilibrium theory argues they are.

Also, to the extent that resources are complementary rather than substitutes, a change in relative prices will have little effect on their use. Such changes may produce larger profits or losses, but are unlikely to increase or decrease their use, so the profit changes are unlikely to indicate either greater or lesser efficiency. Moreover, the existence of increasing returns in real life makes the equi-marginal principle redundant. With increasing returns, prices do not equal marginal costs, therefore the economy can neither reach nor maintain a unique and efficient equilibrium. Hence it can be demonstrated that there is no unique position that can be attained, no matter how much the economy is tampered with. Even if there were a unique position, it is questionable whether it would be socially desirable, as it would not be a position identified with a dynamic, growing economy. Finally, is it socially desirable if it weakens the principles on which a socialist society is built?

5 Conclusions

No one doubts that attempting to improve the working of an economy, any economy, is a useless undertaking. What does need to be thought through more carefully is whether any suggested changes or policies will have the desired results without producing more, unexpected problems in other areas. If anything, the experience of the socialist economies in transition is forcing a rethinking of what an economic system is for, and what it can accomplish, if structured 'correctly'. It is unquestioned that there are inefficiencies and deficiencies in the planned economies. Is the introduction of market pricing and decentralized decision making by newly-privatized enterprises the only way to increase output, improve resource use, minimize costs, speed up growth and raise living standards? Taking only a purely microeconomic focus based on a restrictive idealized vision of economic reality is insufficient; it is necessary to consider the entire range of possible changes within the context of society itself. What needs to be done, and bearing in mind that the history of 'reforms' in the planned economies dates back to the 1950s, is to consider the effects on society as a whole. The ability to change has been shown, but not the ability to implement a coherent new model that improves economic functioning and stabilizes institutional change.

Improving social and economic functioning requires consideration of several issues. First, the information problem must be dealt with: information must be timely, accurate and relevant, and information-providing entities must become aware of this. Withholding information or providing inaccurate or misleading information is one reason for the existence of inefficiencies in the planned economies.

Second is the adjustment/adaptation problem. Flexible responsiveness is important not only to survival, but also to growth and change. Adequate incentives are needed to encourage new research or new innovations.

Third is the environmental problem. Improved economic efficiency can deal with material deficiencies, but material adequacy is meaningless if the environment is befouled and the ecosystem damaged. A system of market prices based on private costs and benefits cannot incorporate this type of information. If the standard of living incorporates both qualitative as well as quantitative considerations, it is essential that some non-market mechanism be adapted to remedy the deficiency.

Fourth is the incentives problem. An acceptable set of incentives must harmonize the actions of individuals, enterprises and collective institutions so as to achieve a socially desirable result; there is no way that this can be done through the operation of a private market system. Incentives must include both material and non-material ones, with their proportions likely to fluctuate depending on the level of economic development, ideological assumptions and overall state policy.

Finally, democratization of both the political and economic sphere seems able to improve economic performance and achieve the ideals of a socialist society. If it does this by providing incentives and motivation as well as a process that encourages socially beneficial behaviour, then the results should be socially stabilizing. Although it is too early at the time of writing to evaluate political changes, the need to change the political sphere has been accepted in the USSR and Eastern Europe, but it is also obvious that the reality of change is extremely difficult. It is to be hoped that the outcome of these recent events will in fact produce the results desired. What is clear is that the immediate replacement of a central planning mechanism by markets (even if that were possible) without due consideration of the specific social environment in which it is done cannot succeed.

Notes

* The author thanks Mark Knell, Gary Mongiovi and Edward Nell for their comments on this paper; any errors remaining are her responsibility.

References

Armstrong, W. E. (1951). 'Utility and the Theory of Welfare', *Oxford Economic Papers*, III: 3.

Asselain, J. C. (1984). *Planning and Profits in Socialist Countries*, London: Routledge and Kegen Paul.

Bergson, A. (1948). 'Socialist Economics', in H. S. Ellis, ed., *A Survey of Contemporary Economics*, Homewood: Irwin.

Dearlove, J. (1989). 'Neoclassical Politics: Public Choice and Political Understanding', *Review of Political Economy*, I:2, July.

Dobb, M. (1969). *Welfare Economics and the Economics of Socialism*, Cambridge: Cambridge University Press.

Dunlop, J. T. and Fedorenko, N. P. (eds.) (1969). *Planning and Markets: Modern Trends in Various Economic Systems*, New York: McGraw Hill.

Galasi, P. and Sziraczki, G. (1985). 'State Regulation, Enterprise Behaviour and the Labour Market in Hungary, 1968-83', *Cambridge Journal of Economics*, IX:3, September.

Gintis, H. (1986). *Democracy and Capitalism: Property, Community and the Contradictions of Modern Social Thought*, New York: Basic Books.

Gintis, H. (1991). 'Where Did Schumpeter Go Wrong?', *Challenge*, January-February.

Hewett, E. A. (1988). *Reforming the Soviet Economy*, Washington: Brookings.

Kaldor, N. (1934). 'A Classificatory Note on the Determinateness of Equilibrium', *Review of Economic Studies*, I, February.

Kaldor, N. (1966). 'Marginal Productivity and the Macro-Economic Theories of Distribution: Comment on Samuelson and Modigliani', *Review of Economic Studies*, XXXIII:4, October.

Kaldor, N. (1972). 'The Irrelevance of Equilibrium Economics', *Economic Journal*, LXXXII, December.

Kaldor, N. (1975). 'What is Wrong with Economic Theory?', *Quarterly Journal of Economics*, LXXXIX:3, August.

Kaldor, N. (1979). 'Equilibrium Theory and Growth Theory', in Michael J.

Boskin, ed., *Economics and Human Welfare: Essays in Honor of Tibor Scitovsky*, New York: Academic Press.

Kaldor, N. (1985). *Economics Without Equilibrium*, Armonk: M. E. Sharpe.

Kornai, J. (1986). *Contradictions and Dilemmas: Studies on the Socialist Economy and Society*, Cambridge: M.I.T. Press.

Kornai, J. (1990). *Vision and Reality, Market and State*, Budapest: Corvina.

Lange, O. (1936). 'On the Economic Theory of Socialism', *Review of Economic Studies*, 53-71 and 123-144.

Lange, O. (1987). 'The Economic Operation of a Socialist Economy', *Contributions to Political Economy*, 6.

Nuti, D. M. (1988). 'Perestroika: Transition from Central Planning to Market Socialism', *Economic Policy*, 8.

Ofer, G. (1987). 'Soviet Economic Growth: 1928-1985', *Journal of Economic Literature*, XXV, December

Pareto, V. (1971). *Manual of Political Economy*, New York: A. M. Kelley.

Samuelson, P. A. and Nordhaus, W. D. (1989). *Economics*, 13th ed., New York: McGraw Hill.

Sawyer, M. (1991). 'Analysing the Operation of Market Economies in the Spirit of Kaldor and Kalecki', in Michie, J. ed., *The Economics of Restructuring and Intervention*, Aldershot: Edward Elgar.

'The Soviet Union', *Financial Times*, March 12, 1990.

Sraffa, P. (1926). 'The Laws of Return under Competitive Conditions', *Economic Journal*, December.

Wicksell, K. (1934). *Lectures on Political Economy, Vol. I*, London: Routledge.

Young, A. (1928). 'Increasing Returns and Economic Progress', *Economic Journal*, December.

Yunker, J. A. (1988). 'On the Morality of Capitalism: In Light of the Market Socialist Alternative', *Forum for Social Economics*, XVII: 2, Spring.

Zaleski, E. (1971). *Planning for Economic Growth in the Soviet Union, 1918-1932*, Chapel Hill: University of North Carolina Press.

Zimbalist, A., Sherman, H. and Brown, S. (1989). *Comparing Economic Systems: A Political-Economic Approach*, New York: Academic Press.

3 Transitions from Centrally Planned to Market Economies

*Christian Gehrke and Mark Knell**

1 Introduction

It was argued in the second essay that the concept of Pareto-optimality is accepted either implicitly or explicitly in most of the literature on the reform of centrally planned economies. The case for reform based on this approach rests on the premise that imperfections inherent in central planning, which keep prices and quantities from adjusting to changes in demand, make it impossible for the planner to duplicate the tâtonnement process in Lange's (1936) sense. Consequently, there is Pareto-inefficient use of resources which appears as disequilibrium, shortage and/or unemployment of resources. To improve efficiency, therefore, it is proposed that these imperfections be removed by replacing the centrally planned economy with a market-oriented one.

Kornai (1980) explains Pareto-inefficiencies in centrally planned economies by introducing the notion of the soft budget constraint. A soft budget constraint is said to exist if the enterprise is a price-maker, can obtain external financing, or is able to negotiate taxes, grants and credit. The consequence of a soft budget constraint is that enterprises can avoid bankruptcy indefinitely. Moreover, because there is no punishment for departing from the plan, there is a tendency for managers to be over-ambitious which creates chronic excess demand and overinvestment at the macroeconomic level. This results in Pareto-inefficient allocation of resources which appears as shortages, widespread product deterioration, and sluggish growth. To improve efficiency, reforms must harden the budget constraint by introducing competitive markets, requiring internal financing and enforcing binding tax, credit and grant contracts.To explain the problem of chronic disequilibrium and shortage in centrally planned economies, therefore, Kornai simply makes small changes in the assumptions of the Walrasian approach to include 'Keynesian features'.[1] Economic reform, therefore, is still derived from the concept of the Paretian optimum.

The inappropriateness of using the Paretian optimum to compare economic systems was raised by Kalecki (1949) in a discussion of a paper by Lange on the realities of the socialist economy versus the theory of the socialist economy:

> The present planned or controlled economies are being compared to the capitalist economy... endowed with perfect equalization of marginal cost and prices, negligible unemployment, optimum distribution of resources, and so on and so forth. In fact, it was an apologistic myth of the capitalist economy and nothing of the sort has ever existed. Prices were never equal to marginal cost; unemployment was considerable, and so on. It is from this point of view that the problems of the present discussion should be considered.

Independently, but taking up similar problems, Adolph Lowe (1942, 1965) challenged the Walrasian-Paretian approach to economic analysis by questioning the validity of the theoretical premises on which the approach depends. He argued that the proposition, according to which the 'free market economy' generates Pareto-efficient outcomes, can only be derived from very strict structural and behavioural assumptions and that it requires substitutability and perfect mobility of resources. These premises, Lowe argued, cannot be sustained in view of the rigidities of modern industrial structures and the diversity of individual motivations, expectations and behaviours.

Lowe's criticism of the Walrasian-Paretian approach was complemented by his subsequent development of a teleological approach to economic analysis which he termed *instrumental analysis* (Lowe 1965, 1976, 1987). According to Lowe (1976, pp. 11-12), the object of instrumental analysis is to *'search for the economic means suitable for the attainment of any stipulated end'*. Instrumental analysis inverts the traditional approach 'by treating some of the knowns of traditional analysis as unknowns and, conversely, by treating the major unknowns of traditional analysis—the terminal states and processes—as known' (Lowe 1987, p. 172). In the instrumental approach, three sets of data must be known: (1) the initial state of the economic system; (2) the macro-goal or terminal state of the economic system (which can be specified either by stipulating numerical values for target variables or by stipulating qualitative interrelations among the target variables); and (3) certain laws, rules and empirical generalizations through which the suitability of means for the attainment of ends can be established. Given these data, Lowe (1987 p. 172) argues, the following unknowns can be determined: '(1) the *path* or the succession of macro-states of the system suitable to transform a given initial state into a stipulated terminal state; (2) *patterns of micro-behaviour* appropriate to keeping the system to the suitable path; (3) *micro-motivations* capable of generating suitable behaviour; and (4) *a state of the environment* including, possibly though not necessarily, political controls designed to stimulate suitable motivations'.

This essay has two objectives: (1) to show the suitability of Lowe's method of *instrumental analysis* to study transitions from centrally planned to market economies; and (2) to show that the methodology underlying the current proposals for restructuring the socialist economies is inadequate. To achieve these objectives, section 2 discusses the instrumental approach as a method for analysing the socialist economies in transition. Section 3 examines the initial conditions of the transition process, including problems caused by chronic disequilibrium and shortage. Section 4 discusses the importance of clearly specifying the stipulated goals and the corresponding means to achieve them. Section 5 deals with the sequencing and pace of the transition process in terms of both structural change and the problem of stabilization. Section 6 looks at the prospects for marketization and privatization. Finally, a conclusion summarizes the main aspects of an instrumental analysis of transitions from centrally planned to market economies.

2 The instrumental approach to economic analysis
The transformation of centrally planned economies to more market-oriented ones can be viewed as a traverse from one growth path to another. Lowe's instrumental-deductive method of analysis is well suited to the study of this transition. In Lowe's view, public controls are seen as the means by which democratically selected macro-goals are achieved and social, political and economic freedom is maintained. Instrumental analysis, therefore, formalizes the design of public controls to establish an 'environment' in which behaviours and motivations are consistent with the desired growth path or macro-goal. This ensures that a 'goal-adequate' transition path that optimizes the use of available technology can be established, subject to certain social, cultural and technical constraints. Thus, both public control and freedom are seen as complementary and as a necessary condition for transitions from centrally planned to market economies.

The reversal of the means-ends nexus creates a distinction between structural and behavioural components of an economic system which appears in Lowe as a separation of *structure analysis* from *motor* or *force analysis* respectively. *Structure analysis* is defined as the study of:

the configurations in which the elements of an economic system—inputs and outputs, employment and income, savings and investments, etc.—must be arranged if the transformation of the initial into the stipulated terminal state is to be achieved. These configurations have two aspects: one, physical or technical; the other, social. *Technical* relations are concerned with the manner in which resources can be combined; the sequence of stages of production through which natural resources are converted into finished output; the coordination of specific sectors of production to assure steady replacement; and, under conditions of growth, the expansion of material resources. *Social* relations, on the other hand, refer to the dominant type of decision making, centralized or decentralized; the order of ownership; and the ruling systems of communication and sanction, for example, based on personalized command or on the anonymous price mechanism. Both types of structural relations operate as constraints on the motion of the respective systems and as such determine the range of feasible *paths* toward the stipulated terminal state (Lowe 1976, p. 17).

The purpose of structural analysis is to determine an optimal succession of macro-states of the economic system that lead towards the stipulated macro-goals which comprise the terminal state. Its focus is on deriving goal-adequate structures and structural changes in the economic system, e.g. required changes in the sectoral allocation of inputs, or in the levels of certain macro-aggregates such as savings, investments, etc. The selection of a goal-adequate structural adjustment path has to take into account that the range of feasible paths is constrained by both technical and social relations.

The *technical structure* of production refers to feasible technological possibilities of adapting the economy's capital stock to the requirements of the desired terminal state. For Lowe, the existing capital stock is the main structural barrier to short-term adjustments in the path of growth. A change in the path of growth is generally connected to a change in technology which necessitates the liquidation of part of the old capital stock and the formation of a new capital stock. This involves both time and financing. As this process takes place, technological unemployment and sectoral imbalances will appear in the short period and will persist in the long period unless appropriate economic policies are adopted which lead to full employment of labour and capital.

Underlying the technical structure of production is a *receipt-expenditure structure* which relates aggregate monetary demand with aggregate monetary supply (Lowe 1976, p. 86). Embodying the principle of effective demand, the interdependence of the production-receipt-expenditure relationship defines the relationship between physical and monetary flows. However, physical relations are treated as conceptually different from monetary relations because 'the validity of these physical relations transcends the socio-political differences of economic systems' (Lowe 1976, p. 42). Likewise, monetary relations, such as those between wages and profits, are dependent upon the supporting social structure of the economic system.

The *social structure* refers to the institutional framework in which decision-making processes take place. The institutional framework consists of the following components: (1) the industrial organization (including market forms and labour organizations); (2) the financial intermediaries (including instruments of money, credit and capital markets); (3) the legal system (including property rights and other legal codes); (4) the social system (including the health care system, the educational system and the welfare system); and (5) the historical context (including cultural and ethical-religious traditions). The range of structural adjustment paths that are feasible from a technical point of view can be further constrained by the existing social relations, i.e. a goal-adequate structural adjustment path must be both technically and socially feasible.

The determination of the required motions of the structural elements that will transform the initial state into the stipulated terminal state is only preliminary to the analysis of behaviour. In order to set the economy at a goal-adequate traverse, patterns of micro-behaviour, motivations and the state of the environment (which includes, *inter alia*, monetary, fiscal, industrial and environmental policy instruments) should be studied. Lowe (1976, p. 17) defines *motor* or *force analysis* as the study of:

> the patterns of behavior and motivation that initiate and sustain the motion of the system along the structurally determined path. These patterns themselves are closely related to the prevailing social structure that defined the institutional framework within which economic activity is to operate. Force analysis has a special significance in market systems, whose goal-adequate performance depends on the interlocking of innumerable microdecisions and on the concordance of these microdecisions with the required macroprocesses.

Economic policies which intend to overcome unemployment and sectoral imbalances must, therefore, engender appropriate behavioural and motivational responses.

It should be kept in mind, however, that it is possible to calculate what is required to maintain a prevailing structure or to achieve a different one without making assumptions about motivations, expectations, or other behavioural responses. The instrumental approach implies a separation between structural and behavioural components. Indeed, if both the current and desired structures are known and the optimal structural adjustment path has been derived, the necessary behavioural responses, and hence institutional arrangements (such as incentive schemes) required to convert the one economic system into another can be derived.

At the level of analysis of structure and structural change, centrally planned socialist and capitalist market economies are basically the same (Lowe 1976, p. 168). Differences in motivations and behaviours are found in the social structure, not in the underlying technical structure. In both economies, the desired state is translated into goals and objectives that take into account the historical, institutional, administrative and financial constraints of the economy. If these constraints are not adequately taken into account and/or the environment is not goal-adequate, then the traverse will not be optimal. However, while traverse is generally defined in a given socio-economic system for mathematical simplicity, it is possible to transform part of the social structure in order to introduce a new range of feasible paths toward the stipulated terminal state. The transformation of centrally planned socialist economies into capitalist market economies is a good example of a traverse between socio-economic systems.

3 The initial conditions of the transition process

The reason for distinguishing between structural and behavioural attributes of the economy is that the difference between capitalism and socialism lies in the stimuli provided by the social structure and public controls. In the centrally planned socialist economy, behavioural and motivational patterns often result in chronic shortages of consumer and producer goods and lengthened construction periods of plant and equipment. Bottlenecks, sectoral labour shortages and underemployment of labour and capacity exist simultaneously. Because the shortage economy is a *sellers'* market, there is little information about the real quantities demanded, the quality of products, quality of services and delivery, which in turn creates little incentive for product and process innovation. The traverse from a centrally planned economy to a market-oriented one, therefore, starts from a particular kind of disequilibrium state and its corresponding behaviours. Moreover, because these behavioural and motivational patterns were not goal-adequate in the actually existing socialist economies of 1989 they will probably not be goal-adequate for the socialist economies in transition.

When embarking on a transition path, the existing physico-technical structure acts as a constraint on the achievable rate of growth. Because the centrally planned economy appears fully employed at the macro-level, as the economy moves on a path of economic growth it tends to encounter *physico-technical* bottlenecks that emerge during the process of restructuring the economic system (Gehrke and Hagemann 1990).[2] The effect of these bottlenecks, which include labour, capacity and material inputs, depends on whether the particular commodity or sector is *basic* or *non-basic* in Sraffa's (1960) terminology, or the extent to which *backward* or *forward linkages* exist in Hirshman's (1958) terminology. If a commodity is *basic*, i.e. is used either directly or indirectly in the production of all other goods, then shortages of this commodity will constrain the entire system unless substitution or importation of the good is possible. In other words, the maximum rate of growth, and hence the level of output, is constrained by the surplus generated by the basic good sector that can be used for accumulation. Similarly, the effects of a shortage of a particular sector can be traced through the forward linkages to all other sectors. In the Soviet Union, for example, bottlenecks were pervasive in many basic industries during 1990, especially in the fuel and energy industries.

The extent of physico-technical bottlenecks in an economy is also determined by the receipt-expenditure structure and the level of investment. If investment is above a technically feasible level, then there is overinvestment or excess effective demand in the Keynesian sense. When prices are inflexible and output is constrained by physico-technical bottlenecks, then overinvestment causes shortages in any or all of the sectors in the economy, and the construction period of fixed capital may lengthen depending on the intensity of shortages appearing in the producer good sectors. In the monetary sphere, shortages appear as repressed inflation and forced savings. For example, in 1989 imbalances in domestic markets were the worst since World War Two in Eastern Europe (UN 1990, p. 134).

Physico-technical bottlenecks are a result, therefore, of both overinvestment and the prevailing social and technical structures. Overinvestment and structural change, on the other hand, are caused by motivations and micro-behaviours engendered by economic policy and the social and economic structures. At least six causal explanations of this overinvestment behaviour in centrally planned economies have been offered: (1) a conscious policy of overinvestment and excess demand (Nuti 1986); (2) existing shortages and lengthened construction periods are self-reproducing (Nell, 1991; Kalecki 1986); (3) the tension between maximizing growth and maximizing consumption (Kalecki 1986); (4) a legal code which does not enforce contracts between the state and state-owned enterprises (Kornai 1980); (5) a principal-agent problem between managers and the state (Berliner 1988; Granick 1975); and (6) the lack of tautness or flexibility (Hunter 1961). All of these explanations can be seen as contributing to the chronic disequilibrium and shortages prevalent in centrally planned economies.

In the short period, it is possible to relax physico-technical bottlenecks in the centrally planned economy by either reducing investment so as to concentrate on the completion of certain projects or by importing goods in short supply. The first solution implies that credit constraints must be imposed by the central bank and the second solution requires relaxing international credit constraints. Prior to 1990, both solutions would have implied a recentralization in order to increase control over investment and the trade balance. Since 1990, the trend toward decentralization created the possibility of introducing new public controls such as monetary and strategic trade policies to relax physico-technical bottlenecks.

Because the centrally planned socialist economy is characterized by chronic shortages, excess demand and repressed inflation, different motivations and social relationships between enterprises, the state and manager, the state and worker, and buyer and seller, have become institutionalized and have engendered particular behavioural patterns which are not easy to change. The results are sluggish growth, a lack of incentive to innovate, and widespread product deterioration. A primary objective of institutional transformation and restructuring is to achieve a new macro-goal in which a higher rate of growth leads to a persistent improvement in living standards.

4 The envisioned terminal state
An important element in the transformation of centrally planned economies is the introduction of new market forms, new financial intermediaries, new ownership structures, etc. In short, a change in the social and institutional context, in which micro-behaviour is formed, is generally considered necessary to increase efficiency. Since Lowe only applied the instrumental approach to the analysis of traverse paths within a well-defined social context, an integration of a changing social structure into Lowe's instrumental approach is necessary for the application of this approach to the transition between economic systems.

Clearly, the role of change in the social structure and the establishment of new institutions cannot be considered as an end in itself because it does not define the desired terminal state or goal that is to be achieved; it is purely instrumental. Institutional change has to serve as a suitable means to the achievement of certain macroeconomic goals (such as the efficient utilization of available resources). An analysis of the transition, therefore, requires that the desired or envisioned terminal state of the economy must be specified and that institutional changes be viewed as *instrumental* to the achievement of clearly specified macro-goals.

The need for specifying the envisioned terminal state of the transition economies comes into sharp contrast with some prevailing views. Lipton and Sachs (1990a, p. 75) argue that these transition economies do not need to choose their desired social structure, but only certain institutions:

> Western Europe offers a wide array of alternative economic models from which to choose, but in practical terms there is little reason *yet* for the Eastern European countries to choose among the variants of Western European political economy. Before such choices have to be made, Eastern Europe should work hard to create the common core of market institutions found in all of Western Europe: private ownership protected by a commercial law, a corporate structure for industry, an independent financial system, and so forth.

It is true that the alternative models of market economies share a number of common institutional features, such as the existence of financial intermediaries and property rights, etc. Yet there are important differences not mentioned by Lipton and Sachs. While the institutional arrangements required for market-oriented *micro-behaviours* are broadly similar, the essential difference between, for example, a Swedish-type and an American-type market economy concerns the role and functioning of *public controls*.

As Gabrisch and Laski (1991, p. 16) pointed out:

> Macro-control is ultimately a question of government attempting with its economic and social policy instruments to prevent excessive inflation and unemployment and giving incentives for structural change—or leaving well alone. In the East European countries this is not a matter that may be left to be solved at a later stage: it is a problem of burning actuality, even in the period of transition. Already the selection of a particular policy of transition constitutes an anticipated decision about the desired market-economic model.

A policy of transition that sees the main goal as the rapid creation of certain market institutions is neither neutral in answering the question of what kind of market economy is ultimately to be adopted, nor is it conclusive. In such a policy proposal institutional changes appear not as the means to the realization of economic ends, but as desirable goals in themselves. By adopting an instrumental perspective to economic analysis it becomes clear that economic and social ends must first be specified as desired macro-goals and that the necessary institutional changes for their attainment must then be derived instrumentally.

Once it is realized that the crucial difference between alternative market-economic models lies in the significance placed upon macro-controls, the non-neutrality of the Lipton and Sachs proposal becomes immediately apparent. For if the desired form of market economy is one that combines micro-autonomy with public controls, comprehensive steps towards establishing the necessary institutional arrangements for such a controlled market system should be made at an early stage of the transformation process. Moreover, the transformation process itself should be guided by governmental macroeconomic policy objectives. A similar view has been expressed in a United Nations (1990, p. 155) document:

> ...rectifying current macro-economic imbalances should be the objective of putting in place proper monetary and fiscal policies, including the institutional and instrumental infrastructure through which such policies can be implemented in an orderly way. Inasmuch as these mechanisms in planned economies are underdeveloped, it will be necessary during the transition to experiment with new policies and their institutions and instruments in order to fine-tune the macro-economics of the transition and eventually of the market-oriented economy.

Most proposals for reform, including Blanchard et. al. (1991), and Lipton and Sachs (1990a), give priority to stabilization and privatization at the start of the transformation programme. However, while it is acknowledged that a totally free economy is 'neither socially acceptable nor economically desirable' (Blanchard et al. 1991, p. xvi), placing priority on stabilization and privatization over restructuring the economy implicitly neglects the need to specify the desired terminal state. By neglecting the technical and social structures of the economy, their proposals create institutions and macro-controls which may lead to a socially undesirable end state. Establishing these institutions before knowing where the traverse is heading also handicaps the establishment of the necessary institutional arrangements for the implementation of macro-controls in Lowe's sense.

Blanchard et al. (1991) and Lipton and Sachs (1990a; 1990b) do not deal directly with the longer-term macro-goal of economic and social development. These goals are generally subsumed into a blueprint of a 'free market' in which there is:

> unhampered entry, exit, and fair competition in the market. The notion of a free economy also implies a certain configuration of property rights and a certain institutional and political structure. The system promotes the free establishment and preservation of private property and encourages the private sector to produce the great bulk of output. It is a system that encourages individual initiative and entrepreneurship, liberates this initiative from excessive state intervention, and protects it by the rule of law (Kornai 1990, pp. 22-23).

Indeed, if the macro-goals are a higher growth rate, structural change, better utilization of labour and capital and/or higher standard of living, then a goal-adequate environment supported by the appropriate public controls must be put into place. It is presumed that there are many desirable aspects of social development that the economies in transition may want to retain, for example, a commitment to the social system. It is presumed also that as well as the various changes associated with marketization and privatization, certain supportive or reinforcing institutional changes will be required. These include the various educational and behaviour-modifying institutions that enable ordinary people to adapt to and cope with the new socio-economic system. Once thinking broadens and moves away from the simple Walrasian-Paretian framework, the immensity of the changes that are needed for acceptable self-generated economic development becomes apparent.

5 The political economy of the transition path

Once the desired terminal state has been specified, the instrumental approach requires that a structural path of adjustment should be defined in terms of a sequence of macro-states. In the current debates on reform in the socialist economies, however, one of the most controversial issues is the sequencing of introducing institutional changes. Because the magnitude of the change from a centrally planned economy to a market-oriented one is so large, it is generally argued that the social structure has to be reformed in stages. Taking a similar position to Kornai (1990), a United Nations (1991b) document suggests a four-stage sequence to: (1) eliminate chronic imbalances from the past and create clear property rights; (2) create public controls for the maintenance of macroeconomic stability; (3) introduce a regulatory environment, liberalize prices, encourage competitive behaviour and create public controls for an industrial policy; and (4) divest most state-owned enterprises. Because price liberalization may intensify inflation and shortage according to Kornai (1990, pp. 146-148), institutions, including property rights and financial intermediaries should be introduced to harden the budget constraint. Only when the budget constraint is hardened, can the market be expected to function in an optimal way.

What is significant about the proposal suggested by the United Nations (1991b, p. 125) is that first priority should be given to the creation of a 'clear set of rules for the distribution of economic returns from property' which creates incentives and motivations 'for property owners to put their assets to the most productive use'. In this sense, property rights are a public control 'guaranteeing private property' irrespective of whether it is owned by an individual, a group of individuals or an institution, including the state. Property rights are an instrument by which desired motivations can be created to achieve certain macro-goals.

The proposal by Lipton and Sachs, and strongly favoured by the IMF, suggests that marketization and privatization should take priority over structural change in the sequencing of market-oriented reform. On the surface, this proposal appears to be similar to the UN proposal. This proposal has three stages: (1) eliminate excess demand; (2) liberalize prices, demonopolize industry and implement austerity programmes; and (3) privatize. However, it appears that the sequence is simultaneous when they argue that:

> The transition process is a seamless web. Structural reforms cannot work without a working price system; a working price system cannot be put into place without ending excess demand and creating a convertible currency; and a credit squeeze and tight macroeconomic policy cannot be sustained unless prices are realistic, so that there is a rational basis for deciding which firms should be allowed to close. At the same time, for real structural adjustment to take place under the pressures of tight demand, the macroeconomic shock must be accompanied by other measures, including selling off state assets, freeing up the private sector, establishing procedures for bankruptcy, preparing a social safety net, and undertaking tax reform. Clearly, the reform process must be comprehensive (Lipton and Sachs 1990a, p. 99).

Thus, Lipton and Sachs argue that marketization and privatization should be simultaneous and rapid in order to create proper motivations and incentives to support the market economy. The result is a sequence which appears to equate privatization to the creation of clear property rights, and is therefore required before public controls are put into place.

These divergent strategies simply reflect the fact that there exists a range of theoretically possible transition paths. To select an optimal path, it is necessary to have a well-defined terminal state and clearly specified macro-goals, given the technical and social relations prevalent in the economies under consideration. What has to be sequenced, then, is the structurally required succession of macro-states during the transformation process that lead towards this state. It is the lack of properly specified macro-goals that is responsible for the ambiguity of the various proposals for the reform process.

It is also important to take into account the speed of the transition strategy. The Lipton and Sachs proposal, known as the *shock therapy* approach, argues that a more rapid transition is necessary because most of these countries are highly unstable politically (and there is the possibility that both prolonged shortages and hyper-inflation may intensify this condition). They argue that the more rapid the liberalization of the economy, the earlier will the fruits of the reform become visible, and that this will have a stabilizing effect on the political situation. Indeed, it is argued by Lipton and Sachs (1990b, p. 297) that privatization should be 'rapid, efficient and equitable' because:

> the current pattern of ownership in Eastern Europe is itself prone to massive inefficiencies. The potential costs of overly rapid privatization must be traded off with the high cost of maintaining the present system in which state-owned enterprises lack clear incentives (or actually have perverse incentives)... [However], the real risk in Eastern Europe is not that the privatization process will be less than optimal, but that it will be paralyzed entirely.

The speed of the transition, however, is constrained by the technical and social structures. Problems in the technical structure have become immediately apparent as the socialist economy leaves the protection of the CMEA. As pointed out by McKinnon (1991), if a socialist economy is opened to the world markets and domestic costs are above world market prices in certain sectors, then bankruptcy will follow in these sectors unless costs are reduced substantially.[3] Because the problem is found in the structure of production, a currency devaluation will not be sufficient to bring about a positive profit rate for the industry. This implies that an innovation must be organizational because it takes several years for capital construction and subsequent learning processes to reduce costs significantly. The only feasible solution, therefore, is to implement industrial and strategic trade policies, which in turn, require time and planning.

A rapid transition may also create large-scale macroeconomic instabilities because expectations are not met. This could then create political instability. There is reason to expect that the shock therapy ap-

proach will create considerable economic and political instability because it does not properly take into consideration that the adaptation
of micro-behaviours to the abrupt change in the social context takes
time. It does not realize that:

> Economic behavior takes place in a definite social context (by which we do
> *not* mean simply the 'market'). This means that the agent must know how to
> perform all the ordinary social routines, must have learned to speak the lan-
> guage, to recognize the relevant stimuli, and to act as expected in his normal
> roles. To say that economic behavior takes place in a social context is to imply
> that a social context exists in which such behavior is possible. The agents have
> been trained, are currently being supported and their roles are tied together in
> a network of duties, expectations and mutual interdependencies (Nell 1984, p.
> 139).

In the Eastern European economies in transition, a well-defined social
context is unlikely to exist. Consequently, the learning capacity of the
microeconomic actors becomes one of the most important factors in determining the macroeconomic outcomes of the transformation programme. As Wood (1990) recently remarked:

> It is necessary to distinguish between nominal reform, meaning official policy
> initiatives, and real reform, meaning changes in how the economy actually
> works. Nominal reform can contribute to real reform (price decontrol being
> an example), but does not do so if it outstrips microeconomic learning capac-
> ity. In other words, the real pace of reform may be limited by how rapidly
> people and institutions can learn to play new economic roles.

The selection of an appropriate structural adjustment path would
have to take into consideration that the range of feasible transition
paths is constrained by the prevailing social structure. This means that
the proposed sequence of macro-states that leads from the initial to the
terminal state must be compatible with the achievable changes in the
patterns of micro-behaviour that result from reshaping the social structure. Therefore, the learning abilities of individuals and their ability to
adapt themselves to the changing social environment, can constrain the
range of feasible transition paths. Hence, a more rapid adjustment path
may turn out to be unfeasible because the necessary changes in micro-
behaviour do not materialize quickly. The result may be both economic
and political chaos.

As the economy is subjected to a transformation programme, institutions and hence motivations change, creating stabilization problems in
the underlying receipts-expenditure structure. Conceptually, the receipts-expenditure structure and the social structure are different.

Consequently, stabilization policies should be distinguished from policies aimed at changing social institutions. In Lowe's approach, however, the macro-goals of the transformation programme are data, and both institutional changes and stabilization programmes are instrumental in achieving these goals. While it is important to distinguish between institutional transformation and stabilization programmes conceptually, it is also important to see the interdependence among them.

This relationship between institutional transformation and stabilization programmes is found in all of the socialist economies in transition. It is best illustrated in Poland, where the shock treatment approach was adopted. Shortly before the end of the last communist government, prices of foodstuffs and some other commodities were allowed to fluctuate according to market conditions (Kowalik 1991, p. 259). This resulted in hyper-inflation during the last half of 1989 because of pervasive shortages and the monopolistic nature of the industrial structure. As a consequence, the Solidarity government was left with only two options: (1) recentralize to control prices and credit, and balance the budget; and (2) introduce a macroeconomic austerity programme to reduce inflation, increase the interest rate and balance the budget. Because the first option was politically unfeasible, a stabilization programme, known as the Balcerowicz plan, was implemented on January 1, 1990. Among other measures, the stabilization programme imposed punitive wage controls, austere fiscal and monetary policies and comprehensive price liberalization. However, the stabilization programme was:

> not only a fight for internal and external equilibrium of the economy, but also for the creation of a different economic mechanism. It is accompanied by [the] construction of appropriate institutional surroundings for the market and for the use, especially in the fiscal and monetary areas, of ever more numerous policy instruments typical of the market economy (Kolodko 1991, p. 4).

While the Balcerowicz plan shifted the economy from a *sellers'* market to a *buyers'* market, thus reducing or eliminating shortages in many sectors, the plan led to unintended macroeconomic consequences. Expecting only a 5 per cent decline in industrial output and a 2 per cent unemployment rate, the programme resulted in a 23.3 per cent reduction in industrial output and an unemployment rate of 6.1 per cent (see table 3.1; Kolodko 1991). Because initial unemployment was negligible, this implies that labour productivity fell by more than 17 per cent. The decline in industrial output was also coupled by a 27.3 per cent decline in real wages during the same period (UN 1991b). These problems were further exacerbated by an inflation rate of almost 585 per cent, five times the expected rate. Although it could be argued that the problem is caused by a lag in the supply response by the business sector, i.e. there were no bankruptcies and the degree of monopoly changed very little, it is mostly caused by policies based on the automatic equilibrating mechanism underlying the concept of the Paretian optimum. If macroeconomic instabilities are inherent in the economy, as suggested by Kalecki, Keynes and Harrod, then demand management and industrial policies are better suited to control instabilities and induce restructuring of the economy. If these macroeconomic instabilities are not addressed within the proper theoretical framework, then institutional changes and stabilization policies will no longer be instrumental in achieving the desired macro-goals as they will slow down the overall long-run growth rate, and hence the path of economic growth.

Table 3.1: Basic economic indicators, 1990 (percentage change).

	Output	Inflation	Unemployment[a]
Czechoslovakia	-3.7	10.1	1.0
German Democratic Republic	-28.1	-2.5	7.3
Hungary	-4.5	28.5	1.7
Poland	-23.3	584.7	6.1
Yugoslavia	-10.3	588.0	13.2

Source: UN, 1991b.
[a]Unemployment rate, December 1990.

Yugoslavia adopted similar measures to Poland in the first half of 1990 to freeze wages, tighten credit, especially to finance the budget deficit, and to liberalize about 90 per cent of the prices of all goods and services. Although institutional change took place, there were considerable unintended consequences. In 1990, the consumer prices rose by 588 per cent as opposed to the target of 13 per cent. During this same period, industrial output fell by 10.3 per cent and the unemployment rate was 13.2 per cent.

While Poland and Yugoslavia have been trying to impose changes to turn themselves into Western-like market economies, East Germany inherited the social structure of the Federal Republic of Germany through an economic and monetary union on July 1, 1990 and a complete political union on October 3, 1990. Completely dominated by the western German markets, industrial output fell by 28.1 per cent in 1990 and unemployment was 7.3 per cent at the end of 1990, not including part-time workers. However, the rate of inflation fell by 2.5 per cent. Perhaps the most intensive shock treatment in Eastern Europe, the cost to western Germany to maintain and transform the social structure is expected to be very high.

Hungary and Czechoslovakia opted for the *gradual approach* and have focused on privatization, demonopolization, industrial restructuring and the introduction of new financial intermediaries, and treat the problem of marketization as secondary. In this approach the reform of institutions, especially financial intermediaries and the legal framework to support these intermediaries, is seen as a necessary precondition of price liberalization. Instead of introducing an austerity programme, Hungary implemented an industrial policy which encourages exports and the creation of private enterprises. The results of the gradual approach are compared to the results of the shock treatment approach in terms of the percentage change in industrial output, rate of inflation and the unemployment rate in table 3.1.

6 The prospect of reform

The prospect of reform is conditioned on whether the structural path of adjustment is optimal. Finding this path is complicated by stabilization problems caused by the ingrained motivations and behaviours engendered by the centrally planned economy and inappropriate macroeconomic policies.[4] The achievement of the macro-goals are further frustrated by policies of marketization and privatization which have led to a fall in output and labour productivity and a rise in unemployment.

In the current debates on the restructuring of socialist economies, it is generally accepted that either a socialist market economy or a capitalist participatory economy is not a viable alternative. In the broad sense, a socialist market economy is one in which there is decentralized decision-making and socialized ownership. A participatory economy is one in which democratically controlled workers' and consumers' councils facilitate growth, economic democracy and justice, and various forms of property ownership are allowed to coexist (Albert and Hahnel 1991). At the beginning of the reform process in Eastern Europe, market socialism was seen by many reformers as a possible alternative (e.g. Brus 1972; Kowalik 1989). However, after the collapse of the centrally planned economies in 1989, the target shifted towards the adoption of a Western type (non-socialist) market economy. Yet, the question of what particular kind of non-socialist economy is finally to be adopted as the desired one is frequently considered as being of minor importance.

The primary objective of most reform proposals is a rapid marketization and privatization of the centrally planned economies. However, because of stabilization problems, few enterprises were privatized in Poland during 1990, and plans to distribute shares of shareholding companies to the adult population have encountered difficulties. By contrast, over 120,000 private enterprises have been created in Hungary, contributing almost half of GDP. There have been relatively unsuccessful attempts to privatize state enterprises, however, but there is a new attempt to privatize approximately 10,000 small service-based enterprises and 20 relatively healthy, large state-owned enterprises in 1991 (UN 1991a).

The inability to privatize quickly has to do with to two fundamental problems: (1) who decides to privatize; and (2) how the value of the privatized enterprises is to be established. These problems are compounded by the question of whether privatization decisions are driven by political needs or by economic needs. In Hungary, for example, the first attempt to privatize was aborted because the nomenklatura controlled the sale and purchase of state assets, leading to a centralization of capital in the hands of the nomenklatura.

It is also not clear whether there is a broad political and social consensus in Poland for the transition to a market economy. A survey taken in mid 1990 suggests that 75 per cent of Polish workers do not want privatization (Kowalik 1991). Lipton and Sachs (1990b, pp. 298-299) are concerned about this sentiment when they argue for rapid privatization:

> Workers' desires to block privatization may also increase rapidly in the near future if, as expected, unemployment rates rise sharply in Eastern Europe. ...Even if workers in a particular enterprise do not actually block privatization, they may attempt to bargain with the government, demanding for example a cut in the enterprise's debts or various guarantees on employment levels, as their 'price' for letting the privatization go forward. ...In Poland, an increasingly powerful coalition of interests that favor worker management is already organizing itself against widespread privatization.

Neglecting workers' desires, however, negates the need for setting macro-goals in the democratic process. Moreover, the establishment of property rights can overcome 'the massive inefficiencies' and 'perverse incentives', without resorting to the rapid, if not desperate, privatization programme suggested by Lipton and Sachs. Labour would not hesitate to support the establishment of property rights, but they would not support a system which does not allow labour to collectivize or allows the nomenklatura to gain special privileges.

There also appears to be no broad political and social consensus in favour of creating a market economy in other Eastern European countries. In Yugoslavia, political and economic instabilities threaten the future of the economy as well as the viability of the post-World War II federation. While the general lack of consensus is probably due to the lack of information and knowledge of how a market economy works, there are many historical similarities. In the United States at the beginning of the 19th century, for example, there was widespread antipathy to capitalist industrialization. The evidence of the dark satanic mills despoiling England's environment led many to oppose Alexander Hamilton's proposals supporting manufacturing as a way of diversifying the American economy.

7 A return to fundamentals
The main problem in dealing with the transformation of centrally planned to market economies is to establish the ends-means relationship properly. A terminal state with an efficient utilization of resources and a higher rate of growth is the objective of the socialist economies in transition, not necessarily the marketization and privatization of the economy. To achieve this goal, changes in the institutional structure are considered necessary to induce motivations and microeconomic behaviours compatible with the desired goals. The terminal state, however, has to be defined in terms of clearly specified macroeconomic goals and the introduction of institutional changes has to be instrumental to their achievement. As new institutions are being introduced, the former social context in which microeconomic behaviours were formed is disturbed in a profound way. The introduction of new institutions in itself is not sufficient to achieve the desired terminal state. Macroeconomic instability is likely to result from the inability of micro-units (or agents) to adapt quickly to the new, not yet established, social context.The problem remains, however, whether the envisioned institutional structure creates the necessary motivations to move the economy to the desired terminal state.

The achievement of the desired market economy requires appropriate policies. The great irony, as pointed out by Nell, is that centrally planned economies did not use demand management policies. Even as these economies become increasingly dominated by demand constraints, supply-side policies inspired by 'New Classical Economics' are being suggested by the IMF and many economists. There has been little discussion about Keynesian fiscal and monetary policies coupled with an industrial policy to stimulate innovation and entrepreneurship. In Lowe's instrumental perspective, democratically controlled economic planning (or industrial policy) is complementary to the market and should not be abandoned. Indeed, planning is an instrument of stabilization which supports emancipation and freedom. The purpose of planning, therefore, is to engender motivations, expectations and behaviours suited to the stated macro-goals. In the current transition from centrally planned to market economies the macro-goals are clear while the means and motivations are not.

Notes

*   We would like to thank Andreas Blaho, Robert Dernberger Tadeusz Kowalik, Edward Nell, Christine Rider and Wenyan Yang for their helpful comments. Any errors in the paper remain the fault of the authors.
1. Kornai's approach is a variant of the non-Walrasian approach which can be traced to Leijonhufvud's argument that Keynesian conclusions can be derived from the Walrasian system if the tatonnement process is assumed away (Knell 1988). It should be noted, however, that Kornai made an important distinction between systemic differences in the structural relationships of centrally planned economies and market-oriented ones. Although Kornai's approach is based on restrictive micro-behavioural assumptions in the ideal system, a wide range of micro-behaviours are allowed for in his distinction between demand-constrained and resource-constrained systems.
2. The significance of physico-technical bottlenecks during the process of restructuring the economic system is shown in Lowe's tripartite production schema (see Lowe 1976). The tripartite system places commodities into three categories: (1) the production of machines used for the production of machines; (2) the production of machines used for the production of consumer goods; and (3) the production of consumer goods. Hence, machines produced in sector 1 are *basic* in that they are used directly in sectors 1 and 2 and indirectly in sector 3. Because sector 1 is *basic*, the production of machines is a bottleneck which any process of accelerated growth must overcome.
3. Because the system requires that a positive profit rate must exist for the system to be viable, domestic prices must be compatible with international prices. When a closed economy is opened, differential profit rates will exist as domestic prices adjust to world prices. If costs are above the world market price in any sector, then the rate of profit will be negative in this sector.
4. It should be noted that inappropriate macroeconomic policies are a manifestation of the inability of theory to explain reality. As noted by Taylor (1988), sometimes inappropriate policies will put the economy on a path toward the desired goal, but appropriate policies will put the economy on the most direct or optimal path. It is often the case, however, that inappropriate policies may put the economy on a path away from the desired goals.

References

Albert, M. and Hahnel, R. (1991). *The Political Economy of Participatory Economics*, Princeton: Princeton University Press.

Berliner, J. (1988). *Soviet Industry: From Stalin to Gorbachev*, Ithaca: Cornell University Press.

Blanchard, O., Dornbusch, R., Krugman, P., Layard, R., and Summers, L. (1991). *Reform in Eastern Europe*, Cambridge: M.I.T. University Press.

Brus, W. (1972). *The Market in a Socialist Economy*, London: Routledge and Kegan Paul.

Brus, W. and Laski, K. (1990). *From Marx to the Market*, New York: Oxford.

Gabrisch, H. and Laski, K. (1991). 'Transition from the Command to a Market Economy', in P. Havlik, ed., *Dismantling the Command Economy in Eastern Europe*, Boulder: Westview.

Gehrke, C. and Hagemann, H. (1990). *Efficient Traverses and Bottlenecks: A Structural Approach*, Research Memorandum #9003, Department of Economics, University of Graz.

Granick, D. (1975). *Enterprise Guidance in Eastern Europe*, Princeton: Princeton University Press.

Hirshman, A. (1958). *The Strategy of Economic Development*, New Haven: Yale University Press.

Hunter, H. (1961). 'Optimal Tautness in Development Planning', *Economic Development and Cultural Change*, 561-72.

Kalecki, M. (1949). 'Discussion on the Paper of Oscar Lange', *Econometrica*, 176-177.

Kalecki, M. (1986). *Selected Essays on Economic Planning*, Jan Toporowski (ed.), Cambridge: Cambridge University Press.

Knell, M. (1988). 'The Economics of Shortage and the Socialist Enterprise: A Criticism of the Walrasian and non-Walrasian Approach', *Review of Radical Political Economics*, 143-148.

Kolodko, G. (1991). 'Inflation Stabilization in Poland. A Year After', in *Polish Economy in Transition*, Warsaw.

Kornai, J. (1980). *The Economics of Shortage*, Amsterdam: North Holland.

Kornai, J. (1990). *The Road to a Free Economy, Shifting from a Socialist System: The Example of Hungary*, New York: Norton.

Kowalik, T. (1989). 'On Crucial Reform of Real Socialism', in Hubert Gabrisch, ed., *Economic Reforms in Eastern Europe and the Soviet Union*, Boulder: Westview.

Kowalik, T. (1991). 'Marketization and Privatization: The Polish Case', *The Socialist Register 1991*, London: Merlin.

Lange, O. (1936). 'On the Economic Theory of Socialism', *Review of Economic Studies*, IV, 53-71 and 123-144.

Lipton, D. and Sachs, J. (1990a). 'Creating a Market Economy in Eastern Europe: The Case of Poland', *Brookings Papers on Economic Activity*.

Lipton, D. and Sachs, J. (1990b). 'Privatization in Eastern Europe: The Case of Poland', *Brookings Papers on Economic Activity*.

Lowe, A. (1942). 'A Reconsideration of the Law of Supply and Demand', *Social Research*, 431-57.

Lowe, A. (1965). *On Economic Knowledge: Toward a Science of Political Economics*, White Plains: M. E. Sharpe. Second edition, 1977.

Lowe, A. (1976). *The Path of Economic Growth*, Cambridge: Cambridge University Press.

Lowe, A. (1987). *Essays in Political Economics: Public Control in a Democratic Society*, New York: New York University Press.

McKinnon, R. (1991). *The Order of Economic Liberalisation: Financial Control in the Transition to a Market Economy*, Baltimore: Johns Hopkins University Press.

Nell, E. (1984). 'Structure and Behavior in Classical and Neoclassical Theory', *Eastern Economic Journal*, 139-155.

Nell, E. (1991). 'Capitalism, Socialism and Effective Demand', in E. J. Nell and W. Semmler, *Nicholas Kaldor and Mainstream Economics*, New York: St.

Martin's.

Nuti, D. (1986). 'Systemic Aspects of Employment and Investment in Soviet Type Economies' in D. Lane, ed., *Labour and Employment in the USSR*, New York: New York University Press.

Sraffa, P. (1960). *The Production of Commodities by Means of Commodities*, Cambridge University Press.

Taylor, L. (1988). *Varieties of Stabilization Experience*, Oxford: Oxford University Press.

United Nations (1990). *World Economic Survey 1990*, New York.

United Nations (1991a). *World Economic Survey 1991*, New York.

United Nations (1991b). *Economic Survey of Europe in 1990-1991*, Geneva.

Wood, A. (1990). 'China's Economic Reform: Nominal Pause, but a Degree of Real Progress', *Financial Times*, October 4.

4 Michal Kalecki and Early Attempts to Reform the Polish Economy

Tadeusz Kowalik

This essay is devoted mainly to the economic reforms and economic programme introduced in Poland in 1956 to 1958 and to the part Kalecki played in drawing them up. International aspects of the reforms will not be discussed for reasons of space, but it should be kept in mind that the Soviet Union established the limits for what could take place. It should also be kept in mind that the language of the time was less a medium of communication than a means to conceal the true thoughts of the speaker. During the course of this discussion, the essay will also challenge some of the views concerning Kalecki's role in the reforms.

1 Towards a theory of growth

Prior to his return to Poland in February 1952, Kalecki spent over 16 years abroad: His travels took him to Stockholm in 1935 on a Rockefeller grant; to Cambridge University in 1937 as a visiting scholar; to the Oxford Institute of Economics and Statistics as a researcher in 1939; and to the United Nations in 1946. During this time Kalecki wrote very little on the social organization and working of a socialist economy, preferring to write about capitalism. What is known is that during the Second World War Kalecki had links to the non-communist-socialist left through the Socialist Clarity Group and had, through this medium, co-authored an essay on centrally planned economies.

It should be noted that because it was co-authored by many people, there is a question about the degree of Kalecki's (1986) authorship of *The Essentials for a Democratic Planning*. It is very unlikely that his lecture differed considerably from the text written by the Group. Undoubtedly, Kalecki tried to persuade his audience that a planned economy and the democratic supervision of planners was a good thing, and that only a planned economy could guarantee full employment. At the same time, however, his emphasis on the difficulties of centrally planned economies rather than the advantages of them may have been his most important contribution, given that the audience was made up

65

primarily of far-left anti-Fabian socialists. It is unlikely, therefore, that Kalecki was the originator of the idea that simultaneous grass roots and top level revolutions were necessary. Moreover, it is also doubtful that Kalecki would have said:

> the administrative measures from above and the workers from below would thus interact with a cumulative effect, sustaining the impetus of the whole planning movement, and bringing about, in fact, a continuing social revolution... The important thing, however, is that labour should not be afraid of the consequences to the social revolution within industry, but should make itself master of the situation, not by trying to damp down the mood of the workers, as did the Popular Front in France, but by directing it against the opponents of democratic planning.

Thus one can argue that the *Workers' Councils and Central Planning* published in 1956 was the first statement by Kalecki on the essentials of a socialist economy.

Kalecki's contributions to the theory of socialism appeared after his return in 1955 to Poland (to become adviser to Deputy Premier, and architect of the six year plan of 1950-55, Hilary Minc). In September 1955, Kalecki delivered a lecture titled *Dynamics of Investment and National Product in a Socialist Economy*, which was essentially technical, neglecting institutional and social questions. Although this lecture was critical of the official doctrine favouring the production of capital goods over the production of consumption goods as a means to increase the growth rate, it was largely ignored. An expanded version presented to the Second Congress of Economists in June 1956, however, generated considerably more interest because of a highly charged public debate over the industrialization model which generated interest in the relationship between investment and national income (Kalecki 1986).

Interest in the lecture, however, was not because of the theoretical ideas it contained, but the rigorous logic free from ideology. Many of the young participants in the Congress found the restoration of the language of scientific inquiry, precise reasoning free of all ideology a refreshing novelty. The Second Congress was a soul-searching event with considerable criticism, much of which was directed toward the government and top Warsaw economists. Kalecki delivered the lecture, however, as if he did not notice these disputes, continuing to analyse basic economic laws the way a mathematician resolves problems. Even Kalecki's (1956, p. 70) conclusion was rigorous:

No general rule is available to describe the dynamics of investment and national product. The decision on whether investment should grow as fast as or faster than national product depends on such factors as the availability of labour reserves, technical progress and on whether the possibly higher consumption figure is to be achieved in the near future or later.

In retrospect, it is now easy to see that Kalecki's methodology was biased. It is also noticeable that this article and the book developed from it, *Introduction to the Theory of Growth in a Socialist Economy,* (Kalecki 1972) neglect the social aspects of development. Yet this was how economic theory was 'secularized' in Poland, paving the way for reasoned thinking instead of the prevailing economiums and condemnations. Had he continued to confine himself to that kind of purely quantitative analysis, he would have found himself out of step with most economists as well as with the general public. However, a short time later, Kalecki was drawn into socio-political problems by the spontaneous grass-roots movement, the movement of workers' councils in factories.

2 Self-management and planning

The most significant and direct political consequence of the events which followed the June 1956 workers' revolt in Poznan was the initiation of the movement of workers' councils. For the first time in Poland a new social force, which gained momentum after the revolt and affected more than half of industrial establishments, entered the political stage as an organized movement guided by the idea of participation in management and in sharing responsibility.[1]

Although economists played a role in organizing the workers' councils, with few exceptions they cannot be credited with actually initiating the concept. Indeed, most economists did not look closely at the workers' councils until after a Commission, headed by Deputy Premier Piotr Jaroszewicz, was appointed in September 1956 by the Prime Minister to 'assist the workforce in developing initiatives in enterprise management'. The Commission was an interesting attempt to bring together theorists and practitioners. To the first group belonged: W. Brus, Head of the Economic Research Center of the State Commission for Economic Planning, E. Lipinski, president of the Polish Economic Society and M. Kalecki. A second group, which was substantially larger, included several ministers and deputy ministers of economic departments, eight enterprise directors, two union representatives, party functionaries and a journalist. Except for Kalecki, all Commission members were party members.

What the authorities wanted to achieve by appointing the Commission is not clear. The composition and name of the Commission suggests that the administration wished to contain the growing self-management movement. Perhaps this signalled also a desire to set up a surrogate of the Economic Council, which the Congress of Economists had demanded. However, the Commission included several individuals whose aim was to decentralize economic management and introduce workers' self-management.

Rapid changes in the political situation, mainly due to the spontaneous emergence of workers' councils in hundreds of enterprises, and Gomulka's triumphant reinstatement, eclipsed the significance of the Commission's original intentions. It helped the councils, and in a matter of weeks prepared three pieces of legislation which, as would be seen later, were the only significant breach ever in the planning and management system, before the collapse of communism. These were:

1. Government regulation 704 (November 10, 1956) granted enterprises the power to decide what products to manufacture, to make minor investments, to acquire the materials freely, to organize work and to set their own employment and wage ceilings. The total number of centrally-determined indicators (quotas) which were mandatory for enterprises was reduced from several scores to just eight.
2. The law of November 19, 1956 on the Workforce Fund authorized enterprises to set aside part of their retained profits for incorporation in the wage fund.
3. The Law on Workers' Councils of November 19, 1956 authorized these councils 'to manage, on behalf of the workforce, the enterprise which is owned by all the people'. This law was a unique law not found in the Soviet bloc.

These three laws were drafted before Gomulka's return at the October plenary session of the Polish United Workers' Party. The reason why these laws were easily approved barely one month later was more a reflection of the enthusiasm in factories and among intellectuals for radical change rather than being evidence of Gomulka's own intentions. But they did help spread the myth of his alleged reformist attitude and made him a symbol of 'the Polish October'.

Gomulka was highly suspicious of the self-management movement and the idea of granting enterprises greater autonomy. At the plenary session, he was strangely reticent on that point: 'Leading bodies in the economic administration, political organizations and state agencies must do their best to assist the workers' initiative in order to introduce, where possible, a certain generalization of the proposed forms. But there is no need to hurry when it comes to doing anything on a larger scale' (Gomulka 1956, p. 20). Consequently, Gomulka treated the movement as an experiment, for 'each new mechanism must be tested for the defects and flaws it usually has. No factory will turn out a new machine without first building and testing a prototype'. Moreover, Gomulka proposed to have those 'prototypes' tested first in the coal mining industry, which was perhaps the least suited for this kind of experiment.

Kalecki's article on *Workers' Councils and Central Planning* may be seen as the theoretical and prognostic recapitulation of work with the commission. Next to Brus and Jakubowicz, who were among the most ardent advocates of the idea of self-management in Poland, Kalecki played the most prominent part in the Commission. The same can be said about two of Kalecki's minor contributions—Kalecki's commentary to a French translation of the law on workers councils, and his article called *Models Are Not That Important*.

In these contributions, Kalecki voiced his belief that the marriage of workers' councils in enterprises with central planning would form a fortunate union. In his view, these two elements of the model were 'indispensable for quick economic development which, however, would be free of the distortions of the preceding period'. His greatest hope was that workers' councils would be able to prevent abuses as far as work conditions were concerned, to see that workers received overtime pay, to 'have a say in preventing overgrown bureaucratization and centralization of the national economy' and in mobilizing worker initiative to an extent central planning could never do. Indeed, Kalecki was certain that the union of workers' councils with central planning was potentially confrontational, whereby one partner seeks to out-smart the other. Kalecki (1982) points out:

> One should not be deluded into thinking that such arrangements are free from inconsistencies and easy to operate. Undoubtedly, there will always be a tendency in them to reduce the prerogative of the workers' councils in favour of greater centralization, as well as a tendency for workers' councils to weakening the position of central planning and bureaucratizing the whole system of management. On the other hand, pressure from the workers' councils may lead to a situation in which it will be necessary to slow the pace of economic development or become dependent on foreign aid. Alternatively, after a period of chaos, 'order will be restored with a return to a system of bureaucratic centralism'.

This article can be interpreted in two ways. First, it can be seen as a general warning against the tendency to either limit self-management or to paralyse the central administration. If it is interpreted in this way, Kalecki had a point. It is also obvious that special interests are behind the two tendencies and that they reflect a permanent conflict between the vested interests of rival groups, rather than just between lack of experience on one hand, and bureaucratic routine on the other; a conflict bound to last as long as self-management and central planning exist side by side.

If the article is taken as a general description of the reality of the times, then it has clearly failed to stand the test of time. In this regard, Kalecki (1986) observed that:

> ...a weakening of central planning, to the benefit of workers' councils, has occurred that contains a serious danger for the economy. I have in mind specifically the renunciation of all controls over employment. In accordance with the resolution extending their rights, enterprises' compulsory plan targets include their total annual wage bill, but exclude their average wage and numbers employed. In many factories in manufacturing industries, the supply of raw materials is the factor limiting production and constraining the growth of labour productivity. In practice, therefore, cost-cutting may lead to substantial reduction in employment.

Kalecki goes on to discuss the allegedly imminent threat of unemployment—a problem that has not occurred until the collapse of the communist system in 1989.

Nevertheless, this was not the most important problem. A more fundamental problem is his evaluation of the Polish economic model of 1956. In retrospect, it is surprising that Kalecki concluded that the emergence of workers' councils with the legislation mentioned above ushered in a new economic model. While acknowledging that it was not a perfect model, he only stressed that it was possible to loosen the ties of central planning and that it was necessary to improve (but not abandon) some indicators.

In this regard, Lange (1973) expressed a more realistic view:

> As regards the socialist state-owed industries, the economic management system is beginning to crystallize. We now have workers' councils which can run enterprises together with the management. That of course, requires greater autonomy for the enterprise. Otherwise the workers' council and the management would have nothing to decide and self-management would be fiction.

Lange realized that if enterprise autonomy and central planning remained as they were in 1956-57, bureaucratic central planning would ultimately prevail, an opinion with which Brus and Pajestka concurred in a later debate within the Economic Council.

3 The founding of the Economic Council

The creation of the Economic Council was proposed at the June 1956 Congress of Economists by P. Ehrlich, an economist from Katowice. Ehrlich proposed that the Council be made up of economists independent of the decision-making process at the central level. However, the final resolution adopted by the Congress stipulated that the Council be composed of both theorists and practitioners. The function of the Council was to provide opinions on economic documents and decisions and to initiate suggestions and proposals.

Interestingly, participants at the Congress expected to be provided with guidelines for economic reform by another temporary institution, the Social Polling Commission, rather than the Economic Council. The Social Polling Commission was to draw up and submit a report on the state of the economy, together with proposals for 'improvement', expressed in rather imprecise terms in the final resolution adopted by the Congress.

After the Congress, the idea of creating the Social Polling Commission was dropped and its functions were transferred to the Economic Council. One reason was that the motive force behind the move was Jòsef Popkiewicz of Wroclaw, who was remarkably critical of the authorities at the time. He linked the motion for the shift with a vote of no confidence in the economic leadership and openly admitted his model to be the pre-war Polling Commission referring indirectly to Rychlinski's well-known book *The Waste of Labour and Capital in the Polish Economy*. There was not the slightest hope that economists as a professional group could force the creation of a commission which would be independent and vested with special powers.

An important question to ask is: Why did the Polish Economic Society not come forward with its own report on the economy? Both the party and the government were in no hurry to create the Economic Council, putting it off until October, perhaps because they wanted to try to get around the troublesome demands made by the economists. Their answer was rather to transform the existing State Commission for Planning from a supreme executive office into an institution dealing with research, forecasts and expert advice, which would leave no room for the Economic Council.

In response to the first public protest against the founding of the

Economic Council, especially in response to an article by Fiera ('Zycie Warszawy', August 29, 1956) Polish Economic Society Secretary, General Miroslaw Orlowski, defended the economists' idea and presented the basics of the proposal to Prime Minister J. Cyrankiewicz in the summer of 1956. The Polish Economic Society suggested that the Council combine expert advice with representation of nongovernmental bodies. It would be made up of over 80 members appointed by the Prime Minister from names submitted by the Polish Economic Society (one third), the Labour Union Federation (one third) and with the remaining names proposed by the Academy of Sciences and the education department, or filled by direct invitation to economic journalists and Parliamentary deputies. A further problem was the range of questions the Council was to deal with. It was widely believed that it was primarily created to prepare a proposal for economic reform or a new economic model. This is what the Council is remembered for, but it was not what the Council was conceived to do or even planned to do.

Orlowski proposed that the Economic Council should assess: (1) the bills affecting the basic economic issues; (2) economic policies; and (3) the organization of the national economy. In his view the Council should initiate and conduct studies and make policy recommendations either at its own initiative or at the request of the government. Indeed, it is remarkable that the Polish Economic Society did not see the Council as the body responsible for outlining a blueprint for the economic reform or a new model for the economy. Some of the areas the Council was supposed to be concerned with were rather detailed, including agriculture, key industries, cooperatives, local industry and small business, price policy, employment, development of backward regions and foreign trade.

It was only after Gomulka was reinstated that more was heard of the new economic model, even though the word reform was used more often. However, it was not expected in 1956 that a group of economists would draw up the guidelines for a new economic model which could be translated into operating instruments. In this regard, Lange wrote:

> The Polish economic model... cannot be formulated from above and worked out at the conference table. It stems from the great movement toward socialist democracy which has permeated the country from the setting up of workers' self-government, from the renewal of the self-governing co-operative movement, from the search for new forms of self-government and of social initiative among farmers... The experience of this great movement must, however, be analyzed scientifically in order to draw practical conclusions from

it, and to enable the Party to make use of it and to direct the construction of a Polish model of the socialist economy. The scientific analysis of this experience will be one of the principal tasks of the Economic Council.

The government, however, did not accept the Polish Economic Society proposal, probably because it had no intention of putting up with an *ad hoc* body vested with so much autonomy, i.e. with no activists from the central party and state apparatus on its staff. Steps were then taken after Gomulka's return to power. This was made easier by the return home from exile of C. Bobrowski, a specialist in economic policy and a good administrator who gained extra credit for having been dismissed early in the process of Poland's stalinization. After considerable discussion, Bobrowski proposed a list of members and an agenda for the Council.

The final composition of the Council was different from the Polish Economic Society suggestions, but was moderately reformist.[2] Oskar Lange was appointed chairman and Bobrowski, Brus, Kalecki, Lipinski, C. Pszczolkowski and K. Secomski were appointed deputy chairmen. The relatively large proportion of high-ranking party officials assured effective control by the party, and the Council could not come forward publicly with proposals which were not approved in advance by the party leaders. Consequently, dissent was not tolerated. Perhaps this was why Lange was chosen as chairman over Bobrowski because the former was more malleable as member of the Central Committee and of the Council of State.

Such a composition of advisory bodies does not deserve to be recommended. Although the Council became a first-rate forum for debate between academic and practicing economists which provided first-hand information on what really occurred in Poland's economy, the presence of so many officials had a paralysing effect. Moreover, the authorities were able to forestall any suggestions that could be embarrassing to the government. This was not the decisive factor affecting the atmosphere of the 'great breakthrough' of 1957, but it was an effective brake on progress in the following years.

4 The Economic Council's reform proposals

The Council had been charged with the task of drawing up efficient economic policies and methods for implementation based on academic research and practical experience in management. Its founding statutes listed four objectives: (1) studies of management organization and methods applied in the national economy; (2) expertise, opinions, evaluation criteria and methods of economic policy; (3) its own research and systematic analysis of the economic situation; and (4) topics for study suggested to other research institutions.

The Council, which investigated almost every facet of the economy, was one of the most active institutions, at least during the first two years of its existence. The Council's *Theses on Some of the Proposed Changes of the Economic Model*, published in June 1957 was its most important paper. In this paper, three principles for the so-called socialist or state-owned industry sector were outlined: (1) national plan targets can be reached by an optimal combination of incentives, economic instruments and obligatory orders, with a trend towards a future reduction in the number of these orders; (2) decision-making should be democratized by having the workforce, workers' councils, local self-management and the Sejm involved in drawing up the plans. The Council said that 'a prerequisite of that participation was (literally) the opening up of economic life as well as such a formulation of plan objectives that would give unofficial representatives at the relevant levels a good view of the feasible alternatives that constitute a realistic objective of economic choice'; and (3) enterprises should form obligatory associations similar to multiplant organizations (trusts) to replace the existing bureaucratic central industry boards.

This proposal triggered a heated debate within the Council. The bone of contention was the question of whether only enterprise directors should be members of these industry associations, or whether workers' councils should also be represented. Some representatives of the economic administration refused to accept the second proposal for obviously political reasons. This is why the wording in the *Theses* was vague, referring only to 'representatives of enterprises and, if needed, also other people'. Differences of opinion on this issue were acknowledged in the economic weekly *Zycie Gospodarcze* version, but never appeared in later editions of the *Theses*.

This was not the only point over which Council members had to reach a compromise. Bobrowski's shrewd and originally rational maxim to 'make haste slowly' and his strong emphasis on the relative nature of management systems in adapting to specific conditions influenced the *Theses*, making it possible to reconcile the advocates of speed with those who barely moved, and those who wanted to slightly improve the existing model with those who wanted an entirely new one.

The *Theses* proposed that the reform be carried out in several stages, which contrasts with later experience, especially in Hungary where reform was essentially implemented in one act on January 1, 1968. As is well known, the Hungarian reform was also the only one in a CMEA country to be at least partially effective and significant.

The conclusion of the *Theses* covers implementation, and is basically a timetable for the first stage of reform for the years 1957 and 1958. It included four important points: (1) a price reform of production supplies to be concluded by the end of 1958; (2) a recommendation for a sweeping reorganization of the central industry boards in the first half of 1958; (3) introduction of new rules in enterprise operation that would enable them to become economically autonomous; and (4) methods used to draw up and implement plans should involve only partial change in the first stage, but radical change later on, although the term 'ultimate changes' was not clearly defined. In a certain sense, the *Thesis* was a 'mixed hodgepodge' of 'well-combined incentives, economic instruments and mandatory quotas which were the best possible under the given conditions', with a wide margin for deciding which would be the proverbial 'half horse' and 'half hare'.

In July 1957 the conclusions of the *Theses* were deemed 'essentially correct' by the Government Economics Committee. At the same time, however, this Committee instructed the Council to specify and expand on the proposals, and, in combination with the Planning Commission and itself, draw up proposals which could be enacted in 1957-58. Although the Council was occupied with many specific problems, it is not clear why they did not draw up a new expanded version of the *Theses*. Perhaps it was not understood that, taking the composition of the Council into account, it would be easier to reach agreement on particular rather than general issues.

Understandably, the reformers interpreted the Government Economics Committee decision as an encouragement to speed up reform. This was expressed in a lengthy editorial 'Approval and Conclusions' in 'Zycie Gospodarcze', which suggested that the Government Economics Committee had recognized the Theses as 'a good foundation for continued work on the reconstruction of the model'. The journal also voiced its confidence that the Government Economics Committee resolution would speed up work on the development of new management and planning models. The editors were sure that 'the work of fleshing out the general contours with specific substance will have to be done by tens of thousands of people—employees at all levels of the national economy, especially since we want... to adjust our policy measures to what the particular industries, regions and levels of economic activity may need'.

The article stated that the *Theses* were conceived as a tentative formulation of a general directive which would clarify 'the main directions of development while being flexible enough not to hamstring the initiative of enterprises'. It went on to say that work at the Planning Commission, in the ministries, central industry boards, enterprises and research institutions was beginning to change the proposed model, especially by introducing changes which were due to become effective early in the following year.

Nothing like that actually happened, however, and in a later article reviewing the events of the year following the Polish October, Brus (1957) accused the authorities of slowing the pace of reform and of lacking a clear idea of what they wanted to accomplish:

> It is upsetting that no concrete plans have been submitted—one year after the Polish October—on the removal of at least the most glaring contradictions... The Economic Council's general *Theses* have, after a wait of several months, finally received official approval, but no tangible effects are to be seen. Nothing has been heard of the reorganization of the central industry boards. Little has been seen of the proposals of the Economic Council on the question of compensating enterprises for plan quotas that had an impact on their cost effectiveness.

There were many 'there is no sign of', 'no preparations have been made', 'too slow', and other similar phrases, followed by a call for speed. Although the Council could not be blamed for the sluggish pace of progress, the general public would still hold it responsible. Brus (1957), in desperation, argued:

> It has to be made clear, especially on the anniversary of the October events, that we are trailing behind other countries. ...If press reports are anything to be trusted, in the USSR, Czechoslovakia, the German Democratic Republic and Rumania, changes of the model have been included in comprehensive and concrete political and economic programmes. ...In Poland, one still has the impression that the model is considered marginal in importance.

The continuing debates in the Economic Council were increasingly technical and professional. Two issues in particular were debated: procedures to set prices, and the creation of a system of incentives based on profit. On the latter, Kalecki proposed as a base increases in profits compared with the three year earlier period rather than just the preceding year, whereas Brus suggested a combination of the share in the profit, and the share of profit in the increase with the aid of a progressive tax formula. However, these were merely discussions of details which did not move beyond the conceptual framework of the *Theses*.

To summarize thus far, the model of a socialist economy in the *Theses* mixed features from different models. It retained the centrally planned commands for enterprises typical of the Soviet model, while stressing the need to rely to a greater extent on economic instruments in order to improve the operations of enterprises. This would provide a certain amount of autonomy, but remain within the framework of centrally managed investment[3] and administratively set or controlled prices.

The so-called decentralized model emerged out of discussions both inside and outside the Economic Council. Called a planned economy with a built-in market mechanism, it was developed by Brus in 1961 and differed from the above by dropping the command system in favour of economic instruments. The best practical example of it was installed in Hungary in 1968. However, the new Hungarian version bore out Kalecki's (1982) prophecy that 'if you believe that management of incentives is going to require no bureaucracy you are mistaken, for various incentives will be applied and different industries will need a bureaucratic machinery to cope with that'. The millions of interventions by such bureaucratic machineries into the details of enterprise operations led to what has been described as neither central planning nor a market economy. The Hungarians called it indirect centralization.

Recently Professor Brus rejected his own model, since it did not work. Recalling the experience of Hungary and Yugoslavia, in particular the calls by Hungarian economists for greater reliance on the market economy because they could not hope for a change in the political system, Brus (1989) wrote:

But at closer watch I found I had been wrong. The great expectations attached to the effects of introducing a market of goods (consumer as well as producer goods) could not become materialized for several reasons: allocation of the bulk of investment expenditures using vertical planning methods presupposes the existence of a strong administrative centres which tends to expand its power to other sectors of the economy; competition and entrepreneurship are unlikely to spread without free entry and exit, and this in turn presupposes a possibility of horizontal capital flows; the lack of capital, in turn, undoes the disciplinary effect of market mechanisms, because that makes it immediately difficult to tell enterprises which are inefficient from those which have become inefficient as possibilities of modifying their product offers are blocked for them, they could not take advantage of new technology, etc. that is why there is good reason for putting the administration which decides the allocation of resources, under pressure. This probably holds true of the capital and labour

markets as well. ...But I just wanted to indicate the general direction of change
of my theoretical reflections as a result of a close watch of the reforming
economies. ...My trip to Hungary and Yugoslavia in 1983 has undoubtedly
helped me get a better view of those matters.

5 Kalecki on the socialist economy

In his otherwise important study of Kalecki as a theorist and practicing
planner, M. Nuti (1986) contrasts Kalecki to Lange and other Polish
reformers in the aftermath of the Polish October. He writes that Kalecki
developed a complete and coherent model of a socialist economy,
distinct from both the Soviet model and from Lange's market socialism.

At first sight, this seems plausible, for even non-economists regard
Lange as the originator of the concept of market socialism, and there
have always been reformers who consider market socialism to be both
feasible and desirable. But Nuti explicitly states that even after the war,
1956-1958 to be precise, Lange remained true to his classical model,
proposing it as the foundation of Poland's road to socialism, and this
was a view reportedly shared by other reformers. This is simply not
true. It is easy to show that after 1956, there were no major differences
between Kalecki and Lange on economic reform. Paradoxically, the
publications Nuti cites actually prove my point, not his.

For example, Nuti (1986) writes:

> Kalecki envisaged in his model—in place of economic decentralization—
> general political decentralization under a guise of workers' councils which, in
> every enterprise oppose excessive bureaucratization and centralization
> tendencies which appear when the enterprise director answers only to central
> powers and exercises initiative under the stimulus of material incentives.

To Nuti, this summarizes the meaning of Kalecki's paper *Workers
Councils and Central Planning* and is unambiguous. Nuti, however,
interprets Lange's (1973) article *The New Economic Model Must be
Developed in Reliance on a Dynamic Working Class and Socialist
Intelligentsia,* which appeared next to Kalecki's as supporting the
position that 'Lange regarded enterprise autonomy extending to prices
and investment as a precondition of workers self-management'.
Contrary to Nuti's opinion, however, evidence suggests that both
Lange and Kalecki held similar, if not the same, views on the question
of prices and investments. Moreover, this view was also shared by
almost all of the reformers on the Economic Council.

On the question of prices Lange (1973, p. 477) wrote:

Price-setting must be used as a principal regulator to apply in the management of national economy. Accordingly, it cannot be turned over to individual enterprises but should basically remain in the hands of the state, that is, the central or local authorities, depending on the nature or importance of the given product to the national economy at large. Only in exceptional cases ... should prices be allowed to be determined freely by the market: yet even then the government should exercise some or other kind of control.

Lange (1973, p. 478) had similar things to say about planning production and investment:

National economic planning must embrace the basic sectors and sub-branches of national economy, that is the production of producer goods, consumer good production, industrial production, agriculture production etc. and sub-branches... Lastly, planning ... must embrace employment of labour and its distribution among the basic sectors of national economy.

In another article written the same month, Lange (1973, p. 484) writes:

Central planning must embrace all investment expenditures, with the fundamental projects being planned directly by the central government and subsidiary projects of lesser importance for the national economy as a whole planned by departments, people's councils and enterprises within the framework of general limits and directives set in the central plan.

When referring to Kalecki's *Do Not Overrate the Importance of the Model*, and by placing him in opposition to other reformers, Nuti seems to ignore the fact that immediately after that article was published, Kalecki co-authored with Lange, Brus and others the *Thesis on the Model*. This represented the common platform of most Polish reformers at the time, and Kalecki regarded the *Theses* as his own reform programme, defending it to the authorities. Three heatedly debated issues represented the Council's stand: the establishment of prices and investment expenditures as an inherent attribute of central planning; full employment as an unquestionable principle of socialism; and the system of workers' councils as a counterweight to the planning and management bureaucracy.

6 The adviser's drama

A short period of activity in the Economic Council was the most hopeful, professionally the happiest time in Kalecki's life. The next years brought him a lot of bitterness and disillusionment. This is true not only with regard to his involvement in economic policy, but also his teaching job. Kalecki's official post was as full-time adviser to the Chairman of the Planning Commission. But his work there was more as researcher than adviser. He organized a team of researchers, which produced *inter alia, A Long-Run Plan of Economic Development of Poland.* This plan—an interesting and pioneering work from many points of view— was not accepted by the government, and thus was not implemented, apparently because it was regarded as too minimalistic in its targets, although now it looks overly optimistic. Its main goal, to which all other targets were subordinated, was to reach the standard of living of West Germany within 15 years.

Open conflict between Kalecki and the authorities emerged in the mid 1960s over the targets of the Five Year Plan for the second half of the 1960s. Kalecki's role as an adviser was very limited in shaping its content, which is why he broke his habit of internal criticism, and published his counter-proposals. His main idea was to shift resources from investment in heavy industry in order to increase output targets in consumption. This was met with furious rebuttal from the First Secretary of the communist party, Wladyslaw Gomulka. As a consequence, Kalecki decided to leave the Planning Commission, and asked for early retirement.[4]

Such a fate as an adviser was not only unfortunate from a personal and social point of view, but was also highly paradoxical. One would have rather expected Kalecki to be an ideal candidate for the central planner's adviser. He was a man of integrity and principle, but simultaneously tried to be as loyal to his principals as possible. Never involved directly in politics (he never belonged to any political party and never aspired to a high post in the state hierarchy), he tried to be useful as an expert adviser and researcher.

Some aspects of Kalecki's interest in economic theory seemed to predestine him for this role. Despite his criticism of the practice of central planning in Poland or in Eastern Europe, to the end of his life he deeply believed in the superiority of planning over the market, and he regarded the amelioration of planning techniques as his life's mission. Kalecki's (1963) major work on the socialist economy, *An Outline of the Theory of Growth of Socialist Economy,* contains the theoretical foundations of planning, namely a consideration of material and human barriers for economic growth. Being interested in the proportionality between economic entities and their interrelations, Kalecki for a long time devoted little attention to the social and political framework of planning. Indeed, his book is totally lacking any consideration of these types of problems. Moreover, Kalecki has thought it possible and fully legitimate to analyse what he thinks are the most fundamental problems of growth of the socialist economy under the assumption of rational action (behaviour) of the central planner. In this way, he isolates the theory of growth from the theory of the functioning of the socialist economy, and still more from the political system of regulation. Thus, it was hardly touched by the most conflicting of political and ideological questions. Taking all this into account, the resignation of such an outstanding, widely known expert must be seen as one of the most glaring examples of the devolution of political power. The end of Kalecki's career as a teacher was even worse. He himself and the Kalecki school of thought became one of the targets of the famous anti-revisionist and anti-semitic campaign of 1968. Many of his collaborators and pupils had to leave the Main School of Planning and Statistics, where Kalecki was teaching; some of them left Poland. At the beginning, Kalecki defended his views and the School, but soon asked for early retirement, and until the end of his life refused to publish anything in Poland. His last publications are devoted to the capitalist economy. Only in private conversations did he stress the need for institutional change in socialist countries, which he labelled a 'crucial reform' similar in its depth to the 'Keynesian revolution'.

Notes

1. The factory committees established right after the War were an ephemeral phenomenon deprived of systemic goals.
2. Of the 29 nominations, 15 were accepted by the authorities who added 19 of their own, chiefly to reinforce the apparatchik faction. Among those removed from the list were J. Frankowski, the only Catholic social activist proposed, L. Gozdzik, the working class symbol of the Polish October, W. Stys, regarded as a bourgeois economist, and T. Kowalik, then editor of the economics weekly, *Zycie Gospodarcze*.
3. Investment made by enterprises would account for only a small proportion of the total.
4. Needless to say, by ignoring the proposals of Kalecki, the government's frozen standard of living led to riots in 1970, and as a consequence caused the collapse of Gomulka's regime.

References

Bobrowski, C. (1985). *Wspomnienia ze stulecia*, Lublin.

Brus, W. (1957). 'Październik-Model-Październik', *Zycie Gospodarcze*.

Brus, W. (1989). 'From Revisionism to Pragmatism', *Acta Economica*.

'Discussion at the 2nd Congress of Polish Economists', *Ekonomista*, 1956, No. 5.

Gomulka, W. (1956). 'Speech at 8th Plenum of the PUWP Central Committee', *Nowe Drogi*, 80f.

Kalecki, M. (1956). 'Dynamika inwestycji i dochodu narodowego w gospodarce socjalistycznej', *Ekonomista*.

Kalecki, M. (1972). *Essays on the Economic Growth of Socialist and Mixed Economies*, Cambridge: Cambridge University Press.

Kalecki, M. (1986). *Selected Essays on Economic Planning*, Jan Toporowski, ed., Cambridge: Cambridge University Press.

Kalecki, M. (1982). *Dziela, vol 3*, (collected works), J. Osiatynski, ed., Panstwowe Wydawnictwo Naukowe, Warszawa. (English version, Oxford University Press [1992])

Lange, O. (1970). *Papers in Economics and Sociology*, P. F. Knightsfield, ed., Warszawa.

Lange, O. (1973). *Dziela, vol 2*, (Collected Works), T. Kowalik, ed., Pastwowe Wydawnictwo Naukowe, Warszawa.

Nuti, D. M. (1986). 'Michal Kalecki's Contribution to the Theory and Practice of Socialist Planning', *Cambridge Journal of Economics*, 333-353.

5 The Failure of Demand Management in Socialism

*Edward Nell**

1 Introduction

The collapse of socialism, implying a much-heralded triumph of capitalism—the 'end of history', by one account—is a profoundly ambiguous event. Socialism collapsed because it failed—yet earlier it rebuilt war-torn Eastern Europe and for two decades grew faster than its rival system, industrializing previously backward societies at a prodigious rate. Capitalism now reigns triumphant, yet it has persistently and disastrously failed its own underclass, and has never succeeded in controlling its instability, which has persisted through several changes of character.

The conservative critics of socialism predicted its failure, while liberals and mainstream economists feared or hoped for its success, or assumed its success and hoped for its reform, but generally discounted the possibility of wholesale collapse. Conservatives now gleefully claim that their predictions have come true. However, it will be argued here that neither conservative nor mainstream economists understood the real economic problems faced by socialist regimes; the conservatives did not correctly predict what happened, nor have the mainstream analysts adequately explained it. When discussing socialism, both Hayek and Samuelson-Solow, for example, normally concentrated their attention on the price mechanism and allocation problems. Hayekians, following von Mises, argued that without an actual market the myriad supplies and demands could not be equated—the problem was too complex for the human mind. Mainstream economists noted that actual markets often fail to clear and are always subject to imperfections. Moreover, as Lange and Taylor had pointed out, the planners could perfectly easily solve the equations; all the more easily now, in the age of computers. The problem was not complexity, it was motivation. The real question was, would the institutions enable the plan to be carried out properly? Markets would provide the profit motives that would ensure proper allocation, allowing for imperfections. But in their absence could the bureaucracy ensure that the decisions of the plan would ac-

tually be carried out? If not, then there would be systematic misallocation and welfare losses.

Both these arguments are based on static, price-theoretic thinking,
whereas the actual problems of socialism arose in the context of aggregate demand and growth, and in particular, concerned the failure of
productivity to grow in pace with rising incomes (even at times to fall),
thereby leading to intensified shortages. Shortage, however, is a relative term; it indicates a shortage of supply in the face of effective *demand*. Aggregate or overall shortages, therefore, imply an excessive
pressure of aggregate demand. The problem has to be examined in a
macroeconomic perspective, and this is what has been missing from
most accounts which have focused too much on prices and allocation.

This paper will investigate some of the typical macroeconomic
problems arising in a shortage economy. It will show that past and
present attempts to improve the efficiency of the planned socialist
economy have not been successful because they have failed to understand the characteristic mode of operation. In particular, by failing to
understand the essentially *macroeconomic* nature of the problem, the
attempt to introduce microeconomic 'solutions' that are used in capitalist demand-constrained economies will be a wasted effort.

2 Harrod-Domar analysis

Capitalist economies characteristically operate with a margin of excess,
not merely reserve, capacity, while socialist economies suffer under
pressure of excess demand. Each economy *normally* operates out of
balance, but they tilt in opposite directions, and this tilt in each case explains many characteristic features of the system.

It will become apparent that there is an affinity here with the famous
Harrod-Domar claim regarding the warranted rate of growth. That rate
just balances aggregate demand and aggregate capacity: aggregate demand, in simplified form, is investment times the multiplier, while total
capacity is the capital stock times its productivity. Equating the two
gives us the rate of growth (investment divided by total capital) that
will keep entrepreneurs just satisfied, namely a rate equal to the productivity of capital times the ratio of withdrawals to income. But a
small deviation from this rate in either direction will be self-augmenting.
For too low a rate will imply that aggregate demand is less than total
capacity—which gives business the signal to cut back investment
spending, thereby reducing demand even further. Too high a rate in
turn signals a shortage of capacity, and thus the need for speeding up

investment. In each case, responding to the market signal worsens the initial imbalance.

This appears to show that capitalist growth is seriously unstable, a claim that has given rise to a great deal of controversy (Morishima, 1975, and Kregel, 1980 both comment on the long debate). But the claim and the controversy are seriously misplaced; the warranted rate is not a potential, satisfactory balanced growth path for an actual economic system. No capitalist system has ever grown for any time at the warranted rate. Capitalism *always* operates with a margin of *excess capacity*. (World War Two is the exception that proves the rule: the Allied economies were planned and developed shortages.) Socialist economies, that is the economies of the former Eastern bloc, always tended to operate with a level of aggregate demand above full capacity. The warranted rate is not an achievable target (although it may be *approachable*, as a matter of policy); instead, it is a *dividing line*, separating two contrasting *modes of operation*. The same economic system cannot cycle around the warranted rate, first below, then at, then above it, and so on. Below the balancing point, the system operates one way, generating one pattern of incentives and results; above, an altogether different pattern holds. The discussion of the Harrod-Domar claim— Morishima termed it 'the Harrodian avalanche'—has always been curiously inconclusive. The attempts to find plausible mechanisms that would, in general, restrain the centrifugal forces have met with little success. The logic of the instability claim is both simple and powerful, but capitalist growth is not that unstable. The argument here is that the original problem was miscast; when reinterpreted, not only do the difficulties vanish, we can contrast capitalist and socialist economies in new ways.

3 Definitions

This paper will compare abstract, idealized versions of the two systems.[1] A capitalist economy will be understood as one in which some own the means of production while others do not; capitalist production generates a surplus through the employment of wage labour, and competition establishes a common ratio of surplus to the value of the means of production used. This is the rate of profit, and every capitalist system is characterized by a 'normal' rate of profit (expressed in the rate of interest on money) which makes it possible to calculate the 'amount of capital' in any sector or industry by capitalizing its net income stream. On this basis, therefore, economic activities can be bought and sold.

Capitalist enterprises compete with one another; and liquid capital, funds conferring ownership of or claims against such enterprises, will actively seek out those with the highest rates of return. Hence there is constant pressure to increase the surplus, i.e. to raise productivity.

Under capitalism the ownership and distribution of wealth is given, and the system generates pressure to operate the means of production most efficiently (productively). By contrast, under socialism the efficiency and productivity of the means of production are assumed, but private ownership is abolished and the system seeks to distribute the gains most fairly, taking account of both the general interest and the interests of all. Ownership is vested in bureaucracies supposedly representing the general interest, run in accordance with an overall plan, and income is distributed in proportion to productive contribution, modified by subsidies to those with special needs. Investment is planned to bring about balanced growth at the highest rate consistent with planned consumption. Job security and a basic standard of living are guaranteed to all. Capitalism is regulated by prices and the rate of profits, socialism by quantities and the rate of growth. In actual fact, both systems develop characteristic patterns of corruption, but this paper will analyse the ideal type.

Both capitalism and socialism are essentially monetary systems: capitalist profits do not count until they are realized in money and socialist incomes must be both paid and spent, before any judgement of fairness can be rendered. Since prices are realized in money, in neither system, therefore, does the money wage—fixed by the wage bargain in the labour market—determine the real wage. In both systems production and distribution are carried out at least partly through market processes—wages are paid and spent, accounts are kept of purchases and sales—although the markets work differently, and socialist markets are not competitive. Further, in both systems production is largely concentrated in the hands of giant bureaucratic organizations, with easy access to funds and well placed to lobby the government. And in each a privileged class or stratum can be identified.

These similarities and differences in the organization of production are fundamental, but do not explain many of the most obvious contrasts between the systems. For this we have to consider each system's characteristic mode of operation, in particular, the way each builds and uses productive capacity.

4 Modes of operation

Capitalism and socialism have traditionally been defined as modes of production, meaning ways of organizing and controlling the means and processes of production, so as to appropriate the resulting surpluses. This traditional approach does not explain either capitalism's combination of wasted capacity and unnecessary products with innovative dynamism or the corresponding mix of high capital construction, shortages and frustration apparent in socialism. To understand these problems we shall examine the characteristic modes of operation of the two systems, which, following Kornai and Kaldor, may be called 'demand-constrained' and 'resource-constrained', respectively, showing that what has been interpreted as the 'instability of the warranted rate of growth' can be better understood, when recast to take account of productivity changes, as the set of pressures that separate these two modes of operation.

The influence of the characteristic mode of operation pervades the economic sphere and colours all aspects of it—and much beyond as well. Expectations of enterprises as to prices, quantities, revenues, and capital values, all will be formed on the assumption of normal demand scarcity or normal shortage. Households will likewise plan careers and education of children with an eye to the normal state of the labour market. Public bodies will shape their expenditure and capital construction plans on the basis of the normal conditions of operation. Even the agenda of public policy and the issues in political debate may be shaped more by the mode of operation than by the mode of production.

In comparing capitalism and socialism it is common to counterpose bureaucracy and the market; socialism is said to be bureaucratically planned, and therefore inefficient, whereas capitalism is a market economy, therefore efficient, except where monopolies and oligopolies have introduced distortions. Market and bureaucracy are seen as two opposed and incompatible forms of organizing economic activity. Nothing could be further from the truth; modern capitalism is highly bureaucratic, and contemporary socialism is equally obviously a market economy, though this has been much misunderstood. Both systems are bureaucratic and both are planned through state agencies, although the nature and objectives of the planning are different. But the production units of all industrialized, mass production economies so far have been run by bureaucracies; no alternatives have yet proven workable on a large scale. Moreover, all modern economies are market economies; the market may be planned by the state or administered privately or through some mixture of state and private, but it is still a market—goods are produced for sale; ownership changes hands through monetary transactions; monetary income, arising from property or from work, confers the power to consume. But the mode of operation of a market system can be demand-constrained or resource-constrained, and that makes more difference than whether production is run by bureaucracies professing to represent the citizenry as collective owners or representing shareholders as collective owners.

The idea that economies have a characteristic mode of operation, either demand- or resource-constrained, runs counter to most current economic thinking. On the one hand it is assumed that aggregate demand in capitalist societies can and often does reach or surpass the level of full employment. But 'full employment' has been redefined— as a 'natural rate' or NAIRU or whatever—to make this possible; capitalist economies almost never reach full capacity—and when they do they develop shortages. On the other, the problem of shortage in socialism is widely held to be due to systemic inefficiency and slackness in production—'soft budget constraints', in Kornai's phrase (Kornai 1986; Davis and Charemza 1989).

There is a sophisticated argument here: for political and administrative reasons—lazy workers cannot be fired, inefficient firms cannot be shut down—bureaucratic socialism is unable to enforce budget constraints. Consequently, enterprises feel no compulsion to cut costs or produce efficiently; so long as they meet their quotas, they will suffer no penalty for being unprofitable or for making costly and unwise investments. Also, being bureaucrats, they will prefer to follow established practices; so they will not innovate. But managers and bureaucrats will regularly try to expand their territory; hence expansion will follow success in bureaucratic manoeuvering, which will bring the required funds, regardless of costs, and the results will often have no economic justification. The process will end in unusable capacity coupled with general shortages.

This argument has the facts correct, but the causality is exactly backwards. As we shall see, shortages result from excess demand, which in turn leads to inefficiency, since everything produced can easily be sold. Budget constraints are soft because the incentives to expand are strong; not the other way around. Costs are ignored because of the intensity of demand. It is competition for sales that provides the incentive to cut costs and produce—and market—efficiently. And it is this same competition that engenders product innovations. Capitalist firms don't face budget constraints that are significantly different from those in socialism—but they do face an altogether different order of competition. (As for the idea that soft budget constraints in themselves engender inefficiency, what could be 'softer' than the budget constraint of a large American corporation? Perhaps only the budget constraint of a savings and loan! For decades many U.S. government-owned firms, such as TVA, were held up as models of efficient operation.) It is competition for scarce demand, not restrictions on current or capital spending, that stimulates cost-cutting.

Is efficiency inconsistent with public ownership? Do private property and markets dissolve bureaucracy? First, bureaucracy is by no means opposed to the market. Some of the largest bureaucracies in the world are private transnational corporations, some of which are efficient, and some not, though all are powerful. So bureaucracy and market coordination are not necessarily opposed; they can march hand-in-hand. It will be argued later that aggregate shortages rather than public ownership create inefficiency, and that new policies rather than a new property system are the answer.

The 'mode of operation' thus refers to the system as a whole; it determines the character of the system, and, in particular, the incentives which govern market behaviour. It follows that a system must be one or the other; demand scarcity and supply shortage cannot easily be mixed without losing the distinctive virtues of each. And as we shall see, these basic incentive patterns, in turn, affect innovation and productivity and thus react back on the system.

5 Prices

But first we must deal with a basic misconception, according to which the problems of socialism have arisen because, lacking a price mechanism, it cannot allocate resources optimally, whereas capitalism does. By contrast, we shall argue that the basic or normal prices in each (idealized) system are set in very similar ways, although the reactions of agents to out-of-equilibrium situations are different.

To study this question, let us compare the economic working of two industrial economies, each using mass production technologies, where one mode of operation will be capitalist, the other socialist. Products and productive equipment are standardized. Worker skills are required, though jobs are also standardized, and the pace of work is set by the machinery; costs are kept down and economies of scale are realized by large plants and long production runs. Prices in both systems have to cover current production costs and contribute to meeting the fixed monetary costs incurred in setting up the mass production plant. In other words, prices are set according to established mark-ups, where these mark-ups reflect the profits required on normal operations in the respective industries. Since these requirements do not change quickly, in both systems normal or long-run prices of manufactured goods will tend to be inflexible. The differences will lie in the way the mark-up is set, and the extent to which cost over-runs are permitted. For different reasons price-cutting and surcharging, when sales fluctuate, will be infrequent in both systems for manufactured goods (Kalecki 1954; Nell 1992; Eichner 1976). Costs and outputs of primary goods (non-produced means of production and basic consumption—farm and fish products, minerals, raw materials, oil, etc.) will, however, fluctuate in both systems, leading to temporary market price changes in capitalism and variations in subsidies in socialism. In neither system, however, do prices reflect relative scarcities.

But prices serve a significant economic function—the same in both systems. At their normal levels they reflect the requirements of reproduction and distribution; when exchanges take place at the correct long-term prices, distribution will be accomplished and reproduction will be made possible. Prices do not reflect relative scarcities—they cannot in capitalism, because with excess capacity and unemployment, factors are not scarce, and they do not in socialism, because planning must ensure that exchanges will accomplish the desired reproduction and expansion.

As an example of such a price system, let A be the input-output matrix showing the average coefficients implied in the existing equipment of present industries, L the vector of average labour requirements per unit of output (expressed in terms of the consumer goods that support labour), p the price vector, r the rate of profit and w the real wage, considered as a percentage mark-up on the basic basket of goods supporting labour. Then, if A has certain properties,

$$p = (1+r)Ap + wL \Rightarrow p = wL[1-(1+r)A]^{-1}$$

will give the prices and the rate of profit, if the normal or long-run real wage is determined by bargaining, custom and social pressures.[2] Of course, this equation reflects the pressure of competition in establishing a uniform rate of profit, which would not exist in socialism. But planners might seek to establish a balanced, uniform rate of growth, and require that every industry set prices to earn the profit to support this growth. Such a socialist plan would then also require a uniform profit rate. However, no difference in principle is made if the rate of profit is replaced by a vector of mark-ups (Gale 1960; Semmler 1984; Pasinetti 1977).

Such prices are based on covering costs and earning normal profits from the operation of presently existing equipment. Choice of technique is therefore irrelevant; a new technique may indeed be more profitable, but it will take time to build new factories, and in the meantime demand will have to be served by current, less efficient plants. Normal prices will be based on normal levels of operation, reflecting normal costs. These will not generally be affected by aggregate shortages or excesses; indeed, within a wide range, variations in demand will tend to have little effect on prices. 'Benchmarks' for normal prices will be established at the time investment decisions are made, based on the prevailing levels of the wage and other costs, on the one hand, and expected market growth on the other. Market prices can be expected to vary around these norms, but in manufacturing sectors even considerable swings in demand may have comparatively little impact. (Kalecki 1954; Eichner 1976; Nell 1992, especially chs. 16 and 17. For a different route to a similar conclusion, cf. Blinder 1988 and Gordon 1990.) Nor would variations in prices tend to correct aggregate imbalances between demand and capacity (Nell 1992, ch. 20; Tobin 1980).

This leads to an important conclusion in regard to the debate over 'socialist reforms': if prices reflect the requirements for reproduction and distribution, and if pricing benchmarks are set in connection with investment decisions, the claim that aggregate demand imbalances are due to price or wage 'rigidities', and can be corrected by restoring 'free markets', cannot even be entertained. (Cf. Eichner 1976; Wood 1976; and Nell 1992, ch. 17, for the relationships between pricing and investment.)

6 Demand in relation to capacity

Capitalism is competitive, so firms must build and carry extra productive capacity for precautionary or strategic reasons; a firm must be able to keep up with its competition, so when markets are growing rapidly, it must be able to expand production (and also capacity) in pace. If it could not, but its competitors could, it would lose its market share, while the competitors would reap economies of scale, leaving it a relatively high-cost producer. (In a slowdown firms must take care in cutting capacity, lest they suddenly need it again.) Also, markets fluctuate; a firm that holds its capacity to the level of average demand will be unable to service peak demand and will lose customers to those who can deliver at any time. Markets grow irregularly and firms must be poised to take advantage of new openings, especially since idle capacity can be adapted to turn out product variations for new or specialized markets. If some carry such capacity and others do not, the carriers will have an advantage at the expense of the others. Firms with reserve capacity will be able to adapt it and plunge right into the new venture; firms without any reserves will only be able to enter after completing a construction project. Firms with reserve capacity can adapt the reserve plant to new product design, while continuing to serve their normal market with the old; firms without reserves will have to shut down their operations to adapt. Competition for market shares thus requires carrying reserve capacity. (But firms will keep inventories and stockpiles trim, adjusted to current demand levels.)

Reserve capacity, however, is not *excess* capacity; yet it is the latter that is really of interest. Competitive planning on the part of each firm requires it to choose the amount of reserve capacity needed to defend its *desired* market position—the largest share it can reasonably hope to secure and defend. Each firm will thus select and build reserve capacity on this basis, and the aggregate level of reserve capacity will be the sum of these plans. But only some firms will achieve their desired market positions—winners imply losers—and the rest will be carrying too much capacity.[3]

Under socialism, by contrast, the plan will normally try to meet large objectives with limited resources; it will try to reconcile competing claims by assuming that output can be expanded. Hence there will be pressure both to produce at full blast from existing capacity and to increase productive capacity as fast as possible. Given these pressures, enterprises will be chronically short of capacity in relation to total demand and, fearing shortages, will stockpile raw materials, inputs, equipment and other supplies.

Each system thus operates in a characteristic manner. Capitalist competition calls for reserve capacity, whether to seize an opportunity or to repel a market invader; but such capacity must be matched by reserve labour, which can be mobilized quickly. Otherwise the extra capacity will prove useless and the costs of carrying it wasted. However, hoarding labour is prohibitively expensive; instead the system itself tends to generate a labour reserve through regular increases in productivity, combined with a tendency to weakness in aggregate demand. (Low income households, in particular, are pressed to offer labour services from all members.) Such reserves make it easier to keep wages within bounds and to maintain labour discipline. Further, the smooth functioning of the system depends upon labour's willingness to accept capital's decisions about employment, job definitions and working conditions; the existence of reserve labour strengthens capital's hand. Given widespread reserve capacity and labour, however, investment will normally be held back until an innovation, providing a competitive edge, can be introduced.

Socialism, on the other hand, is committed to meeting everyone's needs, and so requires a full effort in current production; no reserves can be held back. Such an effort makes it easier for the authorities to grant increases in pay and to support efforts to expand in all spheres, moves which strengthen the hand of authority and improve its image. It also means that capacity will appear insufficient everywhere; investment will therefore be called for throughout the economy.

Stating the contrast schematically, under capitalism money wages will tend to be kept as low and prices as high as possible; under socialism, wages will tend to drift as high, while prices will be held as low as possible.[4] Capitalism constrains real wages, in order to increase profits; socialism lets them expand in order to achieve social objectives. Under capitalism, investments must be withheld until the time is ripe; under socialism, investment must be pushed forward as rapidly as possible. Given this pattern of investment, and that real wages largely determine consumption, aggregate demand in capitalism will tend to lie below, in socialism, above, productive capacity.

7 Characteristic incentive patterns

Each system's mode of operation sets up characteristic incentive patterns, which fit together into a definite style and tend to reinforce the initial condition of demand excess or scarcity. To begin with growth: under capitalism the presence of near-universal excess capacity, required as a strategic reserve for competitive reasons, dampens the inducement to invest, in the absence of technological improvements. Capitalist economies tend to build capacity sluggishly, punctuated by strong bursts of expansion, usually stimulated by innovation. Weak and/or uncertain investment, in turn, tends to keep capacity utilization low and to create a shortage of jobs. By contrast, under socialism, near-universal shortages of goods, engendered by the attempt to run all productive processes at full potential, strengthen the inducement to invest, which in turn further intensifies the pressure of demand on capacity. Socialist economies build capacity rapidly and regularly, but fail to innovate or to produce high quality. Output growth in capitalism chiefly comes from technical progress, in socialism from adding capacity.

A shortage of demand in relation to capacity tends to intensify competition; sales are uncertain—a firm's market could always be lost to competitors. Hence cost-cutting and quality enhancement will be important, perhaps competitively necessary, to attract and keep a share of the limited market. Technical progress in regard to both products and processes is therefore stimulated by the characteristic situation of capitalism, and accounts for a large part of the growth of output.

Such technical development will be of the kind analysed by Adam Smith and Charles Babbage—separation of function and division of labor. Tasks and designs are simplified, clarified, broken down and made more precise, so that tasks and skills are carefully matched and products fit proposed uses. Expensive skilled labour/equipment will not be used for tasks that unskilled workers can perform. By contrast, the excess demand characteristic of socialism means that neither product improvement nor cost-cutting are necessary to make sales; indeed, sometimes good quality is not even required. When shortages are severe enough practically anything will be absorbed by the market. But generalized shortage sets up pressure for innovations that can meet several needs or perform several functions at the same time. In the face of chronic shortages, jobs must be accomplished without the proper tools or materials, which provides an incentive for redesigning products and equipment, and redefining jobs; equipment and work teams must be adapted to multiple functions. So technical progress takes the form associated with the Pentagon: functions are combined, rather than separated, and tasks are multiplied instead of divided. These innovations are often admirable—Swiss army knives, vegematics—but they seldom reduce costs in the long run, for a breakdown in any one function usually incapacitates the whole, so that all functions must be scrapped or shut down for repairs. Thus as functions are *added*, breakdown/repair costs are *multiplied*.

Similarly, since a shortage of demand means competition for sales, costs must be kept down by driving hard bargains. Companies will therefore ride herd on money wages; for the same reasons they will try to keep other material and input costs down. Moreover, they will insist on quality for money, since sloppy work or poor quality inputs can mean uncompetitive, unsaleable products. Socialist enterprises, on the other hand, do not feel such pressure to keep costs down and quality high. Even with declining quality they can sell their products, and rising costs, though a nuisance, will seldom interfere with the enterprise's plans for expansion, since given the widespread shortages, virtually any reasonable expansion plan will be approved; neither prospective nor realized profitability governs or constrains investment. Capitalism hands out harsh penalties—too liberally, for they fall on many who do not deserve them; socialism hands out easy rewards, also too liberally, for they accrue to many who have done nothing to deserve reward.

These arguments must be treated carefully; it does not follow that capitalism will generate progress and turn out high quality goods, while socialism will stagnate, drowning in junk. Producing high quality goods is one important way of competing; introducing marketable innovations is another. But producing cheap goods with hard-to-detect flaws is also a good strategy, as is covering up dangerous defects, pandering to unhealthy desires, building in obsolescence, and distributing advantageous misinformation through advertising. Socialist enterprises must meet plan requirements and deadlines, but are under no competitive pressures to sell. Hence, although they may let quality decline and costs rise, for example, socialist publishers can concentrate on culturally significant works, rather than best-sellers. Socialist medical care could be delivered to those who need it, rather than those who can pay for it—although it might arrive too late. The contrast may be less between high vs poor quality goods than between, say, classics that fall apart and are delivered late, and swiftly produced, elegantly marketed trash.

Although it is overgeneralizing, a schematic presentation of the argument is that under capitalism, waste is generated by 'commission', by actions deliberately made, while under socialism, waste is generated by 'omission', by actions not done or neglected.

8 Multiplier analysis

In a capitalist industrial economy additional investment spending increases employment in the capital goods sector, leading to an increased wage bill, the proceeds of which are then spent on consumer goods, leading to increased activity in that sector. Investment spending thus causes consumption spending to move in the same direction. (But the reverse does not hold; a decline in consumption spending need not always have the same, or indeed, any general effect on investment.) It also causes energy and materials production to vary directly in the same proportion, and it stimulates replacement activity. Each of these in turn leads to increased activity among suppliers, as expressed in the matrix multiplier.

In a socialist industrial economy additional investment spending means intensifying the excess demand for capital goods. Since in general changes in the intensity of excess demand lead to attempts to change output in the same direction, when excess demand for capital goods increases, overtime work will rise, equipment will be overworked more, breakdowns and accidents will rise, etc. Any of these effects may result in additional wage income, the spending of which will further increase the demand pressure on consumer goods. Changes in excess investment demand thus generally cause changes in the same direction in excess consumer demand, and may cause further pressure on suppliers of materials and replacements. But as in capitalism, a decrease in excess consumer demand need have no effect on excess investment demand. Suppose, for example, that a rise in consumer prices relative to fixed money wages caused excess consumer demand to fall to zero; no productive capacity would thereby be released which could be transferred to the capital goods sector. (This point will be important when we come to the question of reform in socialism.)

In both capitalist and socialist economies the multiplier reflects the turnover of funds, which passes along the stimulus to activity. 'Injections' set off activity, and variable costs are passed along in the current period, transmitting the stimulus to further industries or sectors. Funds representing capital charges, depreciation and fixed costs are withdrawn, or turn over more slowly. In simplified form, then, the multiplier rests on the ratio of variable costs to total revenue, modified, if necessary, to take account of worker saving.[5] (The secondary effects on produced means of production follow from the matrix multiplier—if i is a vector of injections, and y one of outputs, then $y = i(I-A)^{-1}$, where A is the input-output matrix—but will be neglected here to concentrate on the aggregate relationship between demand and capacity.)

The principal injections into aggregate demand are gross investment I, current business spending (energy, consumption by overhead labour, office expenses) B, government spending G, and exports E. To get total demand these injections (measured in normal prices) must be multiplied by an expression which takes account of taxes, imports, saving out of wages, the wage rate and the productivity of labour (Nell 1988, Ch. 5,

Appendix). Let the coefficients be $t = t(w)$, $m = m(w)$, and $s = s(w)$, where these show the additional taxes, imports and savings that take place when aggregate income (output) increases as the result of additional employment, prompted by additional demand. Hence they are each positive functions of the real wage; even if the marginal tax (import, saving) ratio to individual income were constant, a higher income would mean higher taxes (imports, savings) when an individual changes from unemployed to employed. Moreover, there are good reasons to think that all three may be progressive in both systems. Hence aggregate demand can be written (Nell 1991):

$$[I+B+G+E] \frac{1}{\{1+t+m-(1-s)wn\}},$$

where t, m, and s are all increasing functions of the real wage w.

Aggregate productive capacity is given by the capital stock, measured at the given normal prices, multiplied by the productivity of the system. This last depends on the normal average ratio of capital stock to the labour force, and on the number of workers required per unit of output, on average. Aggregate capacity can therefore be written very simply:

$$K \frac{1}{(kn)},$$

where K is the total capital stock, k is required capital per worker, and n is labour force per unit of output. Both these coefficients must be measured at established or normal prices.

Now consider these expressions in the light of the earlier discussion. Characteristically, capitalism will find itself with excess capacity, socialism with excess demand (Nell 1988, chs. 5, 8). Hence, for capitalism:

$$[I+B+G+E) \frac{1}{\{1+t+m-(1-s)wn\}} < K \frac{1}{(kn)},$$

and for socialism:

$$[I+B+G+E] \frac{1}{\{1+t+m-(1-s)wn\}} > K \frac{1}{(kn)}.$$

However, care must be taken interpreting these, for they are not the same. When demand exceeds capacity, the multiplier cannot work properly because additional workers can not so readily be hired; however, existing workers can work overtime and sometimes additional shifts can be added. So the rate at which wages are paid and respent is likely to change as output rises above capacity. An increase in demand pressure will tend to raise w and n, thereby increasing the multiplier, intensifying the pressure, even though employment may not have risen. With this in mind let's compare the two.

Under capitalism, the existence of excess capacity requires firms to compete for the scarce demand by cutting costs and improving products. Hence n will tend to decline, increasing the expression for aggregate capacity, while reducing the multiplier. Thus the gap between capacity and demand tends to widen. However, competition may force firms to increase w in proportion to the decline in n, offsetting the impact of increased productivity on the multiplier. But t, m, and s are all increasing functions of w; hence the multiplier will still tend to decline and the gap widen. In any case, however, if overall productivity increases by x per cent, the new level of income is $(1+x)Y$; if wages rise in proportion and are wholly spent on consumption, its new level will be $(1+x)C$. So the new level of demand will be $I + (1+x)C < (1+x)Y$; excess capacity increases.

The competitive pressures arising from demand scarcity will tend to reduce normal investment and business spending, or at least increase their variability. Rising productivity increases capacity under conditions in which excess capacity already exists; this will dampen I. Increased efficiency in the use of energy, labour and materials will cut into B, and as superior or more cost-effective equipment designs become available, so that k falls, the reductions will affect I and G as well. Only exports are affected in the reverse way; if product or equipment designs improve, and costs are cut, then exports become more competitive and may increase. Otherwise, the pressures tend to reduce each of the major injections, intensifying stagnation.

This pattern is reversed under socialism. Excess demand—a state of generalized shortage—creates incentives to push production to the extreme, and there are in-built tendencies leading to further excess. Demand pressure can arise from the attempt to establish fair levels of pay and appropriate differentials, especially between different ranks in both enterprise and state hierarchies. Fairness requires granting regular pay increases when productivity permanently improves as a result of worker efforts. But if a certain kind of blue-collar pay increases in pace with productivity growth, relativities and hierarchical differentials will be eroded; to preserve them the pay of other workers, including management and white-collar pay, must rise. Thus localized increases in productivity can give rise to generalized increases in pay, and consequently in consumer demand.

This can take other forms. New capital goods are normally more productive than old. Thus productivity rises as a function of investment; however workers using the new and more productive goods are normally exercising the same skills, often in the same jobs, as workers in the old. Fairness therefore demands that they be paid the same. If pay rises with productivity for workers using the new goods, and then, out of concern for fairness, rises for workers using the old, demand will increase more than productivity.

As a consequence of demand pressure, bottlenecks develop, older and outmoded facilities are utilized, workers put in longer hours and make more mistakes, so that productivity falls, i.e. n rises. Moreover, demand pressure will tend to call forth basic productive inputs of poor quality, which often only become available in the wrong proportions or at the wrong times. As facilities are pushed harder, previously retired equipment will be brought back into production, and inappropriate equipment will be adapted, all of which will tend to raise capital used per worker k. (This is very much in line with the traditional view that costs rise as production facilities are pushed beyond a certain limit.) Hence, as k and n rise, even though K rises, the addition to capacity will be less than is needed, and the general downward pressure on productivity in all facilities may even reduce aggregate capacity, while the increases in n and w will raise the multiplier, expanding aggregate demand; both effects tend to widen the gap.

It was shown earlier that scarcity of demand promotes product improvement; excess demand, on the other hand, leads to product deterioration. Product improvement/deterioration is often represented as an increase/decrease in the productivity of inputs, which here would be a further decline/rise in k and n, compounding the effects already noted.

As in the capitalist case, both the presence of the gap and the tendency for it to widen, due to its effects on productivity, will lead to pressures on the spending plans of enterprises. Shortages of capacity in relation to demand are a signal to increase the pace of investment spending, to try to bring new capacity on line as fast as possible. Shortages of inputs will lead enterprises to stockpile inventory. Inefficient operation will lead to larger than necessary business expenses. Hence both I and B will increase. The same will hold for G; in the face of generalized shortages and inefficient operation, the government will have to increase its activities, expand its facilities and stockpile scarce items. Again, the impact on exports will be different. If costs rise and the quality of goods declines, exports will tend to fall. By the same token the propensity to import is likely to rise. Moreover, if selling is easy in the domestic market, but competitive internationally, enterprises will prefer to focus on the domestic scene.

For closed economies, then, in capitalism the tendency to stagnation is reinforced by competition, while socialist markets tend to intensify shortages. Capitalist pressures tend to stimulate technical progress in the form of cost-cutting and product improvement; socialist pressures tend to foster inefficiency, cost over-runs and quality deterioration. Capitalist economies deliver services to those with money—which tends to be a buyers' market; socialist economies to those with need— a sellers' market. So again the quality is better under capitalism. For open economies, these conclusions must be modified by noting that the effect on exports (and perhaps imports) will tend to run in the opposite direction in each case; capitalist incentives stimulate exports, socialist ones weaken them.[6] Neither capitalist nor socialist systems are *radically* unstable. Capitalism tends to stagnate, socialism to run shortages, but both tendencies meet countervailing pressures and stay within limits. One source of such pressures is external trade, but others can be found within the domestic economy itself.

9 Shortages and stagnant growth

Paradoxically, excessive demand pressure, arising from planners' desires to grow as fast as possible, can lead to slower growth. Capitalism normally has excess (as well as reserve) capacity available, enabling it to shift resources easily to overcome bottlenecks. By contrast, in an economy in which every sector is operating at full blast, getting the proportions of output correct is both important and difficult. The difficulties are obvious—if there is no reserve capacity, neither aggregate output nor the proportions of output can be adjusted with any ease. There is no room to correct mistakes. It is important because if the proportions are not correct, investment cannot be carried out as planned, with the results not only that growth will be slower than expected, but that some output will be wasted. It may even happen, paradoxically, that excess capacity may emerge!

The maximum rate of growth of the system (with given technique, assumed to be embodied in its plant and equipment), will equal the maximum rate of profit, but will only be attainable if outputs are in the proportions that will produce a physical net surplus consisting of the same goods in the same proportions as the aggregate means of production (Pasinetti 1977, pp. 208-212; Abraham-Frois and Berrebi 1979).

For any wage rate above the basic standard of living, there will be a corresponding rate of profit lying below the maximum, according to the inverse wage-profit rate function. If wages are consumed and profits invested, there will be a maximum balanced growth rate corresponding to each level of the wage—but this growth rate can only be attained if the outputs are in the correct proportions. Thus we have the quantity-growth equations, dual to the price-profit system:

$$q = (1+g)A'q + cL' \Rightarrow q = cL'[1-(1+g)A']^{-1}$$

which gives the relative quantities q associated with the growth rate g for a given rate of average per capita consumption c. If $w = c$, then $r = g$, and q and p will be the corresponding left and right hand characteristic vectors.

If output is produced in any other proportions the system will have to grow more slowly; some goods will be in short supply, others in excess. For each basic good a ratio can be formed, the numerator being its total production minus the amount of it used as input in all the various industries; the denominator being the amount used as input by the various industries. These ratios can be called the 'own-rates of surplus'; when they are all equal, then outputs are produced in the proportions that will enable investment of the surplus to reach the maximum rate of growth consistent with the given consumption/wage level. But when the own-rates are not equal, some will be higher and some lower, meaning that some goods will be in surplus and others in deficit, compared to what is needed for investment. The investment which can actually be carried out will therefore be limited by the amounts available, i.e. the limit will be set by the good most in deficit. The surplus goods are simply excess. So the sustainable rate of growth for an economy operating in given proportions will be set by the *smallest* of the physical own-rates of surplus of the basic commodities generated by production in those proportions.

In the absence of shortage, investment would grow at the same rate as the capital stock, the growth of which in turn will be governed by the plan. If the plan's proposed rate of growth (not to be confused with the earlier symbol for government spending) is G (which for reasons already given, will exceed or at best equal g_w), then dI would equal GI. The presence of generalized shortage, however, will cause investment growth to fall below that rate as capacity is overworked and bottlenecks accumulate. The capital goods sector will be unable to expand its output in accordance with the plan and the bottlenecks and shortages will make it difficult to complete projects on schedule. Demand pressures will lead to the production of outputs in the wrong proportions for investment; production can be expected to respond both to demand and to political or bureaucratic pressure—and it would be remarkable if the ability to muster such pressure were distributed in the exact proportions required for growth at the highest attainable rate, given the standard of living. But if goods are produced in the wrong proportions in response to demand and bureaucratic pressure, some goods will not be usable because complementary goods are not available in the correct proportions.

We can spell out an exact relationship here. With a given technique, there is a unique maximum growth rate; when the system is not producing the output corresponding to this, it can only grow at a lower rate. Putting this another way, we know from growth theory that the maximum rate of growth is reached when the 'own-rates' of surplus (output minus direct plus indirect use as input, divided by direct plus indirect use as input) for every basic good are equal. Let the $q's$ indicate output levels, and the $a's$ be input coefficients—then:

$$\frac{q_1 - [a_{11}q_1 + a_{21}q_2 + ... + a_{n1}q_n]}{[a_{11}q_1 + a_{21}q_2 + ... + a_{n1}q_n]} = \frac{q_2 - [a_{12}q_1 + a_{22}q_2 + ... + a_{n2}q_n]}{[a_{12}q_1 + a_{22}q_2 + ... + a_{n2}q_n]} = ...$$

But the outputs, and embodied productive capacities, of the various basic goods will respond differentially to demand pressure. Hence as shortage intensifies, demand pressure will move the system away from the 'turnpike' proportions, in which the own-rates are equal. Some will rise, responding to demand pressure, which necessarily causes others to fall, since the available labour force will provide a constraint. But the sustainable rate of growth is set by the *lowest* of the own-rates among the basic goods. Hence the effective increase in investment will be reduced by demand pressure.

10 The informal sector and self-employment
Under capitalism if the level of demand falls too far below capacity activity can be expected to increase in the 'informal sector'. This phrase covers the provision of illegal products and services—drugs, liquor, tax-free cigarettes, prostitution, gambling, etc.—but also the production of basic goods and services on an *ad hoc* basis, usually using an earlier technology, and traded in barter. In a severe slump activity in the informal sector will tend to rise, providing subsistence and additional income for the unemployed or partially employed. Such increased activ-

ity results from efforts by workers and entrepreneurs to search out and service latent demand; the initiative comes from the supply side. Insofar as these efforts attract money that would otherwise have been saved or put into financial speculation they clearly add to effective demand and therefore tend to offset stagnation. (Since informal sector activities tend to be highly labour-intensive, even when spending on them displaces other goods, demand will be boosted, since the multiplier in the informal sector will be higher.)

In socialism, by contrast, as shortages intensify, unsatisfied demand will look for new channels, and a black market can be expected to develop in strongly needed services and goods, which will divert activity and resources into the most profitable channels. Since enterprises are in the best position to do this, the emergence of the black market may help to overcome serious production bottlenecks. Improvements and innovations may also be generated, both increasing productivity and absorbing demand. The initiative here comes from the demand side. Thus the informal sector in socialism will also move countercyclically, tending to limit the intensification of shortage.

An interesting contrast should be noted. Although the informal sector in capitalism arises in part as a response to conditions of scarce demand, it is itself (at least its illegal part) a sellers' market. Consumers take what drugs, numbers, etc. they can get; they are not in a position to shop around. The police see to that. A contrasting symmetry can be seen in socialism. The black market arises in response to generalized shortage, but is itself a buyers' market. Unless the quality is good, no one will take the risk of buying illegally.

In both systems the informal sector is a special case of self-employment, which must be understood in relation to the predominant enterprise or corporate labour market. Self-employment means working with small-scale technology and high fixed real costs (including self-household consumption needs). Variable costs will generally be low. Thus when demand is high, so that prices drift up (lowering real wages in corporate employment), unit costs will be low due to the large volume and earnings will be significant. Moreover, with lower real wages in corporate employment, self-employment will be more attractive. Hence the supply of self-employment will respond positively to demand. Thus a shortage economy provides a generally favourable environment, but for the same reasons in reverse, demand scarcity will tend to be disastrous—as the history of the family farm illustrates (cf. Nell 1991).

11 Growth cycles

Both systems have built-in tendencies to exacerbate their characteristic condition—stagnation and shortage, respectively and both also tend to generate offsetting influences in international trade and in the informal sector. But the offsetting influences examined so far have been external to the interaction between the creation of aggregate demand and the building of capacity. That interaction, which determines the extent of excess capacity or shortage, itself tends to preserve the gap between demand and capacity, allowing it to fluctuate, but keeping it within limits. This can be shown by examining simple interactions between two variables—investment and excess capacity for capitalism, investment and shortage for socialism. In each case it is possible to find a cyclical pattern, confining the variation within limits. Admittedly, these models are too simple and abstract to be realistic, but the forces portrayed are present in each system (Nell 1991).

The results can be summarized: In both the case of capitalism and demand scarcity, and socialism with demand pressure, the system sets limits on its characteristic gap between demand and capacity; this gap will never disappear, but it will never reach unmanageable levels either. Each system works within definite boundaries, even though there are no 'floors' or 'ceilings'. Nor does either system ever operate at normal full employment, or grow at the warranted rate. Of course, these two models are greatly oversimplified; but they deal with a central issue— the relation between the capacity-creating and demand-generating aspects of investment—and they show that this relationship can create cyclical behaviour while remaining entirely on one side or the other of the balanced or warranted rate of growth.

12 Inflation

Inflation has different but symmetrical causes in the two systems. In a demand-constrained economy, inflation originates in changes in costs; in a resource-constrained economy inflation arises from the effects of demand or changes in demand. In short, a demand-constrained system has cost inflation, a resource-constrained system has demand inflation.

(There is a major qualification to this, however. While prices of manufactured goods are generally insensitive to changes in demand, primary products may be quite sensitive, especially to large or sudden changes. Thus a sudden, unexpected, or large demand increase may lead to a rise in primary products, which is then passed along as cost inflation, setting off a wage-price spiral.)

In a demand-constrained economy inflation is the market process by which it is determined which groups shall bear the burden of increased costs. In a resource-constrained economy inflation is the market process by which it is determined which groups shall bear the burden of the shortages.

In a capitalist economy, when a cost increases (say oil imports rise in price) the various industries using oil pass along as much as they can in higher prices. Consumers thus face a rising cost of living, and so demand higher wages and salaries, further raising costs to business, which in turn are passed along again in price increases, to the extent possible. But while business will try to pass cost increases along, and workers will try to recoup cost of living increases in higher pay, their ability to do so depends on their respective market positions. Not all businesses and not all groups of workers will succeed; indeed, it could even happen that none are wholly successful, but in general some will do better than others. Those who are relatively most successful, round after round, will escape most of the costs, which the least successful will have to bear. As prices and wages rise, however, the burden is lessened in real terms, and the wage-price spiral peters out when the reduced burden has been distributed between business and labour in proportion to their inability to pass it along.

The process can be illustrated with a single-equation model. Let k stand for means of production per unit (aggregate) output, and n for labour per unit output, with m as the aggregate mark-up. Also let $\$$ be the price of capital goods, w the money wage rate and p the money price index of output. Initially:

$$mks_{(t-1)} + mnw_{(t-1)} = p_{(t-1)}$$

$\$$ then increases and p is increased accordingly, w remains fixed:

$$mk[\$_t - \$_{(t-1)}] = p_t - p_{(t-1)},$$

However, once prices go up, households respond by demanding wage increases to compensate:

$$\frac{[w_t - w_{(t-1)}]}{w_{(t-1)}} = \frac{x[p_{(t-1)} - p_{(t-2)}]}{p_{(t-2)}},$$

where $0 \leq x \leq 1$. The parameter x indicates wage-earners' market power; if $x = 0$ they are not able to raise the money wage at all, and the full burden of the cost increase will fall on them; if $x = 1$ they are able to keep pace fully with price increases, and the wage-price spiral will continue until the original ratio $\frac{\$}{w/p}$ is re-established. Any value in between means that workers can keep up partially, but will end up bearing the larger share of the burden. (In a labour-dominated system workers might be able to keep up fully with any cost increases, but business would be able to raise prices only a fraction. Interchange the *w's* and *p's* in the equation.) In any event the wage price spiral comes to an end when the burden, reduced by inflation, is distributed.

In a resource-constrained context inflation will result from the impact of an increase in excess demand, e.g. a rise in investment; prices will be bid up by the competition for the scarce goods as consumers and enterprises try to shift the burden of the shortage to those who cannot afford higher prices. But as prices rise, workers will demand pay increases, and enterprises in turn will increase output prices as their costs rise. Some groups of workers and some enterprises will be relatively successful; but those in weaker market positions will do poorly, and will end up bearing the burden of the shortages, reduced by the effects of the general price increases. Here, however, the Kaleckian dictum, 'workers spend what they get, capitalists get what they spend,' must be adapted and considered. Workers can only spend more if they receive raises; enterprises, however, will collectively get back whatever they collectively spend—from each other for capital and intermediate goods, from consumers spending their wages on consumer goods. In the nature of things, then, enterprises will keep up with demand pressure.

Let us suppose that some input in short supply is bid up in price, to ration supplies to those who can afford them. Enterprises using the input then try to pass the costs along; enterprise spending in the aggregate returns to them. Households respond to the higher prices by demanding wage increases. If they get them, their wages return to enterprises in the form of receipts from consumer goods sales. To the extent they fail to keep up, real wages are reduced, and workers bear the burden of the shortages. A corollary is that real supply and effort will tend to shift away from the consumer goods sector to production for inter-enterprise transactions. (Trying to reduce demand pressure by cutting back money wages could backfire if, in anticipation, enterprises intensified this shift.) Such processes may be open or suppressed.

In both economic systems inflation is a market response to an external shock, whose function is to determine who will bear the burden— of the cost increase in capitalism, of the increase in shortages in socialism. In each case the rise in prices and wages reduces the burden to be distributed, while shifting it to the weakest, those least able to pass along or keep up with the increases. The more evenly matched the market positions of the various players, the longer the process will continue, and the lower the final burden to be distributed.

13 Policies

An important implication of these different perspectives arises in connection with policies for 'transition'. If the problems of shortage arose from a universal condition of soft budget constraints, we could expect all or nearly all firms to have established procedures and work habits that will prove unacceptable in a more or less competitive market. But if the conditions of shortage are macroeconomic in origin, arising from persistent excess demand, then although firms in general may be lax about costs (especially in regard to feather-bedding) and distribution of managerial efficiency and engineering competence. In the first case, all or nearly all firms would require massive and forced privatization. But in the second case, only the weakest firms would require overhaul, and after stripping the feather beds, the bulk of the firms could be considered a good basis on which to rebuild.

When faced with excessive demand scarcity, capitalism's response, in countries where capital is politically dominant, has been government intervention to maintain the level of demand and to control prices. This has to be planned and coordinated with the private sector and is usually understood to be supplementary; it is supposed to make the system work better. If the private sector is dominant, the activities of the government cannot undermine this. (Hence capitalist governments tend to shy away from a commitment to full employment,[7] fearing that it will strengthen labour too much.) Intervention should not displace or compete with private sector production, or even pre-empt potential private activity, unless a strong case can be made that such private activity will undermine general welfare. (Of course, in countries or periods when labour dominates politics, priorities may tend to be different.)

Interventionist spending should be flexible; it may have to be increased or decreased at short notice. It must be possible from time to time to redirect it from one sector or region to another. The purchases it represents therefore cannot be essential to the operation of the government. Military and aero-space spending (which developed for largely political reasons) fit very well. The products, at least the larger items, cannot be marketed privately, and could not be produced without the active participation of the government. And they are inessential not just in the sense that everyone hopes they will never be used, but that they do not enter into either production or consumption, so for the economy it does not matter whether they are finished and delivered this year or next.[8]

Government spending is essential to limiting unemployment and excess capacity, but there are many other policy instruments: other forms of spending, 'automatic stabilizers', taxes, subsidies, monetary policies, social programmes, and, of course, usually kept as a last resort, direct controls. All of these are designed to control unemployment and inflation, to set levels of activity and offset the side effects of incentives, and to induce the economy to move in desired directions. In addition, of course, regulation is needed to prevent fraud, and the marketing of saleable but dangerous products.

This complex—and much-debated—array of capitalist policies stands in marked contrast to the socialist world. There do not appear to be any consistent and well thought out policy packages for managing shortage, for adjusting the level of demand pressure, or coping with the many side effects, for example, on quality, work effort and other incentives.

Socialist government and military budgets should have the opposite impact of their capitalist counterparts—increasing productivity or capacity, without adding to incomes. Thus the use of the Chinese Red Army in the construction of dams or in reclaiming land, the Cuban literacy campaign and similar mass activities which improve skills or construct infrastructure while adding minimally to demand have exactly the right impact. But Soviet deficits, unproductive transfers and poorly planned or executed public projects, on the other hand, are exactly wrong. Just as western economists have proposed TIP's—tax-based incomes policies—to curb wage-price spirals, SIP's—subsidy-based incentives to productivity—would be appropriate in shortage economies. Increases in the productivity of labour or investment could be rewarded with special subsidies, which, in a shortage economy, could not consist only of income, but would have to include shopping privileges at the head of the queue. Indeed, this should be done in an organized fashion. In addition, 'automatic' penalties for falling productivity should be developed, along with procedures for removing incompetent managements, and shutting down inefficent plants.

14 Queue-jumping: shortage as an incentive

To give an example, rewards could perhaps be arranged by taking advantage of the situation of shortages. Competition is what drives productivity, and competition must be based on some kind of scarcity. What is scarce in socialism is precisely the ability to purchase, to jump to the head of the queue. Hence that is what could be used to reward increased productivity, or improved quality. Queues and shortages would have to be administered carefully (and honestly, with effective enforcement); then a limited number of queue-jumping permits, tied to certain products, and lasting for varying periods of time, would be issued as rewards to workers/firms who increase productivity or improve quality. Successful introduction of new products/new processes would likewise be rewarded. (All or some such tickets could be traded, allowing a market to develop to determine the value attributed to each kind of ticket, so providing authorities with information about the relative strengths of the incentives being provided.)

This approach could be adapted to inter-industry transactions as well. Efficient firms could be rewarded with places at the head of the queue for inputs and capital goods; inefficient ones will thereby be penalized. Firms that rank low in efficiency and/or product quality could be given a bonus for reorganizing and re-opening on the basis of new technology and new management—perhaps making the decision on the basis of a vote by the workers and staff.

But how would efficiency, productivity and product quality be measured? Who would determine the rankings and the rewards? The beauty of the market is that this appears to be done automatically, and even if it is sometimes the result of manipulation, it is still free of the dead hand of bureaucracy. Much of it, however, can be done by market-like processes—points can be given for cutting prices, for meeting quotas, and for reducing labour or other inputs, while points will be subtracted for cost over-runs, or for failing to pay bills, for paying them late, or failing to service state loans. Such points can be awarded or subtracted automatically. Banks will keep point accounts for firms which will be audited annually and can be challenged by those lower in the queue. Queue-jumping tickets will be issued based on points. The market for these tickets, the way they are traded and used, will in turn tell which goods are thought to be of best quality—so quality points will then be issued in proportion to the tickets spent on the goods of a firm.

Of course, a proposal such as this would imply that the

'nomenklatura' would have to give up its privileged access to, and control over, positions at the head of the queues for the most desirable goods. This is not the place to consider the problems of introducing reforms, or develop the details of alternative proposals; the point is that *either* these kinds of policy innovations, using the fact of shortage to set up competition, were needed (but nothing of the sort was ever introduced), or aggregate demand had to be curbed sufficiently to prevent the ill effects of excess demand from emerging. But this never happened either.

15 Market reforms

Instead of developing appropriate policies for managing shortage and its side effects, the favoured course for socialist systems was to try to introduce market 'reforms' or, more recently, to shift to a market economy altogether. Such reforms sought to develop competition, spurring technical progress, within the framework of a planned economy. Soft budget constraints are to be hardened by market pressures, bringing efficiency and responsiveness to profit incentives. Besides incentives, the market is believed to provide a better way to test new products and new processes; its advantage over bureaucratic testing is that it is anonymous and objective. And it provides a simple and automatic way to curb excess demand—when demand is excessive, let prices rise. This will cut real wages, or real investment spending, and therefore reduce pressure on industry. Such market reforms, of course, would have to be coordinated with the responsibilities of the planning system.

There are serious problems with these proposals. First, a major effect of price flexibility and relaxation of controls will be to promote self-employment, which does little to improve the performance of the mass production industries. A second consequence of price flexibility will be inflation of the kind outlined earlier. Thirdly, these price changes are not consistent with the ideal of fairness; price increases to ration shortage are regressive and will be likely to create political tensions. Fourthly, price flexibility reduces (or shifts the impact of) shortage, but it does not create demand scarcity. Hence it will not create the characteristic incentive patterns of western market systems. In particular, it will not put any pressure on the worst firms, since they will still be able to sell whatever they produce. Nor, as we have seen, will the labour markets adjust to eliminate shortages.

The virtues of each system, technical innovativeness and full use of economic resources, respectively, depend on the mode of operation of the system as a whole. These can therefore not be developed in a 'mixed' system (not to be confused with the social democratic 'mixed economy'). Not so the vices and defects appropriate to each—alienation and corruption on the one hand, and technical regress and bureaucratic abuse on the other. A mixed system could easily end up with the worst of both worlds, but is unlikely to get the best.[9]

Market reforms, because they incorrectly attribute the cause of shortages to supply inefficiency and/or to incorrect prices, fail to address the real problems, which are macroeconomic in origin. What is needed are policy instruments to manage and control the degree of shortage, on the one hand, and to offset its detrimental effects on incentives on the other. (Indeed, it should be asked why socialism could not be run under conditions of demand scarcity; to do that, however, would require very considerable policy changes.) And the failure to develop appropriate policies may be socialism's most serious problem.

This can be seen in a related area. Capitalism keeps costs down, among other ways, by systematically overlooking the public costs of damage to the environment. Capitalist incentives also lead to systematic distortions of information, the concealing of scientific and technological breakthroughs, the corruption of product development—making things that will sell rather than things that work and/or last. When these effects become seriously damaging, reform movements are provoked, and take action through the democratic political process.

In much the same way socialism leads to parallel but symmetrically opposite problems: from sloppy work and TV's that explode, to large mistakes frozen into the bureaucratic routine and to an inertia that inhibits change, and also, in the scramble for output, to environmental damage. But until now political repression prevented the development of effective specific reform movements.

When a political movement is provoked that may cost the firms/bureaucracies more than it would cost to prevent or clean up the problems, then it is time for reform. But this may happen well after the point where the additional social costs of damage to the environment or the population exceeds the cost of further abuse. Moreover, new externalities often interact with existing ones; rather than combining additively, they may combine multiplicatively—and it may take time for their effects to show. Thus their effects may be especially strong, but relatively easy to conceal or overlook. Neither system has developed adequate policies for coping with externalities, but democratic capitalism, by providing a political forum in which those affected can protest, does block many of the worst excesses. Once again, real-world social-ism has so far failed to develop any comparable political mobilization.

16 Restoring capitalism

This does away with the problems of socialism, of course, but then we are back with the difficulties of inequality, unresponsiveness to the public interest, and the waste inherent in business cycles, excess capac-ity and unemployment. There are well tried, and well understood, though not always effective, policies for managing these evils. It is not clear that the radical 'free-marketeers' of Eastern Europe fully under-stand the necessity—and the difficulties—of managing capitalism, for if they did they might not be so eager to abolish all the controls and planning mechanisms of the old system, some of which might prove useful in the new.

17 Conclusions

The inherent dynamism of the capitalist market system turns out to be a *macroeconomic* phenomenon; it results from a systematic scarcity of aggregate demand. And the shortages of socialism are not the simple consequence of inefficiency or of soft budget constraints or any other microeconomic factors; shortages, inefficiency and soft budgets all are the results of fundamental macroeconomic pressures. *The characteris-tic micro-behaviour of each type of economy has its foundation in that system's macroeconomic mode of operation.*

This in turn implies that a dynamic market economy cannot, in princi-ple, allocate scarce resources optimally. For if it did, it would be re-source-constrained, and so not dynamically competitive. Optimal allo-cation, it seems, is not consistent with a competitive capitalist system. Uncertainty, on the other hand, is necessarily pervasive, since demand scarcity implies that firms can never be sure of their markets. Conventional price theory, concerned with optimal allocation under conditions of market certainty, would thus, paradoxically, seem more at home in socialism.

Planning for optimal allocation is the central feature of socialism, since it can arrange for the full and best use of all its resources. Such a plan also eliminates uncertainty as to markets. But the price is techno-logical stagnation. Each of these modes of operation has strengths and weaknesses unique to it, and they cannot easily be combined. Government intervention in capitalism runs the danger of upsetting the rule of competition and diluting the effects of demand scarcity. But policy intervention has become sophisticated and effective. Market reforms in socialism contradict the rule of fairness in allocation and distribution. So far they have proved ineffective and may simply be tentative steps towards restoring capitalism. Capitalism has faced its characteristic problems and the Keynesian approach, with help from its many critics, has developed ways of coping. Nothing comparable appears to have emerged for socialism, and, at present, most socialist countries appear to be dismantling their economies.

Indeed, over the years each has tended, often without acknowledging it, to try to borrow from the other, hoping for a taste of its virtues. So long as it is ideals and ambitions that are borrowed, there will be no problems. Capitalism wants full employment and fairer distribution, and needs to be able to plan and administer environmental and other controls. Socialism needs quality control, innovation, and ways of breaking through bureaucratic inertia. But socialism tried to adopt the working institutions of the capitalist system, without understanding how this conflicted with its own mode of operation, and it ended up learning only that borrowing ideas, like borrowing money, is no substitute for developing solutions to problems. Unfortunately, in the process the socialist tradition seems to have lost all hope, and is now rushing to embrace the familiar devils of the marketplace.

Notes

* I would like to thank Mark Knell and Christine Rider for their helpful comments on the paper. The usual provisos apply.
1. When comparing capitalism and socialism it is important to remember that no actual economy will be purely one type or another; all are mixtures bearing traces of their national histories, international relations and political compromises. Nevertheless, analytical study is best carried out at an abstract level in terms of pure types. Prominent features of actual economies will be identifiable as belonging to one system or another and the logic of these features can be traced in the abstract system of which they are a part, where they have free play and full scope. We will treat capitalism and socialism as such abstract systems, and in doing so will draw on a central theme of Kaldor's later years, the distinction between 'demand-constrained' and 'resource-constrained' systems, developed implicitly by Kalecki (1986), but first explicitly defined by Kornai (1986). This distinction requires replacing the scarcity-based theory of value with a classical approach in which manufacturing prices are largely invariant to changes in demand.
2. To assure a unique, positive solution the matrix must be square, non-negative and irreducible. The rate of profit is derived from the Frobenius root, prices from the characteristic vector. The rate of profit is therefore not a price; it is a measure of the surplus. The real wage and the rate of profit will be inversely related (Sraffa 1960; Pasinetti 1977). The price equation can be extended to take account of fixed capital, joint production (of which fixed capital is a special case), and rents for non-produced means of production. (The theory is by no means confined to the case of a 'single factor', labour, as has sometimes been claimed.) When land and joint production are included, however, there will arise cases where demand may appear to play an important role, theoretically, in establishing prices (Schefold 1989). But these cases revolve around the question of 'the choice of technique', an issue taken over from the neoclassical framework. (Since the

changes which take place when techniques shift can easily be 'paradoxical', i.e. contrary to what would be expected on the basis of conventional theory (Kurz 1990; Metcalfe and Steedman 1972; Montet 1979), the argument provides no support for a 'scarcity' theory of prices.) In practice, however, techniques are not 'chosen' in the abstract from a 'book of blueprints'; they evolve historically, under market-generated pressures. Given the techniques embodied in plant and equipment, and in human labour skills, at any time, and given the real wage—the normal and expected standard of living—normal prices and the normal rate of profit will be independent of demand.

3. Suppose a firm deliberately chose a less ambitious market position than its competitive place warranted, and so opted for a correspondingly lower level of reserve capacity. Could it thereby avoid the possibility of carrying excess reserves? Only if by aiming lower it could guarantee certainty of hitting its target, and maybe not then. Suppose a similarly well-endowed competitor also aimed lower, and for the same segment of the market. (The two top middleweights both enter welterweight.) The uncertainty arises because competition is a battle, and the winners cannot be predicted any more than the winners in a sporting contest. In any such struggle the contenders must be prepared to defend their home territories if they lose, and to take possession of new territory if they win. This last, especially, requires carrying a purely speculative reserve.

Each firm can calculate the pricing and investment plans of the representative, average firm, and can thereby determine the amount of additional capacity it should build to maintain its market share. But this determination is subject to two kinds of uncertainty: the future expansion of the market can only be estimated within a range, and the exact impact of technological improvements on costs and output can only be approximately judged. Let us suppose that no firm has any definite technological or managerial advantage, so that no one has a special incentive to try to improve their market position, but there do exist economies of scale, both in production and in marketing. Consequently, firms will have to decide whether to err on the side of overbuilding in relation to expected demand, carrying excess capacity with lower unit costs, or on the side of underbuilding, carrying no excess, but bearing higher unit costs.

Consider the strategic position of a representative firm RF vis-a-vis 'all the rest' of the firms AR. If both firms underbuild, the result will be unsatisfied demand, creating room for entry, so that both RF and AR will suffer losses due to new competitors. If AR underbuilds and RF overbuilds, then RF gains because with lower unit costs, it will be able to increase its share. If AR overbuilds and RF underbuilds, RF suffers a substantial loss in market share. If AR overbuilds and RF also overbuilds, RF suffers only a small and uncertain loss due to carrying excess capacity, which may be partly offset by economies of scale. The best strategy for RF, therefore, is to overbuild, or build ahead of demand. This applies to every firm taken successively in isolation, and considered against all the rest. Hence there will be a tendency to excess capacity.

4. This is not a statement about intentions. Socialist managers would probably like to keep the lid on money wages no less than their capitalist counterparts, and they would certainly like to stimulate productivity. But they lack the tools; the system encourages wage drift, and fails to provide incentives for hard work and innovation.

5. Conventionally, the multiplier depends on the marginal propensity to save out of household income, and it is normally assumed, in theory, that business distributes all income to households, and in practice, that it is *as if* they did, i.e. that business treats retained earnings as a household would have, had those funds been distributed to them. These assumptions are seldom explicitly argued, and, in general, are not justifiable. (Marglin 1986; Nell 1988) However, there are even more serious issues; both withdrawals and injections into the spending stream originate on the business side of the social accounts. Withdrawals are not necessarily savings, if by savings we mean the accumulation of long-term financial assets. By distinguishing withdrawals and savings, it is possible to express the multiplier in terms of the *cost structure* of business - the multiplier can be shown to depend only on variable costs, that is, the wage bill and other inputs (Nell 1988). When other inputs are neglected, and sectors are aggregated, we obtain a multiplier which equals $1/(1-wn)$.

6. The respective systems of international trade work the same way. The Western system puts the burden of adjustment on the weaker nations that run deficits; surplus nations do not have to adjust. To restore balance of payments equilibrium basically requires austerity

and unemployment, thereby lowering imports. Thus demand will be lowered throughout the system, until the deficit nations are all either in balance, or at an acceptable level of imbalance. The Comecon system financed deficits; planners tried to achieve balance, but if an imbalance arose the Soviet Union would finance it. No austerity measures were required.

7. During the entire post-war period, the US economy only twice exceeded its potential output level, and each time only for a short period. (Nor is 'potential output' full capacity, in the sense that demand above that level would cause generalized shortage.) Of course, West Germany and Japan, and others, often operated at or near full employment, as conventionally defined. But these were all open economies with a high ratio of trade to GNP and a strong balance of payments position. They were thus able to draw on the excess capacity and labour reserves elsewhere in the capitalist world. So, though expansionist, they never functioned as shortage economies.

8. Military spending generates demand without adding to capacity or providing consumable goods. It is therefore an ideal, but totally wasteful, supplement to demand. Unfortunately, but not accidentally, it produces at high cost, and stimulates technical progress in directions that will generally not be helpful in market competition—for the good and simple reason that the consumers have no competitive choices, and no effective ways of expressing their displeasure. The military-industrial complex is a planned/bureaucratic *finance-constrained* system with no scarcity of demand—whatever it produces will be acceptable and costover-runs will be managed. It tries to achieve many objectives with limited resources, and faces no penalties from disaffected users, a combination of incentives tending to result in baroque technological development.

9. In connection with reform it is sometimes argued that expanding the planned area of capitalism and the market area of socialism will lead the two systems to converge to a mixed economy, operating at full employment and possessing the best characteristics of both. But the planned area of capitalism is not resource-constrained; it is constrained by the availability of finance, which leads to the same pattern of incentives in regard to technical progress, but does not imply the efficient use of scarce resources. Nor is the market area of socialism demand-constrained. Without shortage of demand there will be no competition for sales; hence encouraging the money motive may simply promote corruption. Socialist technical progress is combinatorial—making limited resources do many jobs; in a capitalist context it tends to become corrupted into creating baroque forms. Capitalist technical progress consists in cutting costs through efficient usage; in a socialist context it tends to become corrupted into cutting corners.

References

Abraham-Frois, G. and Berrebi, E. (1979). *Theory of Value, Prices and Accumulation*, Cambridge: Cambridge University Press.

Blinder, A. (1988). 'The Fall and Rise of Keynesian Economics', Paper presented to 1988 Australian Economics Congress, 28 August, Australian National University, Canberra.

Davis, C. and Charemza, W. (1989). *Models of Disequilibrium and Shortage in Centrally Planned Economics*, London: Chapman and Hall.

Eichner, A. (1976). *The Mega-corp and Oligopoly*, New York: Cambridge University Press.

Gale, D. (1960). *The Theory of Linear Economic Models*, New York: McGraw Hill.

Goodwin, R. (1970). 'A Growth Cycle', in Feinstein, C. H., ed., *Socialism, Capitalism and Economic Growth*, Cambridge: Cambridge University Press.

Gordon, R. J. (1990). 'What is New-Keynesian Economics?', *Journal of Economic Literature*, xxviii.

Harrod, R. (1939). 'An Essay in Dynamic Theory', *Economic Journal*, 46.

Kaldor, N. (1985). *Economics Without Equilibrium*, Armonk: M. E. Sharpe.

Kalecki, M. (1954). *Theory of Economic Dynamics*, London: George Allen and

Unwin.

Kalecki, M. (1986). *Selected Essays on Economic Planning*, Cambridge: Cambridge University Press.

Kornai, J. (1986). *Contradictions and Dilemmas: Studies on The Socialist Economy and Society*, Cambridge, Mass: M.I.T. Press.

Kregel, J. (1980). 'Economic Dynamics and the Theory of Steady Growth: An Historical Essay on Harrod's "Knife-Edge"', *History of Political Economy*, 12.

Kurz, H. D. (1990). *Capital, Distribution and Effective Demand*, Oxford: Polity Press.

Marglin, S. (1984). *Growth, Distribution, and Prices*, Cambridge: Harvard.

Metcalfe, J. and Steedman, I. (1972). 'Reswitching and Primary Input Use', *Economic Journal*, 82.

Montet, C. (1979). 'Reswitching and Primary Input Use: A Comment', *Economic Journal*, 89.

Morishima, M. (1975). *Theory of Economic Growth*, Oxford: Oxford University Press [1969].

Nell, E. (1988). *Prosperity and Public Spending*, London: Unwin Hyman.

Nell, E. (1991). 'Capitalism, Socialism and Effective Demand', in Nell and Semmler.

Nell, E. (1992). *Transformational Growth and Effective Demand*, London: Macmillan.

Nell, E. and Semmler, W. (1991c). *Nicholas Kaldor and Mainstream Economics: Confrontation or Convergence?*, London: Macmillan.

Pasinetti, L. (1977). *Lectures on the Theory of Production*, New York: Columbia University Press.

Semmler, W. (1984). Competition, Monopoly, and Differential Profit Rates, New York: Columbia University Press.

Schefold, B. (1989). *Mr. Sraffa on Joint Production and Other Essays*, London: Unwin Hyman.

Sraffa, P. (1960). *Production of Commodities by Means of Commodities*, Cambridge: Cambridge University Press.

Tobin, J. (1982). *Asset Accumulation and Economic Activity*, Chicago: Chicago University Press.

Wood, A. (1976). *A Theory of Profits*, Cambridge: Cambridge University Press.

6 From a Command Toward a Market Economy: The Polish Experience

Kazimierz Laski

1 Introduction

At the beginning of 1990 Poland began a so-called shock therapy programme supported by the IMF and the World Bank. Its main goals were to accomplish the transition from a command to a market economy and to stabilize the economy, including the suppression of inflation. Available statistical data now make possible an analysis of the results achieved by it and of the economic philosophy lying behind shock therapy. This is important because there is still quite a difference of opinion whether the cure was a success or a failure.

The Polish experience with a stabilization and transformation plan deserves attention for another reason. Czechoslovakia, at the beginning of 1991, started a policy almost identical to the Polish one, although its initial economic situation was quite different from that in Poland. Other previously socialist countries will follow suit. It is evident that a transformation and stabilization policy of the Polish variety becomes a kind of standard for countries forging a transition from a command to a market economy. Under these conditions the study of the Polish experience can give us some ideas about the problems and dangers which other countries might meet if they follow the same prescriptions.

This essay is divided into eight parts. Part 2 deals with the economic situation in Poland at the end of 1989. In parts 3 and 4 the programme for 1990 is discussed, focusing on two main elements: the transition from a command to a market economy and the most important elements of the stabilization plan. Part 5 compares the quantitative goals and results of the 1990 plan. Parts 6-8 deal with the dangers implicit in the programme. In part 6 the factors causing the recession are discussed and a method of evaluating their consequences is presented. In part 7 the problem of real wages as opposed to consumption out of wages is analysed. In part 8 the consequences of neglecting industrial policy are discussed. Part 9 is devoted to ideological considerations as opposed to the required pragmatic approach.

2 The economic situation at the end of 1989

The economic situation in Poland in 1989 was characterized by the following elements:[1]

1. The gross domestic product (GDP) after a trend rise in the preceding years, stagnated or even decreased. Industrial output of the socialized sector declined by over 2 per cent, but a still small private industrial sector expanded rather vigorously.

2. Inflation had already accelerated in previous years but between
1988 and 1989 the rate of growth of prices of consumer goods and services increased from about 60 per cent to about 244 per cent.
Calculated from the beginning to the end of the year, the (point to
point) inflation rate increased over the same time from about 74 per
cent to about 700 per cent (and even to 900 per cent on a December to
December basis). Thus inflation developed into a hyper-inflation. The
main factors feeding inflation were weak financial discipline of state
enterprises, allowing excessive money wage increases to go ahead of
inflation, accommodating credit policies and deficit spending of the
government (central and local budgets plus special funds, i.e. quasi-
budgets), reaching about 3.6 per cent of the GDP.

3. The export surplus in the trade in convertible currencies fell from
about $1 billion (in 1988) to $750 million, i.e. by $250 million, and in
non-convertible currencies (calculated in transferable roubles) increased from about $1 billion (in 1988) to about $2 billion. In volume
terms exports remained approximately unchanged, while imports in
convertible currencies increased, decreasing in non-convertible ones.
Private transfers amounted to $1.2 billion and the current account
deficit (including interest payments obligations of about $3.1 billion, of
which only $1.1 billion were paid) reached $1.9 billion (compared with
$600 million in 1988). At the end of the year the debt (in convertible
currencies) was about $41 billion and (in non-convertible currencies)
about 5.2 billion transferable roubles (cf. Rubel and Wojtowicz 1990).

The Mazowiecki government which took office in September 1989
started a new era in the history of Poland after 1945. The main effort of
this government in economic matters was directed toward preventing a
further deterioration of the situation in the last quarter of the year and
preparing an ambitious programme of recovery for 1990. The main
achievements of the last quarter of 1989 were money wage increases
slowed down, curbed budgetary deficit spending, some restraint of the
credit expansion and the continuous devaluation of the zloty, leading
to the spread between the official and free rate of exchange narrowing.

Real wages, which had increased statistically in the first three quarters of the year, declined statistically in the last quarter of the year (compared with the corresponding periods in the previous year), resulting in a statistical increase of 11 per cent in 1989 in relation to the previous year. Real wages, and ignoring money which could not be spent because of goods shortages, probably remained, on average, at the level of 1988 in 1989. The monthly inflation rate, after reaching a maximum in October 1989 (about 55 per cent), slowed down in November and December (to 22 and 18 per cent respectively). Another important development was the drastic reduction of the real value of zloty assets of the population. While these assets were equal in February to 4 months' expenditures and in June to 3 months', they declined to an equivalent of only 1.5 month's expenditure at the end of 1989.

Although the situation at the end of the year improved somewhat, or rather stopped deteriorating, the general picture was that of a shortage economy, inflation, declining output and a system in a deep crisis. The economy did not function any longer according to the rules of the command economy, but the proclaimed transition to a market mechanism had not materialized either.

3 The transition toward a market economy

The programme of the Mazowiecki government for 1990 was oriented toward two basic targets: (1) the transformation of the existing system into a market economy by basic changes in the ownership structure and in the *modus operandi* of remaining public enterprises, by demonopolization and creation of competitive structures; and (2) the stabilization of the economy by a drastic deceleration of inflation and elimination of shortages by reducing the size of deficit spending, and by restrictive incomes, wage and monetary policies, including an exchange rate policy.

The two targets—systemic changes and a working market mechanism—are interlinked and interdependent. If enterprises are to follow the profitability criterion but get false market signals, specifically non-scarcity prices, the market mechanism would not work. If, conversely, the market produces the right signals in the form of scarcity prices, but the enterprises do not react appropriately because they pursue other aims than profitability, or are prevented from proper reaction by the existence of physical constraints (e.g. poor communication, inefficient banking system etc.), then the market will not work either.

The programme is intended to introduce a wide range of market-economy institutions within the next two to three years. The most important steps are:

1. Transformation of the ownership of enterprises so as to establish a property rights structure similar to that of Western industrialized countries. This meant first of all privatization, basically by transforming state-owned firms into joint stock companies and selling the shares to private persons and institutions, including foreign investors, which could even become majority shareholders. At the same time the creation of private and (authentic) cooperative firms would be supported, including joint ventures with foreign capital and direct foreign investment. The sale of state assets, especially in small-scale production and services, was envisaged too. All restrictions on the sale and size of private farms are to be abolished and private agriculture will be granted equal access to inputs and credits.

2. Transformation of directly or indirectly state-owned enterprises, which for some time to come will still include the majority of Polish firms, into autonomous units, subject to a 'hard budget' constraint, meaning an unconditional long-run dependence of expenditures of a firm on its earnings. At the same time bankruptcy procedures would be simplified and used mercilessly when necessary.

3. Promotion of competition by anti-monopoly policies, first of all by breaking up the existing agglomerate corporations created artificially in the command economy in order to facilitate their administration from the centre.

4. Establishment of a capital market (including a security exchange board) and a labour market.

5. Reform of the banking system aiming at creating business banks independent of the central bank and oriented toward profitability. These banks together with the central bank would create the basis for an efficient monetary and credit policy. The establishment of an independent financial institution for economic restructuring was also envisaged.

6. Preparation of a comprehensive reform of the budget and tax system. The main elements of this reform are the introduction of a uniform value-added tax replacing the differentiated (positive and negative) turnover taxes, and the establishment of corporate and personal income taxes as well as the elimination of a number of extra-budgetary funds.

It is quite clear that all these measures aim at creating an institutional environment which is absolutely necessary for the proper functioning of a market mechanism. It is, however, also certain that these measures cannot produce results immediately, and that a couple of years will pass before the required structure comes into being.

4 Main elements of the stabilization programme

The stabilization programme embraced measures aimed at liberalizing prices and foreign trade on the one side and fighting inflation on the other.

On January 1, 1990 most remaining controls were removed, giving way to free price formation of goods and services. The few exceptions concerned coal, coke and electricity, as well as public transportation fares and rents, in total no more than 10 per cent of prices. Energy prices were at the same time increased 3 to 6 times to a level covering the average costs of production plus a significant mark-up. They still remained below the world price level, but it was intended not to allow this difference to increase in the future. Liberalization of prices aimed at balancing demand and supply, putting an end to chronic goods shortages and making the prices the right signals for economic decisions concerning allocation of resources between consumption, investment and foreign trade.

It does not make sense to liberalize prices inside the country while retaining the foreign trade monopoly and non-convertibility of the national currency. Indeed, the achieved level and structure of scarcity prices would not be adjusted to world conditions and would have to be revised anew when foreign trade became liberalized in the next step. It was thus decided to link price liberalization with the liberalization of foreign trade and the simultaneous introduction of internal zloty convertibility. On January 1, 1990 a uniform exchange rate was set at 9,500 zloty per dollar, which was a substantial devaluation of the national currency.

Together with internal zloty convertibility, all quantity restrictions on imports (with a few exceptions) have been eliminated and a uniform customs tariff has been introduced. The export trade regime has been liberalized too, and the number of exports subject to quota has been curtailed to 50 basic commodities, mainly to prevent the re-export of raw materials imported from the CMEA countries or to secure an adequate supply of basic food. According to the new rules all firms were obliged to sell their hard currency earnings to banks, but they also got the right to buy foreign exchange from banks for imports. Private persons, too, were entitled to import and to buy hard currencies for this purpose. The central distribution of foreign-exchange, foreign exchange auctions and foreign exchange accounts (except for private persons) were abandoned. The turnover in state foreign exchange shops (Pewex, Baltona) were to be gradually diminished and completely eliminated during 1990. The private exchange offices ('kantory') introduced in March 1989 were expected to continue selling and buying foreign currency at a free rate. The government would, however, closely monitor the spread between the officially set rate and the free rate, and not allow this spread to exceed a limit of about 10 per cent for a longer period.

The second and most important part of the stabilization policy was directed toward fighting inflation. Here also a two-pronged strategy could be discerned: first, control of the level of production costs, second, control of effective demand.

As far as production costs are concerned, the plan set two anchors: limitation of money wage increases and stabilization of the exchange rate. As production costs, given technical and labour coefficients, depend—disregarding the prices of raw materials, which are mainly demand-determined—on these factors, the choice of nominal anchors seemed correct, at least as an anti-inflationary measure, assuming that their relative stability held, at least for some time. The plan stipulated that money wage increases should be limited to a small fraction (20-30 per cent) of price increases between January and March 1990 and to a partial, although much higher, indexation for the rest of the year. Thus a substantial reduction of real wages over the whole year, especially the first part, was directly envisaged in the plan.

The exchange rate, fixed at the beginning of 1990, was intended to be constant at least for the first quarter of the year. The officially set rate was to be defended by the National Bank using a stabilization fund of $1 billion established by Western governments (of which: US: $200 million; Austria: $20 million) and by a 13 month standby loan of $710 million granted by the IMF. $300 million of the stabilization fund will not be repaid. After any major intervention, the National Bank must buy dollars for zlotys and re-transfer the money to the Federal Reserve Bank of New York, which kept the account. By the end of 1990, the original amount of $1 billion was to be restored.

It should be stressed that the two nominal anchors did not exclude major cost increases provoked by drastic increases in energy prices. Their purpose was to prevent a cost-price spiral which would develop in their absence.

A fundamental part of the fight against inflation was to reduce effective demand by cutting government deficit spending. It was the intention to achieve an approximate balance in the general government account for 1990 as a whole. This target was to be achieved both by reductions in expenditures and increases of revenues. On the expenditure side subsidies were to be cut with total elimination of subsidies for food and agricultural inputs, and with curtailment of the subsidies for coal. (Subsidies as a share of GDP were to be cut by 8 percentage points.) At the same time current expenditures for goods, services, wages (which in real terms were to decline in line with other wages), transfers to social insurance funds etc., as a share of GDP were to increase (by about 5 percentage points). Total expenditure, as a share of GDP, was thus expected to be cut by about 3 percentage points. On the revenue side the most important change was the planned increase of income tax revenues from the enterprise sector as a share of GDP by about 5 percentage points. The reduction of expenditures and the increase of revenues was to eliminate the deficit in government spending, estimated, according to the IMF method, at about 8 per cent of GDP in 1989.

Another measure to control the excessive expansion of demand was a restrictive credit and monetary policy. It aimed at restoring the attractiveness of the zloty as a store of value and strengthening the financial discipline of enterprises. The plan stipulated a positive real interest rate, thus increasing the attractiveness of zloty assets in relation to goods as well as to deposits in foreign currency. The growth rate of the money supply was to remain less than that of prices. Many preferential interest rates (e.g. for exports) were abolished and others (e.g. for housing and agriculture) substantially reduced. The National Bank of Poland (NBP) was to become more independent and charged with full responsibility for the internal stability of the zloty.

5 Quantitative goals and results of the stabilization plan

The stabilization programme represented a completely new approach to the problems facing Poland, and the reaction of the economy to these measures was quite uncertain. Nevertheless some estimates had to be made with respect to prices, output, employment, government budget and foreign trade.

According to the stabilization plan the rate of inflation between December 1990 and December 1989 should have been no higher than 140 per cent. The highest price increase of about 45 per cent was expected in January 1990 to be followed by the slowing down of inflation in February and March. Already, in the second quarter of the year, the inflation was to be reduced to about 1-2 per cent per month.

The sharply limited increases in money wages with anticipated inflation were to lead to a reduction of real wages. According to the plan, real wages were expected to fall by about 15-20 per cent between 1989 and 1990, with most of the reduction taking place in the first quarter of the year. At the same time real consumption was to fall only slightly because it was assumed that shortages of goods and services led to forced savings in 1989. Thus losses in real wages were to be mostly of a statistical nature.

Industrial output was expected to decline by about 5 per cent, and national income by about 3.1 per cent. Unemployment was to reach a level of about 400 thousand people, representing about 3 per cent of total employment. The Government budget was to be balanced, at least toward the end of the year. More or less constant exports were expected in trade in convertible currencies; combined with an increase in imports of about $1 billion, this would change the export surplus of 1989 into a trade deficit of about $0.8 billion in 1990. In trade with CMEA countries, the export surplus was expected to decrease to about 0.54 billion transferable roubles.

One of the main goals of the stabilization plan achieved in 1990 was the restoration of basic monetary functions to the zloty. Hyper-inflation was replaced by inflation. Prices reached the market clearing level and most of the shortage phenomena, typical of a command economy, were removed. There was some improvement in the structure of prices, caused by the lowering of subsidies and by their exposure to a demand constraint. The exchange rate of the zloty was kept constant over the whole year, the government budget closed in surplus and in both convertible and non-convertible currencies a considerable trade surplus was achieved.

However, the macroeconomic goals of the stabilization plan were not met, resulting in costs much higher than anticipated (e.g. Kolodko 1991). As table 6.1 indicates, GDP fell in 1990 by 12 to 16 per cent, i.e. over four times more than anticipated. Similarly, industrial output (including private industry) fell 23.3 per cent when it was expected to decline 5 per cent. Prices of consumer goods increased from December 1989 to December 1990 by a factor of 3.5 instead of 2.4. The monthly rate of growth of the CPI in the fourth quarter of 1990 was still 5.5 per cent instead of 1.5 per cent targeted in the stabilization plan. Real wages decreased by 28 per cent instead of the 15-20 per cent assumed in the plan.² And unemployment reached 1.126 million at the end of the year—almost three times the number expected. Only in foreign trade were results better than expected. In trade in convertible currencies, exports increased considerably and although imports increased also, a significant export surplus of $2.2 billion was registered. In trade in non-convertible currencies, especially with the Soviet Union, a large surplus (7.1 billion transferable roubles) was also achieved, however, exports decreased slightly and imports decreased dramatically. It should be stressed that a large trade surplus in face of a sharply declining GDP was an additional limit on internal absorption. Indeed, consumption financed by private households decreased in 1990 by 24 per cent compared with about 1 per cent (sic!) provided by the plan. Consumption decreased more than GDP because a considerable export surplus reduced the internal absorption relative to internal output.

The demand curtailment of private households directly influenced industries producing consumer goods. Indeed, while total industrial production decreased by 23.3 per cent, the light and food industries declined by 37 and 25.7 per cent respectively.

Table 6.1: Average annual growth rates: goals and results (in per cent, unless stated otherwise).

	(a) Assumption	(b) Results	(a)/(b)
1. GDP	-3.1	-14.0	4.5
2. Industrial output	-5.0	-23.3	4.5
3. Consumer prices			
(a)12/90 over 12/89	140	249	1.8
(b) IV quarter 1990	1.5ᵃ	5.5ᵃ	3.7
4. Real wages	-15 (-20)	28.1	1.6
5. Unemployment			
-in thousands	400	1126	2.8
6. Trade balance			
(a) in billion of $	-0.8	2.2	-2.75
(b) in billion of TRᵇ	0.5	7.1	14.2

Source: Kolodko 1991; Glowny Urzad Statystyczny 1991.
ᵃaverage rate of growth per month, in per cent. ᵇtransferable roubles.

An important factor of the recession has become residential building. The number of apartments built during 1990 fell by 11.7 per cent. In that year only 3.5 apartments were built per 1000 inhabitants compared with 4.9-5.4 in the 1980s. The decline in residential building occurred although the housing shortage in Poland is acute.

Efficiency of production, already very low, decreased further in 1990. While industrial production (in state-owned and cooperative firms) decreased by 25 per cent, employment declined by only 8.2 per cent. This means either that output per employee declined by about 18 per cent and/or that redundant labour in enterprises increased further instead of decreasing.

It should be added that the suppression of inflation was only partly successful because the programme dealt unilaterally with demand-induced price rises and almost totally neglected the cost-induced price rises—a problem implied in the shock-therapy itself.

There are several important causes of the negative features of development in 1990 and of the visible gap between the goals and results of the stabilization plan. Perhaps the most important was an excessive concentration on monetary and fiscal policy with almost complete neglect of the real sphere. Two grave mistakes have been made in monetary policy. The drastic rise of the interest rate at the begining of 1990 gave an initial impetus to the sharp decline of production. The devaluation of the zloty was also excessive: indeed the exchange rate was kept constant although the internal price level increased during the year by 250 per cent. This is the best proof that the devaluation was excessive and resulted in an initial acceleration of inflation. As far as fiscal policy is concerned, a serious fault consisted in tolerating a large budget surplus over much of the year. This factor was an additional constraint on the level of effective demand. Only at the end of the year was the budget surplus reduced.[3]

6 The first danger implied in the programme: Recession was unavoidable, but how deep?

1. In 1989 the Polish economy moved from inflation to hyper-inflation and the fight against this danger was rightly chosen as a task of first priority. There is—in the short run—no other way to crush hyper-inflation than to limit excess effective demand and adjust it to the size of potential supply. As in 1989 the level of effective demand was evidently too high, so its reduction was necessary. The reduction of effective demand, if it is indeed limited to the *excess* demand only, must not reduce *per se* the level of real GDP. This point will be discussed in the next section.

The reduction of effective demand foreseen in the programme should, however, go further in order to decrease the degree of utilization of production capacity. This decrease is directly related to the transition from a supply-determined command economy to a demand-constrained market economy. In a supply-determined system factors of production including the labour force are utilized very intensively, although in a rather inefficient way. In a command economy demand always outruns supply, creating a permanent state of 'suction' (Kornai 1980). There is no other way to replace 'suction' by 'pressure' than to limit effective demand to a level below potential supply. The resulting decrease of real GDP and recession expose the economy to the demand constraint. At the same time some reserve capacity and unemployment arise which allows for the necessary degree of flexibility of production (in the sense of the ability to adjust the structure of supply to that of demand). Thus some recession must be part and parcel of every programme to transform an economy from a supply-determined into a demand-determined system.[4]

It is not easy to estimate the necessary reduction of effective demand in Poland in 1990. It can, however, be arbitrarily assumed that real effective demand in 1990 should not exceed 95 per cent of GDP in 1989.[5] Thus, a reduction of GDP by about 5 per cent is obtained, a magnitude of the order implied in the programme. The depth of the recession was, however, not explicitly dealt with in the programme and seems to represent its most important weakness. In particular, no effort has been made to evaluate, even approximately, the combined effects of the proposed curtailment of total demand on the level of output and employment. This, and not the difficulties in making correct provisions under existing circumstances, is the main reason for the wide gap between goals and results.

2. An important question that needs to be answered is whether the different measures proposed were consistent with a reduction of real GDP of about 5 per cent. In order to find out the order of magnitude, an appropriate method of estimation is proposed. For this purpose a very simplified model is used. First, actual savings of the enterprise sector and of private households for 1989 are calculated. Expected savings for 1990 are also calculated assuming that provisions of the plan for this year are fulfilled. In the next step we shall calculate the actual share of savings in the GDP in 1989 and try to find out in which direction this share may have changed in the year 1990 under the circumstances foreseen in the plan. As a result an order of magnitude of the decline of GDP implied in the plan can be roughly estimated.

Ex post (gross) savings S, defined as above can be written as:

$$S = I + E + D \qquad (1)$$

where I denotes (gross) investment in the enterprise sector, E stands for the difference between exports and imports, and D represents the budget deficit, the difference between government's expenditures (on goods and services) and revenues. Let s be the share of savings in GDP; the savings rate will then be:

$$s = \frac{S}{Y}$$

or

$$Y = \frac{1}{s} S \tag{2}$$

where Y is GDP (at market prices).

If s is constant, the change in GDP can be obtained from (2):

$$\Delta Y = \frac{1}{s} \Delta S \tag{3}$$

and if s is not constant, i.e. in the general case:

$$\Delta Y = Y(g_S - g_s) \tag{4}$$

In equation (3) the term $1/s$ denotes the multiplier measuring the impact of changes in savings S, i.e. of the sum of investment, deficit spending and the export surplus upon the GDP. In equation (4) g_S and g_s denote the rate of growth of S savings and of s, the rate of saving, respectively.

When annual changes in S and s are large, equation (4) cannot be used, in which case we obtain from (2):

$$1 + g_Y = \frac{1 + g_S}{1 + g_s}$$

where g_Y is the rate of growth of GDP. Rearranging, we obtain:

$$\Delta Y = Y \frac{g_S - g_s}{1 + g_s}, \tag{5}$$

a formula which can be used when yearly changes of S and s are large.

3. In 1989, according to provisional data, GDP was Zl 118.3 trillion (i.e. thousands of billion), and included investment of the enterprise sector of Zl 38.6 trillion, an export surplus of Zl 4.6 trillion and a budget deficit of at least Zl 3.6 trillion. (According to the methodology used by the World Bank, the budget deficit was much higher.) Total savings S were therefore Zl 46.8 trillion and the share of savings s was 39.6 per cent.

There is no estimate in the programme for the investment of the enterprise sector in 1990 but it was evident that it would decrease. If it is assumed that the estimated reduction is 10 per cent, then the expected decline in investment would have been -3.9 trillion Zl. Further, the export surplus foreseen in the stabilization plan was negative (about -1.0 trillion Zl), thus the expected decline of the export surplus in 1990 would have amounted to $\Delta E = -1.0 - 4.6 = -5.6$ trillion Zl. And lastly the basic assumption of the plan was the balancing of the government's budget; this meant a reduction of the deficit by $\Delta D = -3.6$ trillion Zl. Hence, the expected reduction of total savings (ΔS) in 1990 is -13.1 trillion Zl (see column (5) of table 6.2).

If the share of savings s in 1990 were to remain the same as in 1989, the decline of GDP could be calculated using formula 3:

$$\Delta GDP = \left(\frac{1}{0.396}\right)(-13.1) = -33.1 \text{ trillion } Zl$$

or a relative decline of about 28 per cent of GDP. This is a rough estimate of the combined results of the measures anticipated in the stabilization plan. In reality, leaving aside investment, neither the export surplus nor the budget deficit are independent of GDP. Thus, if GDP were to decline more than anticipated in the plan, then imports, being an increasing function of GDP, would decline (or increase less than expected) and the import surplus should have been assumed smaller than estimated above. This factor would moderate the expected fall of the GDP. The same applies to the budget deficit. If the GDP were to decline by more than anticipated, then budget revenues would be smaller (because of taxes related to income and output), and expenditure larger (because of unemployment benefits). As a result the budget could not be balanced and the remaining budget deficit would moderate the expected decline of the GDP. If proper account were taken of both factors the resulting estimate of the decline of GDP would have been much less than 28 per cent.

It is necessary, however, to come back to the assumption concerning the constancy of s, the rate of savings. At the beginning of 1990 nobody knew for sure how the rate of savings would change and in what direction, if at all. However, factors which influence these changes were known and could and should have been analysed. First, because the share of the sum of direct and indirect taxes in GDP in 1990 (according to the budget projections) was to increase by almost 4 percentage points, the share of value added after taxation would correspondingly decrease. Given the distribution between wages and profits, and the propensities to save out of these incomes, this factor should have diminished the coefficient *s*. Second, it could be expected that the propensity to save out of wages (and in the case of peasants, out of their earnings) would probably decrease because forced savings would disappear and real income would decline. Under these conditions the second factor should have acted in the same direction as the first one, although it should be stressed that private households' propensity to save in Poland was rather low. Third, it could be expected that the distribution of value added after taxation between wages and profits would change and the share of profits would probably increase. Indeed, when subsidies are reduced, profits correspondingly increase, even if prices increase only by the amount of subsidies withdrawn. It was known that prices would increase also in relation to unit labour costs because real wages were expected to decline absolutely and in relation to labour productivity creating opportunities for additional profits. As the propensity to save out of profits is much higher than that out of wages—and out of profits in state-owned enterprises it is almost equal to one—this redistribution of value added toward profits would increase the value of the coefficient *s*. Taken together the first two factors seemed to act in one direction, the third one in an opposite one. It could be expected that the third factor would play an important role and might prevail, leading to some increase of the rate of savings. An opposite result could, however, not be excluded either. As there are forces acting in different directions, it was admissible for the plan to assume that changes in the coefficient *s* would not be very large.

This conclusion means that changes in the rate of savings could positively or negatively influence the expected decline of GDP provoked by the assumed decline of savings, but not by very much. Thus the recession implied by the plan was very deep indeed, and in any case much deeper than the assumed decline of GDP of the order of 3 per cent.[6]

4. The data recorded for 1990 (see table 6.2, column (2)) support to a great degree our forecast for the same year (see table 6.2, column (5)). Savings decreased by 7.2 trillion Zl compared with 13.1 trillion Zl estimated in the forecast. As expected, the import surplus did not materialize and instead quite a large export surplus was recorded: a difference of 2.6 trillion Zl as against -5.6 trillion Zl assumed in the forecast. This is the main cause of the gap between the actual and the forecast decline of GDP. Another factor was a larger fall of investment while the budget surplus declined according to the forecast.

Table 6.2: Gross domestic product in Poland (in trillions zloty 1989 prices).

	1989 (1)	1990 (2)	(2)-(1) (3)	(3):(1) (4)	1990 (5)[a]
GDP *(Y)*	118.3	107.7[b]	-16.6	-14.0%	
Investment *(I)*[c]	38.6	32.7	-5.9	-15.3%	-3.9
Export surplus *(E)*	4.6	7.2	2.6	56.5%	-5.6
Budget deficit *(D)*	3.6	-0.3	-3.9	-108.3%	-3.6
Savings *(S)*[d]	46.8	39.6	-7.2	-15.4%	-13.1
Savings rate *(S/Y)*	39.6%	38.9%		-1.8%	

[a]Changes in *I*, *E* and *D* as forecasted in February 1990.
[b]Our estimate, a mean value between the officially published decline of GDP of 12 per cent, most probably arrived at by assuming a large increase of unrecorded economic activities, and a decline of 16.2 per cent of GDP estimated at the end of 1990 without the unrecorded economic activities.
[c]Investment of the business sector, including changes in inventories.
[d]Savings of the business sector and private households.

An important point is the relative stability of the rate of savings. It decreased by 0.7 percentage points, i.e. by less than 2 per cent, reaching 38.9 per cent in 1990. This decline somewhat modified the decline in GDP provoked by the fall of *S*, but was by far too weak to play any substantial role. The relative stability of the rate of saving—if it can be assumed—means that there is a simple method of evaluating the joint influence of different measures affecting investment, export surplus and budget deficit upon GDP, and it cannot be claimed that such a forecast is impossible.

7 The second danger of the programme: Standard of living and real wages

A recession provoked by a reduction of savings means of course a decline of GDP and employment. It leads also *ceteris paribus* to a decrease of real consumption but not necessarily to a reduction of the real wage. Indeed, if the relation between nominal wages and prices remains unchanged, i.e. the real wage remains constant, real consumption—disregarding unemployment benefits—would decline *pari passu* with employment. If, in addition, the real wage decreases, then real consumption falls more than employment and deepens the recession.

Thus it is not clear why a recession seen as an unavoidable measure on the road from a command to a market economy should combine a reduction of employment with a reduction of the real wage. If for whatever reasons such a decline is nevertheless intended, its effect upon effective demand should have been taken into account when cuts in factors determining savings *S* are planned.

Some doubts may arise as to whether the constancy of the real wage can also be defended when a hyper-inflation of the Polish type is being fought against. In order to analyse this problem in a pure form, the reduction of effective demand discussed previously will be ignored, and attention will concentrate on the possible ways of removing excess demand which existed in Poland in 1989. This excess demand was caused mainly by two factors: uncontrolled increases in the nominal wage not supported by any gains in labour productivity (although justified by concurrent rises in consumer good prices), and increasing subsidies to prices, financed by deficit spending. A specific feature of Polish hyper-inflation was the fact that most prices were not freely determined, thus their level was not a market clearing one.

Now assume that the wage bill is 50 (monetary) units, there is no voluntary saving out of wages and consumption out of wages equals only 40 units, because prices are not free to attain the market clearing level. Thus forced savings equal 10 units, representing excess demand for consumer goods, or a monetary overhang amounting to 25 per cent of their total value at existing prices (the accumulated overhang of the past being ignored). Now imagine that half of the monetary overhang is due to nominal wages being too high, and the other half to subsidies being financed from the budget deficit and in addition keeping prices too low. In this situation there is a difference between the 'statistical' real wage and real consumption out of the wage (or 'real' real wage).

Assume further that the excess demand for consumer goods is to be removed in a kind of shock therapy by introducing at one time market clearing prices and simultaneously abolishing all subsidies in order to balance the government budget. It is assumed also that the shock therapy should remove inflation but let the level of real consumption remain the same.

By doing this exercise several conclusions can be reached. Prices, given nominal wage rate and the volume of consumer goods, increase by 10 units, i.e. by 25 per cent. Profits of enterprises (which by assumption are totally saved) increase by 5 units, and the other 5 units of additional earnings compensate the subsidies withdrawn. Savings decrease by 10 units (forced savings) and increase by 5 units (additional profits), resulting in $\Delta S = -5$. At the same time the budget deficit changes by $\Delta D = -5$ because of elimination of subsidies. Under these assumptions savings S and the rate of savings s change in the same proportion and according to formula (5) the volume of GDP does not change. Excess demand has been removed by a fall of the 'statistical' real wage by 20 per cent, but real consumption out of wages (or the 'real' real wage) as well as employment have remained constant.

This is of course an extremely simplified presentation of the problem. In practice some losses in real consumption or greater than anticipated price increases, for different reasons not taken into consideration, would surely occur. An important factor may be represented by the assets of forced savings.[7] The main message should, however, be clear enough: while the 'statistical' real wage must be cut, real consumption out of wages can and should be defended. It is not at all clear why in Poland the reduction of the 'real' real wage was intended. The ideas presented above were quite popular at the end of 1989 when the stabilization plan for Poland was discussed and—as was said above—were part of this plan. They disappeared from the discussions for reasons which are not clear, at least to this writer, after the shock therapy was started, giving way to an argument that a drastic fall of real consumption out of wages was an absolutely necessary measure in the successful battle against inflation.

The actual plan severely limited the increase of money wages, allowing, over the whole year, only a partial compensation for price increases. Although not really necessary, this is a very effective policy, at least in the short run, because wages, on the one hand, constitute the greatest part of total demand and, on the other, are the most important factor determining costs. This policy thus attacks inflation from both the demand as well as the supply side. Partial compensation of price increases (with a correction coefficient of the order of 20 or 30 per cent at the start of the programme) means, however, a sharp decline in the real wage and of living standards, especially when coupled with diminishing employment. This policy can be maintained only when workers and employees are ready to accept the sacrifices it requires from them. But even in this case the patience of the population should neither be overestimated nor overstrained. Sacrifices acceptable for a short time may become intolerable if they continue for longer periods.

Inflation, and especially hyper-inflation, must be cut by lowering demand, but a decline in output, especially of consumer goods and food, may increase the danger of inflation by cutting supply. It should be clear that for any longer period an effective control of inflation requires not only measures cutting demand but also, and perhaps in the first place, those increasing supply.

8 The third danger of the programme: Lack of an industrial policy
In the last instance the success of any stabilization and transformation
policy depends on its ability to modernize and restructure the economy. It is an open question whether a successful realization of a plan
resulting in reduced inflation to a tolerable level while causing at the
same time a deep recession would create the proper conditions for
achieving these goals. Restructuring requires enterprises to modernize
their production, to improve quality, to lower costs, to start new ventures, to adjust the economy to the requirements of internal and external demand. A recession *per se* does not create conditions for these activities. On the contrary, a low level of economic activity and hence of
profitability, may lead to a cumulative decline of investment and output, going beyond the recession administered by the plan.

For a long time the Polish economy will be a mixture of a market
mechanism with a prevailing sector of state-owned firms. Thus a structural policy aiming at an expansion, as fast as possible, of private firms
and an acceleration of the privatization of state-owned enterprises
must include a clearly defined policy for the remaining state sector. This
policy is lacking in the Polish shock therapy, resulting in a lack of any
perspective for the managers of state-owned enterprises. They try to
muddle through from one day to another and concentrate their efforts
on paying wages and keeping employment. It is quite possible that for
the kind of mixture represented by the actual Polish economy, the
purely market instruments foreseen in the plan would not be able to
produce the necessary structural changes. What may be required are
policy measures which may be superfluous (or not absolutely necessary) under normal conditions, but may be badly needed in a system in
which the market coexists with a large state-owned sector. These measures may include preferential interest rates, control of investment decisions when managers making these decisions cannot be made responsible for their financial results or, in exceptional cases, even direct
investment decisions.

The need for state activities is caused also by structural problems
facing socialist countries on their way to a market economy. The share
of services in total employment and output has to increase, and that of
agriculture decrease. The industrial sector must be basically restructured and modernized in order to reduce its material- and energy-inten-
sity. The opening of the economy to the outside world and the expansion of export capacities is another fundamental requirement. Last but
not least, the environmental situation is almost everywhere critical. To

believe that all these problems can be solved by spontaneous market forces is a dangerous illusion.

Foreign trade is a good example of an area where macroeconomic and industrial policies have to work together. There is no doubt that the exchange rate, being a key macroeconomic parameter, should be set at an equilibrium level and not below it. At the same time the setting of the exchange rate above the equilibrium level (prompted for example by a desire to keep, at least for some time, this rate constant in order to increase confidence in the stability of national currency) may negatively influence the economy. Indeed, too large a depreciation of the national currency may lead to an export surplus, mainly through cuts in imports, and hence to a reduction of internal absorption which magnifies the adverse effect of a recession.

On the other hand a unique exchange rate coupled with convertibility, introduced from one day to another, may ruin whole branches of industry or agriculture or whole regions. The structure of production inside command economies came into existence almost without any consideration for world market conditions and the international division of labour. The quality of locally produced goods is often very low. The abrupt exposure of such economies to world competition may be quite a dangerous experiment, as the example of the former German Democratic Republic has proven. In this situation the liberalization of foreign trade should be rather gradual and accompanied by a selective tariff policy sheltering those branches of production which can become competitive in the future or be liquidated when the necessary conditions are present. Also, different quantity restrictions, tolerated even in most developed countries, should be used when necessary.

The strengthening of the position of the formerly socialist countries in the world economy is a major problem in their transition to a market economy. These countries require an active policy facilitating imports of modern technology and promoting exports and changes in export structure toward manufactures, especially machines and equipment of an up-to-date technological standard. This policy cannot simply follow the conclusions of the conventional theory of comparative advantage of the Ricardo and Heckscher-Ohlin type, supporting a free trade policy. It should rather concentrate on a factor which is missing in all these static theories: technical progress.

Luigi Pasinetti gives an example of two countries: one developed, the other one underdeveloped, but both having exactly the same structure of prices. Under these conditions foreign trade in the pure form is not appealing for either country. Let us imagine, however, that labour productivity in the developed country is 10 times higher than in the less developed one. From the point of view of the latter country, international trade linked with the process of learning from the former is an extremely interesting proposition. The main role of international interaction in this case lies not so much in the choice of an optimal point on the production possibility curve, but instead in the shift of this curve outward from the origin of the coordinates system. Pasinetti (1988, pp. 139-147) concludes that the major and primary source of international gains is international learning, not international trade. This is a rather fundamental proposition, not only for less developed countries but for the previously socialist countries as well, when they turn toward a more market-oriented economy.

An industrial policy is not meant to replace spontaneous market forces which are absolutely necessary, but a sound policy may and has to support (not replace) the market mechanism. It is said that Japan and the NICs have followed two basic rules in their policy of choosing and supporting export-oriented industries: First, the chosen industries should be those which are the most promising from the point of view of expected rate of growth of labour productivity; as a rule these are young industries where the potential for further technical progress is still unexploited. Second, export promotion should concentrate on goods which are characterized by an expected high income elasticity of demand.[8] These two rules do not have much in common with the traditional theory of comparative advantage or with the postulate of state abstention from economic life. They seem, however, to deliver the results.

The transition from a command to a market economy requires, as well as macroeconomic policy, an industrial policy of export promotion (and import substitution) which at the same time must be strong enough but not too strong. State support has to be strong enough to help the development of promising firms, but not so strong as to permit the survival of firms which cannot ever become self-supporting. This is easier said than done. There exists, however, no other solution.

9 Ideological considerations

Ideology played a decisive role in the rise of central planning and in the destruction and sufferings caused by its functioning. Central planning was introduced as a remedy against the illnesses of capitalism, but this medicine proved to be worse than the malady itself. The medicine almost killed the patient, and has been rejected, but this does not mean that the patient was not ill in the first place.

It is obvious that the transition from a command to a market economy is based on an anti-communist and uncritically pro-capitalistic ideology (cf. Jan Drewnowski 1990, pp. 4-6). This is understandable, but may become dangerous if it leads to a doctrinaire attitude in the practical reconstruction of the economy. The generation of economists now directing the transition in Eastern Europe has no direct experience of the pre-war capitalist economy. They know capitalism mostly from microeconomic textbooks and from visits to the most developed Western countries. Their consciousness has been moulded by the absurdities of the Soviet-type economy in their countries; they are inclined to identify every economic activity of the state with these absurdities and to promote a purely capitalistic system with a marginal role of the state in economic matters. The social climate is propitious to this attitude; it is supported also by foreign experts, mostly monetarists, who in the majority of cases have no detailed knowledge of the economic situation of these countries, and by such potent institutions as the IMF and the World Bank.

The main goal of the IMF is to solve short-term problems in the balance of payments of different countries. The World Bank on the other hand tries to solve longer-term problems mainly through 'structural lending'. Both institutions grant repayable credits linked with some conditions to be fulfilled by the recipient countries. It is a rule that recipient countries oppose these conditions and the result is some compromise between the often severe requirements of the international financial institutions aiming mainly at the international balances, and the national interests of governments aiming mainly at the level of domestic production and employment. This, to some degree natural, contestation is rarely observed in the relations between IMF and the World Bank with the previously socialist countries. On the contrary, in many cases the severe conditions of a shock therapy are further strengthened, and deficit spending is not only being abolished but replaced by budget surpluses, and import surpluses are not only cut but replaced by export surpluses. It happens that high officials of those countries complain that the requirements of international financial institutions do not go far enough.

The transition from socialism to capitalism is without any precedent. No sure theoretical background exists for the policy of transition.[9] The liberal and conservative economists now in a position of power in the previously socialist countries pretend, however, that they know the right answers. They are convinced that it is enough to liberalize prices, including the rate of exchange, to enforce a restrictive monetary policy and to keep the budget in balance and then wait till market forces do the job. What is badly needed, however, is to replace ideology by a pragmatic approach, to observe the situation continuously in order to introduce necessary corrections when necessary, to remain open to new solutions, and, most importantly, not to neglect economic policy in times when it is more than ever needed.

Notes

1. Compiled from Glowny Urzad Statystyczny (1990a, 1990b) and the data bank of *The Vienna Institute for Comparative Economic Studies*.
2. Jeffrey Sachs (1990), one of the architects of the Polish shock-therapy, said: '...fears of plummeting take-home pay abound, though the average industrial worker earned the equivalent of $131 in October (1990 added K.L.), compared with $108 in October 1989'. Indeed, between October 1989 and October 1990 monthly industrial wages in zloty increased by a factor of about 5, while the exchange rate of the dollar measured in zloty increased only by a factor of about 4. Jeffrey Sachs forgot, however, to add that prices of consumer goods in the same period increased by a factor of about 6. Thus, the purchasing power of one US dollar on the consumer goods market in Poland decreased by about 50 per cent.
3. In the first half of 1990 the budget registered a surplus of Zl 6.5 trillion, while in the second half of the year the budget closed with a deficit of Zl 5.6 trillion.
4. There exists an important asymmetry between transition from a command economy toward a market economy and *vice versa*. The transition from a demand- to a supply-determined system, as proved by the experience of socialist countries, allows for a better utilization of resources which previously were not fully employed. This leads to a quick increase in production and consumption. These short- (or even medium-) term advantages are overcompensated by losses in efficiency and creativity in the long-run, which make, however, the transition very attractive. In the opposite case the intensity of utilization of resources must be diminished. This means immediate losses in production and consumption. These short- (and even medium-) run losses, which should be overcompensated by an increase in efficiency and creativity in the long run, make, however, the transition to a demand-determined market system quite difficult.
5. It should be stressed that in Poland, at the end of the 1980s, capacity utilization was already very low. Indeed, while in 1989 national income was lower than in 1980, the stock of fixed capital was higher by about 40 per cent (Glikman 1990).
6. In February 1990 a forecast of the expected decline of GDP was undertaken by Laski (1990) using available data for 1989, but did not impress anyone in the Polish government at the time.
7. It has already been stressed that the accumulated forced savings in Poland were almost annihilated through the hyper-inflation of 1989. At the end of 1989 these savings practically did not exist or at least were unimportant. Thus an argument that 'real' real wages at that time were much smaller than real wages is not very convincing.
8. Strangely enough the electronics industry, which seems to be both a young industry and characterized by a high income elasticity of demand, has become one of the first victims of the ultra-liberal shock therapy in Poland.
9. Paul W. McCracken said at the beginning of 1990 at a conference in the Hudson Institute: 'At a recent annual conference, the members of the American Economic Association and sister associations found themselves in an unusual situation. There was a major issue of public policy on the agenda, and they found themselves comparatively uncertain and even a bit empty-handed about what advice to give. We economists are usually quite confident that we have the right answers. This time we were concerned about our own shortcomings

and limitations.

The policy issue was, of course, what some have called transition economics. Granted that the liberal, market-organized economies have been providing more rapidly rising and widely shared material levels of living than the centrally planned, state-managed economies, how does one get from the latter to the former?' (McCracken 1990, p. 13).

References

Bugaj, R. (1990). 'Rzad kocha makro', *Gazeta wyborcza*, June 15, 1990.

Drewnowski, J. (1990). 'Paradoksy polskiej gospodarki, Trybuna', *Political Quarterly*, London, Nr. 65/121.

Glikman, P. (1990). 'Recesja i rozwoj', *Zycie gospodarcze*, nr. 21 (2013), May 27.

Glowny Urzad Statystyczny (1990a). 'Komunikat o sytuacji spoleczno-gospodarczej kraju w 1989 r.', *Statystyka Polski*, Nr. 2 (9), 1 lutego 1990 r., Dodatek Rzeczpospolitej.

Glowny Urzad Statystyczny (1990b). *Biuletyn statystyczny 1*, Warszawa

Glowny Urzad Statystyczny (1991). *Informacja o sytuacji spoleczno-gospodarczej kraju. Rok 1990.*, Jan 25.

Gomulka, S. (1990). 'Stabilizacja i wzrost: Polska 1989-2000', paper presented at a conference organized by Institute of Finance in Poland, on May 30-31, 1990, mimeographed.

Kolodko, G. W. (1991). 'Transition from Socialism and Stabilization Policies. The Polish Experience', presented at the International Studies Association, 32nd Annual Convention 'New Dimensions in Internal Relations', Vancouver, March 19-23, mimeographed.

Kornai, J. (1980. *Economics of Shortage*, Amsterdam: North Holland.

Laski, K. (1990) 'O niebezpieczenstwach zwiazanych z planem stabilizacji gospodarki narodowej', Warszawa, *Gospodarka narodowa*, No 2/3: 5-9.

McCracken, P. W. (1990). 'Thoughts on Marketizing State-managed Economies', *Economic Impact*, No 71, 1990/2.

Nuti, D. M. (1990), 'Internal and International Aspects of Monetary Disequilibrium in Poland', presented at the Working Group on Aid Programs for Hungary and Poland, Brussels, February 6, mimeographed.

Pasinetti, L. (1988). 'Technical Progress and International Trade', *Empirica. Austrian Economic Papers*, Vol. 15, No 1, 1988.

Rubel, M. and Wojtowicz, G. (1990). 'Bilans platniczy 1989', *Zycie Gospodarcze* nr. 14 , April 9.

Sachs, J. (1990). 'A Tremor, Not Necessarily a Quake, for Poland', *International Herald Tribune*, Nov. 30.

7 The Market Transformation of State Enterprises

Branko Horvat

1 Introduction

The 1980s were years of deregulation and denationalization (Hanke 1987); deregulation was more or less common in all economies while denationalization was usually associated with right-wing parties coming to power. This trend is often associated with the efficiency of enterprises, whether state or private. Although state *enterprises* need not be less efficient than comparable private ones, the state *sector* often is, for reasons explored elsewhere (Horvat 1985). In extreme cases, entire economies are organized as state economies and are often erroneously called socialist; erroneously because socialism implies a radical decrease of state control and oppression ('the withering away of the state'), and an elimination of wage labour and class polarization ('the emancipation of the working class'). But to the contrary, in state economies, the state is almost the only employer with monopolistic powers, and because one-party rule increases state oppression, state control is pushed to an extreme. For this reason, such economies are called ètatist or statist in scholarly literature (for a comprehensive treatment of the problem see Horvat 1982).

The breakdown of ètatist command economies in the late 1980s occurred because these economies proved to be less efficient than contemporary capitalist market economies. Consequently, it is generally believed that ètatism must be replaced by some sort of capitalism, which presumably implies privatization. To do this, it is widely believed that state enterprises must be sold. In ètatist economies, however, the state owns 80 per cent or more of the national capital. Because of this, it is impossible to sell this amount of capital because there is no market for it. This problem challenged the ingenuity of economists, and numerous privatization schemes were designed. The common feature of all of these schemes was a privatization period of twenty or more years, implying that these economies would be saddled with inefficient state enterprises in the meantime.

The deteriorating performance of ètatist economies in the 1970s suggested that they were bound to collapse before 1995. Even a simple extrapolation of productivity trends would have predicted that event. For that reason, the possibilities of their transition to socialism were explored in *The Political Economy of Socialism* (Horvat 1982, chap. 17). The present study is a continuation of that enquiry.

2 Confusions in the debate over privatization

When discussing the transformation of state enterprises, two considerations are important. First the goal of improving economic efficiency, and second, ethical, political and other ideological considerations. The present enquiry is exclusively confined to the problem of efficiency. In the debate on transformation, the concepts used are often not defined and participants often argue at cross-purposes. To avoid this, the seven most common errors encountered will be analysed.

1. Privatization is opposed to nationalization. In the late 1940s, everything was nationalized. This trend was not confined to the present ètatist economies. In the 1990s everything is to be (re)privatized. If the justifications offered are examined, one finds that advocates of nationalization really wanted deprivatization, mainly because of the adverse economic and social effects of uncontrolled accumulation of private wealth. Believing that this aim could be achieved by what turned out to be inadequate means, the results ranged from inefficiency to monstrosity. Similarly the advocates of privatization now really want destatization and deregulation in order to increase efficiency, and to save democracy from the oppressive domination of the state. By trying to turn the time arrow backward, they too are bound to become deeply disappointed.

2. A great diffusion of stock ownership is considered to be important for establishing a capital market and improving the efficiency of management. In fact, there is either no relation between the assumed cause and effect or the effects are detrimental. Some concentration of stock ownership is necessary for the effective monitoring of joint stock companies, but this concentration does not require the private ownership of shares or institutional investors.

3. Closely related is the confusion between private property and a well-functioning market. Many believe that no market is possible without the existence of private property. However, it is possible to have private property and a very imperfect market, resulting in misallocations and economic stagnation. It is also possible to combine non-private (social) property with viable competition and fast growth.

Privatization by itself solves no economic problem.

4. Privatization in the social sense as the property of a physical person is confused with privatization in the legal sense (private as opposed to public in law). Instead of requesting that the state be expelled from the market, which is legitimate on efficiency grounds, it is required that state property be transferred to physical persons. This is not justified, because if one accepts the verdict of the market, one must allow the market to determine the forms of ownership.

5. It is mistakenly believed that ownership is one and undivided: if one is the legal owner, one must manage the enterprise. This was certainly true up until the late 19th century, but not in the contemporary world. One of the most characteristic features of the modern economy is the separation of management from ownership. In large joint stock companies, managers are not owners (except symbolically), and owners are not allowed to manage enterprises unless they happen to own a majority of voting shares, and even then to do so only indirectly through the appointment of the board of directors.

6. There is a mistaken belief which survives from the time of Adam Smith that only an owner will be properly motivated to manage efficiently. Closely connected is the misconception about entrepreneurship. An entrepreneur is not an owner of capital, as Joseph Schumpeter pointed out long ago. Owning the capital is a function of the capitalist who may also be an entrepreneur, although that is not necessary. All that is necessary for entrepreneurs to function efficiently is that they are legally free to engage in a business venture of their own choosing and can obtain capital.

7. As a consequence of the separation of management from ownership, the owner is no longer a single agent. The owners appear in pairs: in a market economy, property such as machines or buildings is owned by the enterprise, and the enterprise itself is owned by a secondary or final owner such as another enterprise, a physical person or the state. The primary owner (the enterprise) is legally registered, incurs debts on its own behalf and is liable for them. The primary owner is the productively active owner and is therefore of crucial importance to the economic process. This is where entrepreneurship is to be found. The secondary owner is anonymous and passive, engaging in capital transactions by buying and selling securities.

If these seven distinctions are not clearly understood, a hopeless confusion is bound to be created. This is indeed the case in Eastern Europe, as the series of privatization laws demonstrates. A powerful barrier to the communication of ideas and the solution of real problems has thus been created.

3 What makes a market economy relatively efficient?

Different institutional arrangements in various countries make possible a comparative analysis which reveals the basic sources of efficiency. Again abstracting from political conditions and cultural specifics, economic efficiency seems to be determined by the following factors:

1. *Free initiative*. This is the basis for entrepreneurship. For this to emerge requires political democracy which guarantees civic rights, and a legal state which makes the outcomes of economic transactions predictable, and, therefore, the profitability of business ventures calculable. Free initiative implies not only action but also its absence. For instance, shareholders are legally entitled to take certain decisions, but they usually leave them to the managers, because they do not want to be bothered, because they are technically difficult or for some other reason. But the mere fact that it is possible to act generates important productivity effects.

2. *The independence of enterprises in business transactions*. This has three effects. First, adaptability to ever-changing conditions in the market; second, it produces an information economy because the detailed knowledge of the situation may be fully exploited in decision-making; and third, powerful motivation, because success and failure, with the corresponding rewards and penalties, depend on one's own (individual and collective) ingenuity and effort.

3. *Cooperation within the enterprise*. This eliminates unproductive conflicts and further enhances motivation. The enterprise must be 'ours' (all employees') and not 'theirs' (the bosses').

4. *Unhampered competition between enterprises*. This eliminates monopolies and unearned privileges. Since economic gain is the main motive for business operations, competition acts as an automatic regulating device. No one needs to tell the enterprise what to do. Neither can management or the working collective abstain from innovative efforts and lapse into the tranquility of a leisurely life without being brutally reminded by an impersonal market of their productive duties.

5. *An economic policy that eliminates market failures*. A laissez faire market is very imperfect and its consequences are unemployment and slow growth. There are two types of market failures: misallocation of resources and unequal business conditions. Such distorted proportions must be corrected in order to achieve stability and economic

growth. Moreover, the conditions for competition must be made equal for every participant in order to elicit maximum efficiency.

A full discussion of these five points requires a book on the design of an efficient economic system (cf. Horvat 1982). Here the purpose is much more modest. These five factors provide a framework within which an efficient substitute for ètatist enterprises can be found.

It hardly needs mentioning that economic institutions cannot be designed as mathematical models based on arbitrarily chosen assumptions. They evolve from historically given conditions and are, therefore, historically constrained. Bearing this in mind, it will be helpful to consider how and why the joint stock company evolved from the private, family-owned, enterprise.

4 The contemporary managerial corporation

A private family enterprise starts as a small enterprise. As it grows, it encounters three obstacles. First, after it has achieved a certain size, the owner-manager no longer knows all the employees personally. Authority must be delegated to family members if they are around. If they are not, or when the enterprise becomes sufficiently large, it must be organized differently. Second, private enterprises grow slowly because investment is financed out of internal accumulation, and large bank loans are undesirable because they increase the insolvency risk sharply. The solution is to issue shares and sell them in the capital market, thus mobilizing external accumulation. Third, when the original owner-manager dies, a continuity crisis exists. There may not be heirs willing to continue managing the family business, and the enterprise could be sold, which, as a rule, implies its conversion into a joint stock company. Or heirs-managers may exist, but are not competent, in which case efficiency deteriorates and the enterprise will be destroyed in the process of market competition.

As a result of these three forces, the large private enterprise tends to be less efficient than its competitors. More and more, management is separated from ownership and the function of the entrepreneur is separated from that of the capitalist. A rapidly developing capital market parallels the market for commodities and services. The modern managerial corporation emerges.

Existing legal regulation of corporations is rather simple. The law provides for annual meetings of shareholders who elect the board of directors (the supervisory board in the continental Europe), which in turn appoints the general manager and other senior executives (the management board). The board of directors is supposed to maximize the profits of shareholders; if they become dissatisfied, they are supposed to fire the directors, and appoint a new executive subject to the constraints of possible contracts that the executives may have with the enterprise. Occasionally the corporation may behave as assumed; in the vast majority of cases it behaves very differently.

Those who make daily decisions and who have access to all relevant information—director-managers and senior executives—are the dominant group in the corporation. The actual practice is well described by R. Marris (1964, p. 14):

> It is sometimes supposed that in the corporate sector boards of directors may be regarded as trustees for shareholders, that they are, in fact, akin to watchdog committees set up to keep management in its place. This view, however, is not supported by legal authorities, and in any case the managers have themselves considerably assimilated the directorial system. Legally the function of the board is to operate the company. For the purpose, it employs executives who may...themselves be directors. But board members who are also full-time employees command the power of organization and hence must in general dominate: In the U.S. the majority of all directors are in this position. Thus, by combining the functions of employee and employer, the management body is considerably freed from direct external restraints, a condition which is emphasized by the fact that the vast majority of board nominations are proposed by existing directors. In practice, in many firms, the board itself recedes into the background and operations are taken over by committees of senior executives, not all of whom are necessarily directors.

In other words, managers manage without asking either the board or the shareholders for clearance. Managers are empowered to make decisions and in this way they behave like traditional owners. They are not appointed; they practice self-appointment. In the same way they themselves decide on their own salaries, bonuses and stock options.

In principle, all the directors in a corporation can be removed by simple majority at a meeting of shareholders. This legal possibility is practically never used—except in take-over raids—since shareholders diversify their own risks and so do not own a majority of shares. In 1951, for example, the median percentage of votes held by the 20 largest shareholders was 22 per cent in the largest British corporations (ibid., p. 312).[1] Management holds only between one and three per cent of the votes, but effectively controls the corporations. R. A. Gordon (1945, p. 311) notes:

Wholesale purges of executive ranks are rare, and top management, usually securely in control of the proxy machinery, seldom has to worry about retaining its position.

Despite the absence of direct control by private owners, managers work relatively satisfactorily because of inducements and deterrents provided by the market. Executive mobility is extremely low: In a survey it was found that senior officers had on average changed employment less than twice since the beginning of their career (Marris 1964, p. 67). Thus, they are dependent on their enterprises and are vitally interested that the enterprises prosper. Managers tend to identify with *their* enterprises, feel the approbation of their class if the price of shares is high, rise faster within the company if openings become available through expansion, and increase their power as the company grows.

Market deterrents are equally powerful. Larger institutional shareholders may successfully monitor the corporation by threatening to sell their shares, and such sales may inflict a mortal blow on management. The share price will decline, which makes possible a hostile take-over. If a raid is successful, top management is dismissed, losing jobs, prestige and very substantial material remuneration.

It is this administrative independence and market control that make the corporation tick. Clearly, it is not necessary to slavishly imitate *private* institutions in order to achieve the same or better economic effects. All that is necessary is to identify the two crucial preconditions, as mentioned above, and to design a solution in such a way as to exploit the full potential of the initial position.

5 The social corporation

If the goal is to increase efficiency, it is quite obvious that large state enterprises will not have to be transformed into private enterprises but into corporations. And, of course, the administrative state interventions of a command economy must be replaced by the self-regulating market. For that, no sale of enterprises, no distribution of shares or other fancy schemes, and—most important—no long periods of time are necessary. The whole process of transformation need only consist of some formal legal procedures, which can be performed rather quickly, and of creating market institutions and educating capable managers, which takes longer but is unavoidable in any case. Historically, private family enterprises gradually evolved into managerial corporations which may be called private corporations. Similarly, state enterprises may be expected to evolve into more efficient *social corporations* (previously described as 'participatory corporations', Horvat 1985). The process implies transforming state ownership (with administrative subordination of enterprises) into social ownership (which makes enterprises independent).

A social corporation is a joint stock or limited liability company ruled by its employees who elect a workers' council and appoint the general manager. Persons not working in the company may also be elected to the workers' council. The same considerations apply also to limited liability companies. The process of transformation will then proceed as follows.

The capital of the enterprise is assessed and transformed into internal shares kept in an indivisible Fund of Social Capital (FSC). The workers' council is elected, and nominates a general manager. If the enterprise covers its costs, it is ready to engage in market operations immediately like any other corporation. If it makes losses, it will be put into receivership by a special agency, which will appoint the general manager and suspend self-management until the enterprise is reorganized and put on its feet again, or it will be declared bankrupt and sold. Statistically, only a small number of enterprises are likely to be genuinely unprofitable.

Once in the market on its own, the corporation can supplement its working capital with short-term loans from commercial banks. An increase in fixed capital can be financed by issuing bonds and shares and by long-term loans from investment banks. Shares appear to be internal (FSC) and external (floated on the capital market or sold to the employees at a discount). Whether internal or external, they earn dividends, and dividends determine the market rating of the enterprise. In this way market discipline is imposed and any government control becomes superfluous.

Dividends safeguard the minimum profitability and in this way solve the problem of the distribution of income into wages and profits (accumulation) without any administrative interference. Internal dividends accrue also to one owner, society: these are used for investment and are, therefore, added to social capital. If there are also undistributed profits, the value of share capital will appreciate. In its business policy, the enterprise will choose the best combination of an increase in dividends and capital appreciation.

Enterprises may merge and combine their capital and management. One enterprise may invest in another on a contractual basis, or it may invest by buying its shares. Shares give voting rights, and if profitability falls, the value of shares will drop as well, and that may make possible a hostile take-over. This danger will discipline both workers and managers because the take-over means suspension of self-management, reorganization and dismissals.

A social corporation may also go bankrupt. In this case the law prescribes a standard procedure describing how the property is to be sold in order to compensate creditors. The bankruptcy may be prevented if the Development Bank (a counterpart of the National Bank, see Horvat 1969) decides that it is in the national interest to bail the enterprise out. In this case self-management is also suspended and a new management is appointed by the Bank which undertakes to reorganize the enterprise and make necessary dismissals.

Most of the time, social corporations will have mixed ownership with the social capital fund representing the controlling amount of shares. Nothing changes if mergers and take-overs occur among social corporations. If a social corporation buys a private corporation, the latter becomes social, with self-management introduced, and the story ends. If a private corporation buys a social corporation, the latter becomes private, self-management is suspended, and the Development Bank, as the custodian of the social capital, becomes the owner of internal shares. These shares may now be sold on the capital market. Competition in the market will determine all these changes and it would be counterproductive to impose any particular scheme in advance. The government should only take care that the market is not distorted and that everybody can compete on equal terms. The market will then automatically select the most efficient organization, financial and ownership forms.

The system described above *may work efficiently without any private share ownership*. Therefore, it appears that the emphasis laid on reprivatization is determined by *ideological* and not economic *efficiency* considerations. If only social corporations have access to the capital market, then institutional investors are the only investors since the rest of the economy would be composed of unincorporated entities. This would not be much different from what is happening elsewhere, because *75 per cent of the world stock market is already institutional* and this percentage is increasing. Although private shares are not necessary, they may increase the flexibility of the market and for that reason may be used as well.

The main institutional investors are insurance companies, pension funds, and investment trusts, which means that a sizeable capital market can be started immediately. This is not all that can be done to establish a viable capital market. A common feature of ètatist economies is a huge amount of unsettled debts. A legal requirement may be imposed that, at the time of incorporation, all debts falling due must be settled. Since this cannot be done in cash, it will be done by issuing securities. As a byproduct of this process, the economy becomes financially interconnected and in a rather natural way the efficient enterprises will become centres of economic restructuring and engines of growth. Thus, the entire transformation from an ètatist to a market economy, if undertaken along the lines suggested, will take no longer than five (in Yugoslavia, two) years.

Transforming state enterprises into self-managing social corporations means a genuine deregulation in the shortest possible time. In this way an ètatist economy will be transformed into a more efficient market economy.

6 Comparing private and social corporations

Suppose the profit and loss account of a private corporation is as found in table 7.1. The *upper* limit for depreciation is determined by law. Profit taxes in various countries vary between 35 and 50 per cent. The profitability of the corporation examined is 20 per cent gross and 10 per cent net. Somewhat more than one half of the profit is distributed to the stockholders (6), and the remainder is retained as undistributed profit (4) which leads to an appreciation of the stock.

Table 7.1: Profit and loss, private corporation (hypothetical data; in dinars).

Sales	110
Minus: material costs and depreciation	50
Minus: wages and salaries	40
Gross profit	20
Minus: profit tax (50 per cent)	10
Net profit	10
Dividends	6
Undistributed profit	4
Capital owned	100

Suppose now that the same enterprise operates as a social corporation. In order to safeguard competition on equal terms, the amount of tax remains the same (1), but as table 7.2 shows, the accounting is somewhat different.

Since capital is socially owned, a *lower* limit is legally set for depreciation. In order to avoid complications, it is assumed that the depreciation charges remain the same under both corporate regimes. The participatory social corporation does not have fixed wages set by collective bargaining, but practices profit-sharing. A private corporation can also introduce profit-sharing, but this runs into various difficulties (Wadhwani and Wall 1990) not applicable to a social corporation. Two important consequences follow: (1) gross profits increase appreciably (from 20 to 28) which increases the scope for a flexible business policy; and (2) if wages are increased by 25 per cent through profit-sharing, this must produce a powerful incentive effect.

Table 7.2: Profit and loss, social corporation (hypothetical data; in dinars).

Sales	110
Minus: material costs and depreciation	50
Minus: wages and salaries	32
Gross profit	28
Minus: sharing in profits (25 per cent of the wage bill)	8
Minus: tax on additional wage bill (125 per cent)	10
Net profit	10
Dividends	6
Undistributed profit	4
Capital owned	100
Internal shares (FSC)	60
External shares	40

Again, since capital is socially owned, a profit tax makes no sense, being replaced by a progressive tax on extra wages distributed (assumed here to be 125 per cent). Three important consequences follow: (1) a graduated *profit* tax is practically never applied because it is administratively difficult and for that reason the profit tax used is proportional, and so is usually the capital gain tax; the design of a progressive *wage bill tax* is relatively simple (cf. Horvat 1976, chap. 11); (2) a wage bill tax stimulates investment; and (3) there is a powerful brake on inflation.

Internal shares represent also a new feature. Since dividends amount to 6 per cent of net profit, internal dividends will be 60 x 0.06 = 3.6 dinars, increasing the share of internal stock in the total stock. Undistributed profits cause capital to appreciate proportional to internal and external stocks. In some other respects too, a social corporation is bound to behave differently regarding workers' dismissals, inventory changes, price formation and economic policy during business cycles etc. (cf. Horvat 1971).

In general, it may be observed that private ownership created historical conditions in which the private corporation emerged. Similarly, state ownership represents a socio-economic environment in which the social corporation is likely to evolve. Both are market creations. Simply mimicking the first would make little sense.

7 How will the transformation of state enterprises work?

The previous analysis demonstrated, without any doubt, that it is possible to convert state enterprises into social corporations rather quickly. Yet, how will such a market economy work? Fortunately, there are numerous empirical studies and a 20 year Yugoslav macroeconomic experience[2] that make tentative answers possible:

1. Participatory enterprises tend to act in a stabilizing way by dampening swings in aggregate demand (Horvat 1971).

2. Empirical research in various countries shows positive effects on productivity resulting from participation and profit-sharing (Steven 1982; Defourny et al. 1985; Jones and Svejnar 1985; Estrin et al. 1987; Cable and Wilson 1990; Wadhwani and Wall 1990).

3. Management in the social corporation is subject to the dual control of employees and the capital market which is a logical consequence of the strict separation of management and ownership. Masahiko Aoki (1990, p. 20) describes a similar duality as characteristic for Japanese enterprises and as one of the sources of their efficiency:

> The corporate management decisions of Japanese firms are subject to the dual control (influence) of financial interests (ownership) and employees' interests rather than to unilateral control in the interests of ownership.

4. Compared with the hierarchically organized private corporation, the participatory social corporation may be expected to reduce social conflicts, increase the motivation of employees and provide a more efficient non-market control. Employees live from the enterprise and with the enterprise, are vitally interested in its success, have first hand information, and may intervene instantaneously through the workers' council if something goes wrong. Besides, participation is congenial to modern technology which requires cooperation of different experts in teams producing custom-designed products and, by establishing economic democracy improve human rights.[3] The historical process of separating management from ownership is brought to a logical end: self-management is based on labour, and (financial) ownership on capital.

5. In the first, uncompleted, attempt to apply similar institutions to the entire Yugoslav economy in 1952-1970, the results were surpris-

ingly good: rates of growth of GNP, real wages and global productivity of resources were among the highest in the world, sometimes the highest in absolute terms (Horvat 1982, chap. 6).

6. The social corporation is designed in such a way that it can do anything a private corporation can do. In addition, its social and economic design make it more flexible and, therefore, potentially more efficient.

The large amount of state capital that remained after a period of ètatist development need not be regarded as a cause for despair. By intelligent action it may be turned into levers for fast economic development. If an institution is designed so as to increase human freedom, it is bound to produce impressive effects. Even if someone is in a pessimistic mood and does not believe in the potential efficiency of the new institution—as Adam Smith and English legislators did not believe in the efficiency of the emerging corporation two centuries ago—one does not risk anything. The social corporation may simply be envisaged as an instrument for quickly transforming an ètatist economy into a market economy. By the very design of complementary institutions, the social corporation cannot be unprofitable. In the case that it does become unprofitable, it is put into receivership and all possibilities remain open. Since even pessimists are prepared to accept the verdict of the (fair) market, competition will automatically select the most efficient forms of business organization. What is achieved is a natural and not a paper evolution of an institution.

Notes

1. There is no comparable figure for the United States. In 1936, the median percentage of votes held by the 20 largest holders were 35 per cnet and 28 per cent in large U.K. and U.S. companies respectively (Marris 1964, p. 312).
2. From 1952-1970 self-management gradually expanded and the organization of the participatory firms came close to that of social corporations. Administrative planning was replaced by planning of global proportions and prices were liberalized up to 60 per cent. But shares and a capital market were not established and firms did not become fully market independent. Instead of completing market transformation, for political reasons the trends were reversed towards ètatizations in the 1970s and then, as a reaction, towards privatization in 1990.
3. In Poland, where the present government is committed to privatization for political reasons, 59 per cent of workers and 65 per cent of managers considered participatory joint stock companies beneficial for the economy (Gruszecki 1990, p. 78).

References

Aoki, M. (1990). 'Toward an Economic Model of the Japanese Firm', *Journal of Economic Literature*, 1-27.

Cable, J., and Wilson, N. (1990). 'Profit-Sharing and Productivity: Some Further Evidence', *Economic Journal*, 550-55.

Defourny, J., Estrin, S., and Jones, D. (1985). 'The Effects of Workers'

Participation on Enterprise Performance', *International Journal of Industrial Organization*, 197-217.

Estrin, S., Jones, D., and Svejnar, J. (1987). 'Productivity Effects of Worker Participation', *Journal of Comparative Economics*, 40-61.

Gordon, R. A. (1945). *Business Leadership in the Large Corporations*, Brookings: Washington, D. C.

Gruszecki, T. (1990). *Privatization*, Warsaw: Stefan Batory Foundation.

Hanke, S. H., ed. (1987). *Privatization and Development*, San Francisco: Institute for Contemporary Studies.

Horvat, B. (1969). 'Development Fund as an Institution for Conducting Fiscal Policy', *Economic Analysis and Workers' Management*, 247-54.

Horvat, B. (1971). *Business Cycles in Yugoslavia*, New York: M. E. Sharpe.

Horvat, B. (1976). *Ekonomska politika stabilizacije* (The Economic Policy of Stabilization), Zagreb: Naprijed.

Horvat, B. (1982). *The Political Economy of Socialism*, New York: M. E. Sharpe.

Horvat, B. (1985). 'Efficiency of the Public Sector', *Economic Analysis and Workers' Management*, 195-203.

Jones, D, and Svejnar, J. (1985). 'Participation, Profit Sharing, Worker Ownership and Efficiency in Italian Producer Cooperatives', *Economica*, 449-65

Marris, R. (1964). 'The Economic Theory of Managerial Capitalism', New York: Free Press.

Steven, F., ed. (1982). *The Performance of Labour-Managed Firms*, New York: St. Martin's.

Wadhwani, S., and Wall, M. (1990). 'The Effects of Profit-Sharing on Employment, Wages, Stock Returns and Productivity: Evidence from Micro-Data', *Economic Journal*, 1-17.

8 Failure of Monetary Restriction in Hungary and Yugoslavia: A Post Keynesian Interpretation

Shirley J. Gedeon

> We must learn from those countries, as well as from monetarist and neo- and post-Keynesian economists and practical experts, who have studied experiences collected in market economies over the past decades. We ourselves must also try to find the solution best suitable for us (Tardos 1988, p. 69).

On January 1, 1987, Hungary introduced banking reform which established commercial banking operations. The intent of the reform was to separate central banking activities from commercial lending and to introduce Western-type instruments of monetary control. Within a year of the reform, however, Hungary began to experience many of the same frustrations with monetary regulation that have plagued Yugoslavia, namely an endogenously growing money supply and the inability of central monetary authorities to control spending and inflation.

This essay explores the reasons why the money supply tends to grow endogenously, responding to changes in the behaviour of economic entities rather than being subject to the control of monetary authorities. It is divided into three parts. It begins with a discussion of the post Keynesian theory of the endogeneity of money in market systems and the problem of central bank control of the money supply. Next, it describes and comments on the effect of monetary restriction in Hungary and Yugoslavia, analysing especially the conflicting economic and social goals which belie effective monetary regulation. Bearing in mind the caveats of the post Keynesian analysis, the last section explores the implications of a demand-determined, credit-driven money stock for monetary regulation and suggests directions for further institutional reform.

1 The post Keynesian theory of endogenous credit

A major theme for post Keynesians is that monetary authorities do not have complete control over the supply of credit and hence cannot effectively control aggregate spending: business borrowers and banks together, at least in the short period, determine the amount of credit supplied, and in this sense, the demand for credit creates its own supply.

The essential argument in the post Keynesian theory of credit money is that the supply of money is endogenously determined within the banking system through the interaction of corporate borrowers and bank lenders, rather than exogenously determined by the central bank open market operations and the money multiplier. As captured by the well-known equation, $M = mB$, where M is the money stock, m is the money multiplier, and B is the monetary base, the orthodox view of money is that the amount of bank reserves is exogenously controlled by the central bank. The direction of causality runs from B to M. The post Keynesian argument reverses the direction of that causality (Arestis and Eichner 1988, pp. 1006-7).

The post Keynesian argument is built on the assumption that the demand for credit is determined primarily by the wage bill and resource costs. When wage or raw material prices increase, current production costs rise. If business production schedules are to be maintained, additional working capital to finance current production must be secured. This is accomplished through an increase in bank finance and/or a running down of liquid assets. If bank accommodation is forthcoming (which is generally the case due to such things as credit supply agreements, refinancing agreements, revolving credit lines, and the like), then bank deposits increase and thereby the money supply. In other words, 'as long as banks' liabilities retain their moneyness, banks can always satisfy the demand for credit by issuing their own liabilities' (Wray 1989, p. 1186).

Deficit reserves in the banking system must be made up. As banks issue liabilities, they must obtain reserves to meet legal requirements. The demand for bank reserves is met through the discount window, as it is generally assumed that the central bank operates as a lender of last resort and responds in a way so as to protect the liquidity of the banking system (Kaldor 1982; Moore 1988b).

The argument that banks grant credit in advance of prior saving supports the post Keynesian view that gives causal priority of investment and passive adaptation of saving. In economies with credit money, in-

vestment determines saving: credit permits firms to buy without selling
or accumulating reserves.

Kregel amplifies the post Keynesian theory of money by severing
the link, so important to the transmission mechanism in the monetarist
argument, between real savings in the economy and investment expenditure. He points out that new demands for credit necessary to finance
an autonomous increase in investment demand *require* the banking
system to issue loans *without limit* at a given rate of interest:

> Since current investment expenditures always equal current savings...the
> amount of cash coming into the banks will be sufficient to replenish the pre-
> existing revolving fund of finance and offset the direct or indirect lending
> against the new securities issued in prospect of the increase in investment. In
> stable conditions exactly the same value of investment will be coming into the
> long-term market to be financed as is being saved out of income from current
> investment expenditures... The role of credit expansion is either to reduce in-
> terest rates sufficiently to convince entrepreneurs to hold additional productive
> assets or to keep interest rates from rising and thus causing entrepreneurs to
> change their assessment of profitability. All that is required is that the banking
> system be willing to supply enough liquidity at the given rate of interest to al-
> low this adjustment to take place without producing an increase in the rate of
> interest (Kregel 1984-5, p. 151).

Reversal of the Causation in MV = PQ. Post-Keynesians argue that
the underlying core rate of inflation is determined by the excess rate of
growth of money wages over the rate of growth of average labour productivity. The rate of inflation and the rate of change of the money
stock are therefore driven by the exogenously determined rate of increase of nominal wages.

This is in contrast to the monetarist view which holds that the causal
link in market economies runs from exogenous changes in the money
supply to demand and then to prices, among them wages. Monetarists
argue that the money stock is determined exogenously by the central
bank. Excess money balances cause wages to rise and thereby the
price level. Inflation is explained by the excessive rate of increase of
the nominal money stock.

> One of the core propositions of the quantity theory, an exogenous money
> supply, is strictly appropriate only to commodity money economies. The no-
> tion of the money stock as exogenous leads directly to the Monetarist expla-
> nation of inflation as essentially a monetary phenomenon—too much money
> chasing too few goods. Inflation is viewed as caused primarily by too high a
> rate of increase of the nominal money stock. The underlying notion is of an
> excess supply of money that spills over into demand for other goods and ser-
> vices (Moore 1988b, p. 444).

Conflict Between the Commercial Banks and Central Bank. Conflict between the banking system and the central bank over access to means of payment is brought directly into the post Keynesian analysis. It is the penultimate of 'animal spirits', perhaps best called a game of chicken.

If bankers' 'animal spirits' remain high (they desire to accommodate the credit demands of their clients) but the central bank moves to tighten liquidity in the system, bankers can respond by selling time deposits which carry lower reserve requirements and/or disregard reserve requirements, anticipating that political pressure will eventually be placed on the central bank to reverse the policies. The failure of the monetary authorities to accommodate the reserve needs of the financial markets in general, and of the banks in particular, will give rise to one of the following effects: (a) a financial crisis, (b) a cyclical downturn, or (c) a rise in the level of interest rates.

Arestis and Eichner argue that of these three possible consequences of a non-accommodating policy by the central bank, the rise in the interest rate is usually the one felt most immediately. However, this is unlikely to reduce the demand for loans. For this reason, the central bank is likely to pressure banks to cut back on lending activities through credit rationing or forcing banks to deny credit to entire classes of borrowers. But this may backfire:

> It is this cutting off of credit, even more so than the rise in interest rates, that is likely to lead to a cyclical downturn in the level of economic activity. The cyclical downturn, by reducing business and other cash flows, *will create an ever-greater demand for credit*; and if the monetary authorities, in an effort to continue limiting the growth of the 'money supply', refuse to provide the necessary bank reserves, a financial crisis—with the loss of liquidity by the banking system and widespread insolvency—is likely to ensue (Arestis and Eichner 1988, pp. 1007-8; emphasis added).

Conflict Between Enterprises and Banks. Bankers have a profit-making operand. When banks can make a profit by lending to firms, they will do so. However, when bankers' 'animal spirits' wane—when loans become too risky—they may refuse to accommodate demand for additional finance. In this event, firms may attempt to create their non-bank forms of credit. According to Lavoie, firms may choose one of two alternatives. They may create their own *non-bank* forms of payment such that the amount of circulating media—composed of both bank money and private instruments—will meet entrepreneurial demand. Or, they may economize on the use of currency and checking accounts by reducing their demand for money. In either case, firms can be expected, according to the theory of endogenous supply of money, to independently satisfy their needs of trade.

How can they do this? Lavoie explains that firms: (1) borrow from each other; (2) extend credits to each other (presumably through voluntary trade credits); or (3) create new kinds of money (Lavoie 1984). This third category can include such responses as the issuing of bills of exchange that can be endorsed and passed on to other buyers as would be a cheque, the creation of involuntary trade credit (for example, simply letting accounts payable accumulate), and the selling of accounts payable to other non-finance institutions. Other responses that we may also expect from firms in a credit crunch may include a reduction in the amount of money traditionally held as idle balances, a transfer of assets from non-monetary to monetary deposits, or an abandonment of sound principles of corporate finance, with a decrease in liquidity based on their estimation of likely political or economic sanctions against illiquidity (Gedeon 1985).

These actions permit enterprises, at least in the short run, to undertake production schedules despite 'official' money supply restrictions. However, debt must eventually be paid in currency or bank deposits. If debt cannot be retired, pressure is placed on the state either to inject fresh credit or to administer an eleventh-hour bail-out. Inflation may be fed through an endogenously growing money stock for essentially political reasons: it is not politically palatable or perhaps politically feasible to enforce credit contracts including the use of harsh sanctions in the case of insolvency, bankruptcy, forced merger, or sellout.

Hence we see that the expansion of the money supply is essentially a symptom, rather than a cause, of inflation. It results from state expenditures that socio-political pressures make necessary or from the fear of the socio-political consequences that would follow if it did not.

2   Inflation and endogeneity of money in Yugoslavia[1]
The Yugoslav banking system currently operates on a fractional reserve system. However, the National Bank may not pursue its own goals. Monetary policy is the subject of parliamentary debate and negotiation as one aspect of overall development. In this way, monetary policy is brought into the planning process and is by design under the control of state institutions. The instruments available to the National Bank for injecting or withdrawing high-powered money—what is called primary emission—include the monetization of banks' portfolios,

discount of the bills of exchange of enterprises, the issue of direct credits to banks, and the institution of programmes of selective crediting. The most important difference between Western banking systems and the Yugoslav is that open market operations are not an instrument available to the central bank; the most important similarity is that there is an exogenous *PQ* and endogenous *MV*.

Monetary policy is viewed in Yugoslavia as one of a number of policy instruments to be used to impose financial discipline on enterprises, to curtail an endogenously growing money supply, and to halt the spiralling inflation rate. In 1979, as a prelude to implementation of a comprehensive stabilization programme designed to halt the wage-price inflationary spiral, monetary restriction was imposed (Komisija 1982). However, despite the fact that bank loans fell from 28.2 per cent annual growth rate in the first quarter of 1979 to 16.1 per cent at the end of the fourth quarter in 1983, inflation persisted.

In 1984, Rogic showed a consistent trend for the growth of the social product to outstrip that of the money supply during the five years following monetary restriction. Table 8.1 summarizes his findings. It traces the quarterly rates of growth (stated in annual rates) of industrial production, retail prices of industrial production, the money supply, domestic bank loans, primary emission (high-powered money), and mutual crediting. Mutual crediting consists of debt issued by buyers and accepted by sellers, both uncovered claims as well as claims secured by guarantees and letters of credit, but not circulating bills of exchange.

As can be gleaned from tables 8.1 and 8.2, monetary restriction was most severe in 1979 and 1983. Table 8.1 shows that loans fell from a 27.6 per cent annual growth rate in the second quarter of 1981 to 14.5 per cent annual growth in the third quarter of 1983. Table 8.2 shows that despite monetary restriction, the social product grew. The restriction manifested itself as a widening gap between the growth of nominal social product, especially its price component, and the relatively stationary movement of the official monetary-credit aggregates (e.g. Jaksic 1984; Rogic 1984). The experience of monetary restraint in Yugoslavia lends support to the post Keynesian thesis that reverses the direction of causality in the quantity theory. Inflation explains changes in the money supply rather than the reverse. In a recent study using Granger causality tests, Chowdhury, Grubaugh and Stollar have also confirmed this. They show that money has not played a direct role in influencing real activity in Yugoslavia and that the money supply can be characterized as growing endogenously (Chowdhury et al. 1990).

Table 8.1: Movement of Quarterly Interyear Rates of Growth in the Period 1979-1984

		Industrial production	Prices of Industrial Production	Money Supply	Bank Investments in Dinars	Primary Emission	Mutual Crediting
1979	I	9.67	28.38	26.86	28.19	16.26	48.32
	II	8.79	21.27	19.63	28.29	11.92	53.61
	III	5.89	26.87	14.76	24.54	13.47	44.22
	IV	7.44	24.90	16.54	25.24	18.14	31.13
1980	I	5.47	26.64	19.31	25.24	25.17	48.67
	II	3.30	27.84	22.40	25.67	24.05	48.99
	III	3.09	31.80	25.60	26.40	23.10	52.46
	IV	4.90	39.48	23.73	25.34	21.65	49.29
1981	I	2.12	51.80	23.78	25.71	18.85	55.39
	II	5.97	56.18	26.36	27.64	28.05	52.33
	III	6.44	47.67	27.35	26.87	31.67	44.66
	IV	2.28	43.81	26.93	25.22	30.25	39.47
1982	I	2.69	29.15	24.77	23.21	29.98	40.22
	II	-0.27	25.23	22.92	20.52	24.79	41.29
	III	-0.55	30.51	21.86	19.33	19.36	33.94
	IV	-1.27	29.53	22.58	17.97	19.70	48.92
1983	I	0.00	29.37	25.05	16.44	21.08	59.11
	II	0.29	34.96	22.84	15.22	19.09	52.22
	III	1.56	37.17	25.18	14.53	25.57	69.36
	IV	3.34	53.01	24.16	16.11	28.12	73.45
1984	I	3.79	62.65	23.42	19.21	21.15	71.96
	II	5.34	58.00	30.78	21.98	33.97	66.81

Source: Rogic 1984, p. 159

Table 8.2: Growth of social produce and the money supply (chain index at current prices)

	1978	1979	1980	1981	1982	1983
Social product	122.8	129.2	133.3	142.2	132.0	140.0
Money supply	125.6	118.9	123.1	126.6	126.6	120.0
Difference	2.8	-10.3	-10.2	-15.6	-5.4	-20.0

Source: Jaksic 1984, p. 1276.

What is interesting from the standpoint of the post Keynesian endogeneity issue is the growth of mutual crediting and the creation of non-bank forms of money, especially the bill of exchange, in the face of monetary restriction by central authorities. Knight and Ujdenica have both remarked on the burgeoning growth of bills in Yugoslavia. As we can see from table 8.3, the percentage of material costs and investment paid by endorsed bills of exchange—substitute money—grew from 47 per cent in 1978 to 75 per cent in 1982 (Knight 1984; Mirko 1983). Schonfelder has recently argued that ZOP-bills, bills of exchange backed with a bank guarantee and hence most liquid, served throughout the 1980s as an accepted means of payment.[2] He notes that if one redefines real balances as the aggregate of M1 and ZOP-bills, one finds that real balances did not decline after 1980. So widespread in use, Schonfelder reports that in June 1989, the stock of ZOP-bills in Yugoslavia was nearly $3 billion, considerably larger than the reported M1 (Schonfelder 1990).

Table 8.3: Growth of bills of exchange (substitute money; in billions of dinars).

	1975	1978	1979	1980	1981	1982
Material costs	683	1146	1492	2099	2881	3774
Total substitute money	530	543	963	1433	1933	2815
per cent of material costs	76	47	65	68	67	75

Source: Ujdenica 1983, p. 63.

3 Monetary restriction in Hungary: Emerging trends

Many of the problems which have recently emerged in Hungary since the institution of two-tier banking parallel those in Yugoslavia. A number of Hungarian economists have commented on the failure of monetary restriction since 1987. The consensus among them is that, like Yugoslavia, monetary restriction has not controlled spending (Antal and Suranyi 1987; Bokros 1987; Tardos 1988; Varhegyi 1989).

According to Varhegyi, the most striking effect of the monetary restriction imposed in 1987 was the increase in enterprise debt, manifested in delays of payment and increased enterprise illiquidity.

The restriction led to a drastic decrease of liquid resources at several enterprises... The deterioration of enterprise liquidity positions produced solvency
problems more serious than ever: a considerable part of money orders
(remittances) presented to the banks could not be paid out because they were
not covered. Only the very important and long-standing uncovered money orders are summarized by the monthly bank statistics. Their total amount in
December 1988 was three times as much (HUF 46 billion) as the year before.
The total of delayed payments may be essentially more than this (Varhegyi
1989, p. 407).

These processes can be traced by an examination of the changes in
the structure of enterprise assets and liabilities (see tables 8.4 and 8.5).
Together they show the extent to which Hungarian firms increased
their debt with each other and the foreign sector. For the economy as a
whole, the decrease of enterprise monetary assets of 18 per cent was
followed by an increase of their buyers' debts of 15 per cent. Looking
at enterprises' and cooperatives' current liabilities, it can be seen that
the circulating fund credits fell by 13 per cent, while their debts to their
domestic contractors increased by 10 per cent, and to their foreign
partners by 15 per cent.

Table 8.4: Changes in some current liabilities of state enterprises and
cooperatives, 1988 (previous year = 100)

Sectors	Working capital credits	Domestic contractors	Foreign contractors
Mining	127	171	167
Electric energy	1623	78	91
Metallurgy	46	278	190
Engineering ind.	63	232	164
Building material ind.	100	197	113
Chemical industry	81	156	113
Light industry	88	199	136
Food processing ind.	78	175	371
Industry, total	76	194	171
Building industry	106	181	65
Agriculture	97	176	222
Transport and comm.	49	182	105
Trade	93	152	109
Material branches	83	175	121
Non-material branches	191	101	114
TOTAL:	87	110	115

Source: Varhegyi 1989, p. 407.

Table 8.5: Changes in some assets of state enterprises and cooperatives, 1988[a] (previous year = 100).

Sectors	Monetary Assets	Claims on: All	Domestic	Foreign	Capitalist
Mining	76	111	128	116	122
Electric energy	63	130	117	99	99
Metallurgy	123	176	229	172	173
Engineering ind.	73	129	179	104	98
Building material	129	151	175	142	135
Chemical ind.	91	141	161	125	123
Light industry	110	131	172	102	102
Food processing	127	195	160	192	212
Industry, total	92	145	170	122	121
Building industry	95	155	173	102	103
Agriculture	70	151	155	148	149
Transport/comm.	52	163	175	150	163
Trade	81	146	170	130	129
Material branches	82	148	167	126	126
Non-material branches	82	109	101	120	123
TOTAL:	82	115	109	122	124

Source: Varhegyi 1989, p. 409.

[a]Balance sheets of state enterprises and cooperatives.

What was taken away by one hand was given back by the other. Chronic payment troubles and the (unintended) lengthening of the maturity date of trade credit—the direct results of the monetary restriction—were ameliorated by the expansion of public finance; the state intervened in an *ad hoc* manner when illiquidity and debt threatened too many enterprises.

> Analysing the position of domestic money holders separately, it appears that the fiscal restriction in 1988 failed to affect the single most important money holder: the state finance sector. A considerable part of the enterprise and private spheres was afflicted by the bank credit restriction, whilst the budget handed over more money than ever to a number of enterprises and private people, behind closed doors. The debts of the government sector to the central bank grew by HUF 41 billion in 1988... while those of the commercial banking sector decreased by HUF 26 billion (Varhegyi 1989, pp. 411-413).

This behaviour of 'give with one hand and take away with the other' can also be seen in the Hungarian central bank activities. The tools available to the central bank to reduce the monetary base include reducing the amount of refinancing credits (reserves) available to commercial banks and restricting the central bank purchase of bills of exchange held by commercial banks (see table 8.6). What we find is that central bank behaviour was contradictory: while refinancing credits to the banking system from the central bank fell 52 per cent between 1987 and 1988, the rediscounting of bills of exchange grew by 24 per cent (Varhegyi 1989).

Table 8.6: Central bank claims on the commercial banking sector[a] (billions of forints).

	January 1, 1988	December 31, 1988	Change
1. Refinancing credits	235	183	-52
Short term	74	31	-43
Medium term	48	41	-7
Long term	113	111	-2
2. Rediscouted bills	4	28	24
3. Total claims (1+2)	239	211	-28

Source: Varhegyi 1989, p. 414.
[a]Excludes the National Savings Bank and the State Development Institute.

4   Failure of monetary restriction in Yugoslavia and Hungary

What ultimately explains the source of endogeneity in Hungary and Yugoslavia is a contradiction built into the basic premise of market-based socialism. The contradiction is that the state has conflicting objectives—to maintain employment, to maintain macroeconomic stability, and to mediate competition for investment resources.

In both economies, the enterprise response to efforts of the state to control inflation through a restriction of the money supply is to continue production and permit inventories to accumulate rather than lay off workers. Finance for inventory accumulation and other working capital needs in many firms takes place through involuntary trade credit and price increases. Delinquent debtors and bankrupt firms use political muscle to bargain for eleventh-hour bail-outs. The imposition of discipline on firms when sales are slack does not, therefore, usually take the form of bankruptcy and shut-down, but rather state-directed bail-out and rescheduling of debt made possible by the infusion of fresh credit from the banks. In this way, the state, through its monetary institutions, ends up validating endogenously caused inflation rather than exogenously controlling it. These bail-outs occur because the state fears that multiple bankruptcies would undermine one very basic right of socialism—the right to employment and income.

The single thread that runs through the post Keynesian analysis as well as the Yugoslav and Hungarian case examples is the argument that 'needs of business' ultimately determine the amount of money which circulates in the economy. It is assumed that the state can or must provide a sufficient amount of money and credit to allow various groups of people in the economy to realize their target income. Hence, price pressure from group/enterprise demands ends up being validated by state action.

Political needs of business, as it were, determine the volume of money circulating in the economy. The status quo is thereby maintained by inflationary finance.

But why has the state and its central bank in Yugoslavia and Hungary capitulated to the group demands of enterprises for monetary accommodation despite *resolve* to maintain a tight monetary regime? Understanding some of the underlying political issues that explain why the central bank behaves as the lender of last resort may shed some light on institutional reform.

Hungary and Yugoslavia can both be characterized as economies in which the investment-savings decision is politicized. This is due largely to the bypass of the capital market due to the institution of social property.[3] In both countries, workers are not owners of the means of production but rather 'stewards' of the capital stock, responsible for its productive use and for its constant increase in value (Miller 1989, p. 434). In both countries, capital is not treated as a scarce factor of production but rather as a free gift provided to enterprises to enable them to earn an income. The reason for this is that when capital is treated as a social good, it permits political interests—especially those which maintain a full employment agenda—to intervene in the affairs of the firm. This is the essence of social property.

The effect of this is that enterprises learn to bargain for subsidies and tax concessions in the face of losses, capital is prevented from seeking out its most productive use throughout the economy, and enterprises learn to jealously guard income earned and to quickly vote its distribution to wages and incomes of enterprise members (Miller 1989; Swaan 1990; Bechtold and Helfer 1987).

With reference to Yugoslavia, Miller (1989, p. 437) has recently explained that:

> The mixing of property rights and entitlements through the abuse of the conception of social property has had a particularly deleterious effect on the operation of the economy. It has led to what some economists call the 'privatization of gains and the socialization of losses', often with the connivance of the workers themselves. It is not uncommon for workers in a loss-making enterprise to continue to vote themselves relatively high incomes, in spite of their enterprise's parlous financial condition, in the expectation that society at large will bail them out, using the overall stock of social capital or 'primary emission' (the printing press). Self-management agreements among

enterprises are employed to jack up prices or guarantee markets for their products, often abetted by local and republican political leaders, for whom 'profitable' enterprises are an important source of revenue and prestige. ...This is tantamount to strangling the industrial 'goose' which is the primary source of 'golden eggs' for the satisfaction of societal requirements and often does not allow enterprises to accumulate sufficient funds for operating expenses, let alone investment.

Writing about the Hungarian economy, Swaan (1990, p. 257) makes a similar point:

First, the *soft budget constraint* is extremely important. Enterprises confronted with (imminent) losses have a good chance of arranging some kind of subsidy or exemption from regulators, although much bargaining effort on the administrative market is necessary to convince central organs. The softness of the budget constraint forces the authorities to exercise strict control over enterprises and may be owing to 'regulation illusion', On the other hand, the stronger the paternalism of the authorities, and the more they intervene, the less the enterprises feel themselves responsible. In spite of their recurring complaints about excessive state interference, the enterprises know very well the advantages this has: bad results will also be compensated for.

Laky refers to this process as the hidden mechanism of recentralization (Laky 1980). Because market participants are not fully responsible for their decisions and know that they will not fail, they often act in economically irresponsible ways. Their behavior calls forth additional bureaucratic intervention. Thus, as Swaan notes above, despite recurring complaints about excessive state interference, enterprises fully know what advantages this holds, namely, that poor performance will be compensated.

What this points out is that there is an obvious contradiction in Hungary and Yugoslavia between the processes striving to institute market-type relationships (among them macroeconomic monetary control) and the retention of social control through a property rights system based on social ownership. This manifests itself in the impossibility of solving the question of the right proportion between incomes according to work and social benefits according to needs. In short, there is no mechanism, except through *ad hoc* bureaucratic intervention, to determine the 'social' distribution of wages.

The obvious contradictions between these two processes—the movement toward market-type relationships with a simultaneous retention of the elements of central control—reflect the tension between the ideological commitment to planning as one of the principal advantages of socialism and the drive for greater flexibility and efficiency. On a broader level they reflect the inbuilt fears and doubts of the 'input society' syndrome; namely, that reliance on the 'unseen hand' of the market will lead to increasing socio-economic inequalities and uncontrollable social and political processes and, by extension, the diminution of the party's ability to exercise its leading role. Hence, the continuing efforts to restrict the use of hired labor and the development of a free labor market in general, to constrain the free flow and use of capital and to control the process of price formation (Miller 1989, p. 443).

The effect of this is that investment flows to the strongest firms (from a bargaining viewpoint) and not necessarily to those which are most efficient (from a market viewpoint).

5 Directions for further institutional reform

It is clear that the infatuation with the market and the current drive toward privatization does not negate the role of the state in economic affairs. Market processes are unpredictable and unstable. As the post Keynesians have pointed out, when financial stability is threatened, entrepreneurs (and especially the bankers among them) use their political power to seek protection from the central bank, as well as other state agencies, under the banner of 'lender of last resort'. Bail-outs, loans and monetization of corporate debt become entitlements. At the heart of monetary control is the political problem of resolving conflicts among bankers, industrialists, workers, the state and the international community over the distribution of income.

Ultimately both the capitalist and the market-socialist economies must deal with the question of who is ultimately responsible for bank lending. This is because in both types of economies chronic inflation is explained by the inability or unwillingness of monetary authorities or the state to prevent rival claimants for limited social resources from creating money to realize their target expenditures. The benefits of the market are undeniable, yet the costs, especially inequality of distribution, socially destructive.

The insight offered by the post Keynesian school is that the solution to monetary control—or inflation in general—lies in the striking of some *binding* political accord among major economic groups in the system which outlines the share of income each group is willing to accept. This would suggest the development of collective bargaining institutions which would negotiate at the plant as well as the national level. It would also imply the creation of political parties pledged to represent the interest groups and prepared to enter coalitions to mediate conflict and reach political accord.

To stop the process of continuous, *ad hoc*, enterprise-specific intervention in enterprise policies, and in general to harden budget constraints, Hungary and Yugoslavia must also move in the direction of instituting capital markets and forcing market participants to become fully responsible for their decisions. The 'stick' of bankruptcy as well as the 'carrot' of profits must be upheld.

6 Conclusion

There are limits to the process of privatizing and monetizing the economy. For monetary policy to work in reforming socialist economies such as Hungary and Yugoslavia, there must be an institutional setting in which conflicting interests can be reconciled through open negotiations. That is to say, the undesired income distribution effects associated with the operation of the market economy must be mediated by institutions that provide for open negotiations among interest groups, especially labour groups. Furthermore, enterprises must be held accountable for investment decisions, this accomplished first and foremost through a capital market. But the effects of 'market discipline' must be mediated in order to maintain political stability. Therefore, with the introduction of monetary policy as a tool of management, there must also be policies which provide a guiding hand in the labour market and relieve enterprises from the agony of considering the social costs of unemployment. Unemployment benefits, retraining programmes, new employment options which encourage labour mobility and the setting up of new businesses must be made available to those who lose jobs through bankruptcy or redundancy. In these ways, budget constraints can be hardened, market discipline can be imposed, yet the socialist values of protecting those who fall through the cracks can be maintained. With workers, entrepreneurs, and the state represented in nationally-based interest groups or political parties, the possibility of building political accord may be possible.

Notes

1. The discussion in this section is drawn from Gedeon (1985-6).
2. ZOP is an acronym for Zakon o Osiguravanju Placanja (Law on Insurance Payments).
3. For a recent discussion of the history and meaning of social property, see Miller (1989).

References

Antal, L. and Suranyi, Gy. (1987). 'The Prehistory of the Reform of Hungary's Banking System', *Acta Oeconomica*, *38*, 3-48.

Arestis, P. and Eichner, A. S. (1988). 'Theory of Money and Credit', *Journal of Economic Issues*, 1003-1021.

Bechtold, H. and Helfer, A. (1987). 'Stagflation Problems in Socialist Economics', in *Crisis and Reform in Socialist Economies*, Boulder: Westview

Press, 11-31.
Bokros, L. (1987). 'The Conditions of the Development of Businesslike Behavior in a Two-Tier Banking System', *Acta Oeconomica, 38*, 61-79.
Chowdhury, A., Grubaugh, S. and Stollar, A. (1990). 'Money in the Yugoslav Economy', *Journal of Post Keynesian Economics*, XII:4, 636-643.
Gedeon, S. J. (1985). A Comment on and Extension of Lavoie's, 'The Endogenous Flow of Credit and the Post Keynesian Theory of Money', *Journal of Economic Issues*, 837-842.
Gedeon, S. J. (1985-6). 'The Post Keynesian Theory of Money: A Summary and an Eastern European Example', *Journal of Post Keynesian Economics*, VIII:2, 208-221.
Jaksic, M. (1984). 'Kritika Monetarizma', *Socijalizam, 27*, 1262-1277.
Kaldor, N. (1982). *The Scourge of Monetarism*, Oxford: Oxford University Press.
Knight, P. (1984). 'Financial Discipline and Structural Adjustment in Yugoslavia: Rehabilitation and Bankruptcy of Loss Making Enterprises', *World Bank Working Papers*, No. 705, Washington D.C..
Komisija za Probleme Ekonomske Stabilizacieje, *Polazne Osnove Dugorocnog Programa Ekonomske Stabilizacje*, Sarajevo, 1982.
Kregel, J. A. (1984-5). 'Constraints on the Expansion of Output and Employment: Real or Monetary?', *Journal of Post Keynesian Economics*, VII:2, 139-152.
Laky, T. (1980). 'The Hidden Mechanism of Recentralisation in Hungary', *Acta Oeconomica, 24*, 95-110.
Lavoie, M. (1984). 'The Endogenous Flow of Credit and the Post Keynesian Theory of Money', *Journal of Economic Issues*, 771-798.
Miller, R. (1989). 'Theoretical and Ideological Issues of Reform in Socialist Systems: Some Yugoslav and Soviet Examples', *Soviet Studies*, 430-448.
Mirko, U. (1983). 'Novcani sistem i neka pitanja drustvenoekonomskih odnosa', *Planiranje*.
Moore, B. (1988a). *Horizontalists and Verticalists*, Cambridge: Cambridge University Press.
Moore, B. (1988b). 'How Credit Drives the Money Supply', *Journal of Economic Issues*, 443-452.
Rogic, Z. (1984). 'Analiza Efikasnosti Monetarno-Kreditne Politike u Razdoblju 1979-1984', in *Aktuelni Problemi Privrednih Kretanja i Ekonomske Politike Jugoslavije*, Informator, Zagreb.
Schonfelder, B. (1990). 'Reflections on Inflationary Dynamics in Yugoslavia', *Comparative Economic Studies*, 85-106.
Swaan, W. (1990). 'Price Regulation in Hungary, 1968-87: A Behavioral-Institutional Explanation', *Cambridge Journal of Economics*, 247-265.
Tardos, M. (1988). 'Can Hungary's Monetary Policy Succeed?', *Acta Oeconomica 39*, 61-79.
Ujdenica, M. (1983). 'Novcani sistem i neka pitanja drustveno-ekonomskih odnosa', *Planiranje*, 1-2.
Varhegyi, E. (1989). 'Results and Failures of Monetary Restriction (Some Lessons of Hungarian Financial Policy in 1988)', *Acta Oeconomica, 41*, 403-420.
Wray, L. R. (1989). Review of Basil Moore, 'Horizontalists and Verticalists', *Journal of Economic Issues*, 1186.

9 State Monopolies and Marketization in Poland

Helena Sinoracka

1 Introduction

January 1990 was a turning point for the Polish economy. Since then, the entire economy has undergone extensive change, and the process of intrinsic economic reform has begun to influence the basic elements of economic and social life. At the core of the economic reform is the *Balcerowicz plan*, which includes the following objectives: attaining market equilibrium; ending inflation; demonopolization of the economy; and changes in the forms of ownership.

Changing the economic system in Poland into a new, more efficient one is the main objective of the reform, because the previous economic system proved to be inefficient. The reasons for this included: a permanent state of economic disequilibrium; monopolistic structure of the economy; and state ownership of the means of production.

In order to introduce market mechanisms, three steps should be followed: (1) make the transition from a supply-constrained economy to a demand-constrained one, because permanent excess demand, characteristic of most socialist countries, is a key problem preventing the realization of the plan; (2) achieve the destruction of monopolistic and oligopolistic structures; and (3) introduce a massive privatization effort to include almost all state property, and to a lesser extent also cooperative property. This essay will focus on problems created by the transition from a centrally planned economy to a market-oriented one.

There are three important problems which Poland must deal with in this transition. Section 2 focuses on the difficulties involved in achieving market equilibrium, especially those accompanying the demand-reduction policies of the Balcerowicz plan. Sections 3 and 4 look at the problems associated with the inherited monopolistic structure of the Polish economy, and will point out the difficulties of achieving an effective demonopolization policy. Specific examples of this will be described in section 5: agriculture, automobiles, textiles and housing. Section 6 further elaborates on the difficulties of demonopolization by describing the defences some enterprises have adopted to further strengthen their established position.

2 Market equilibrium

The achievement of market equilibrium required reducing the large and growing state budget deficit. To deal with this problem, tax rates for enterprise sectors were raised, and large cuts in state budget expenditures were made. These were aimed at limiting wasteful production, especially in state-owned firms, investment outlays in the sector of enterprises in general and expenditures in the non-productive sector. Tax policy was aimed at reducing the overall level of demand. Its major features were higher taxation, especially a progressive tax imposed on excessive wage increases, and a high tax on state property owned by enterprises. As part of the overall aim of encouraging privatization and individual enterprise, it should be mentioned that these taxes have been paid only by state-owned enterprises.

In addition, subsidies from the state budget that had supported inefficient enterprises were almost entirely reduced. Traditionally, the main recipients of these enormous subsidies were the mining industry, especially coal mines; heavy industry (metallurgic industry and shipbuilding); the food processing industry; housing construction; and management of housing cooperatives.

By December 1990, 86 per cent of total sales of consumer goods and services were freely negotiated; prices of procurement goods were liberalized 89 per cent (Kolodko 1991, p. 7). The previous system of fixed prices based on costs was, therefore, abandoned, and market-determined prices for goods introduced which resulted in repeated price rises. This drained the financial resources of enterprises and households, and tapped their accumulated savings. Simultaneous implementation of these policies enabled a consequent liquidation of excess demand. Thus, it was due to the plan that the Polish economy, for the first time in almost half a century, has faced demand restrictions, altering the former situation of supply constraints.

An important focus of the Balcerowicz plan was to shift the supply-constrained economy into a demand-constrained one. This involves three steps: (1) establishing the conditions in which the marketization of the economy could take place. This is thought to be necessary as a market pricing mechanism would not be able to function in a situation where acute shortages exist, shortages which were permanent in Poland and getting larger until the end of 1989; (2) disadvantageous economic behaviour and social institutions accompanying the shortage economy should be eliminated, and behaviour patterns appropriate to a market economy encouraged; (3) introducing policies to stabilize the exchange rate.

After an attempt to achieve equilibrium by increasing supply in the 1980s was unsuccessful, the 'shock therapy' treatment was used in early 1990. This led to a 23 per cent decline in output. While the stabilization programme may have overshot the intended goals, which may result in unintended consequences if the proper policies are not undertaken, it did create a demand-constrained economy (see Kolodko 1991).

The initial stage in this transition to a demand-constrained system was also accompanied by adverse changes in the distribution of income, such that an estimated 20 per cent of the population now owns as much as 80 per cent of the financial resources of the country. Ten per cent of the urban population owns up to 70 per cent of the private, non-farm property warrants which were secured or issued in the Polish People's Republic. This increasing income inequality, the result of systemic change, is a problem in Poland which is a society used to the generally accepted idea of social egalitarianism, although this was never completely realized. The potential for conflict that results is aggravated by common opinion, which believes that this small privileged group comes from the former nomenklatura, those high-ranking officials who seemingly have received most of the nation's property as a 'prize' for ruining the country. There is also a threat that this former nomenklatura is capable of creating a 'political capitalism' which would become a driving force in the economy as a kind of substitute for a middle class-dominated capitalism. This could have serious political implica-tions and lead to political unrest. Up untill now, public sentiment has been held in check by widespread social support for the Solidarity government, which supports *parliamentary* methods for accomplishing political change. However, the more extreme positions of some social groups converged around political parties during the presidential campaign.

3 Monopolistic structures in Poland

The removal of monopolistic and oligopolistic structures is extraordinarily difficult in Poland, as state ownership has dominated the economy for about half a century. The economic aspect of state monopoly was accompanied by institutional monopoly which promoted the emergence of powerful lobbies. These groups have become accustomed to their own privileges for many years, and they constantly defend them. The current monopolized structure of the Polish economy is the result of several long-lasting microeconomic and macroeconomic tendencies.

The macroeconomic cause of excessive monopolization resulted from the preference for concentration of production. Plans of socialist industrialization were aimed at building big socialist enterprises. This 'megalomania of the centre' was justified by socialist ideology and the advantages resulting from the economies of large-scale production. This inclination to build big enterprises was supported by similar preferences from the enterprises themselves, as firms soon found that the larger their production potential, the easier it was to obtain additional benefits. In fact, enterprises in a centrally planned economy found exclusion of competitors from the market to be to their strategic advantage, so they wanted to achieve a monopoly position. Being aware of the resulting advantages was the cause of the desire for more investment on the part of socialist enterprises.

Because Poland was a supply-constrained economy, both the nature of competition itself and the competitors differed from those in a demand-constrained economy (Lipton and Sachs 1990; Kornai 1986). First, enterprises did not compete with each other, and the struggle was of a vertical nature as enterprises faced the decision-making centre. The object of this competition is different from that in a market economy. Its purpose is not to gain a larger share in surplus value, but to be given priorities in attaining scarce goods. Above all, enterprises competed for scarce hard currency in order to purchase new technologies and to get preferences in the allocation of scarce raw materials and spare parts. Enterprises also struggled with the centre for subsidies and investment allocations. There was also competition to gain legal priorities, such as getting a reduction of or exemption from different types of taxes.[1] Because the centre's decision-making was effectively arbitrary, vertical competition was a better way of realizing particular objectives than horizontal competition. In practice, the centre often gave in, enterprises stressed their needs still more strongly and more numerous lobbies came into being. This process intensified in the 1970s, when the idea of 'industry Poland' appeared, to indicate a differentiated approach of the centre towards individual industries. This process continued in the 1980s: the stronger the industry lobby, the easier became its struggle with the centre. It is hardly surprising that competition between enterprises is not found in Poland. There was, instead, a tendency among enterprises to integrate. This process consisted of individual enterprises identifying their common interests in their struggle with the federations, while the federations in turn defended the interests of the industry to an industrial ministry. It is not surprising then that state enterprises fought the Ministry of Finance over the taxation of excessive wage increases—such a struggle with what used to be the central authority is simply a continuation of their old behaviour patterns.

The organizational structure of the economy made this concentration of interests very easy. The centralized system by which the economy was managed depended on the existence of the federation as an intermediate level between enterprise and ministry. But then a weakening of the centre combined with the concentration of power of industry lobbies and stronger enterprises, contributed to the increasing danger of excess demand appearing. This was the result of the allocation of excess investment over and above the amount specified in the plan, which meant that some enterprises ended up with more hard currency, subsidies and tax exemptions or reductions. Hence the resulting inconsistency: the actions of the centre in giving in to these demands showed up in the growing deficit of the state budget, and the larger loans from the central loans from the central bank to the government, which exceeded need and were never paid back. Excessive money issue caused a sharp decline in the purchasing power of money. Additional funds were then 'extorted' from the centre and allowed to cover the investment needs of enterprises. Paradoxically, by being able to obtain more resources from the centre, enterprises not only expanded their economic potential, but also increased their bargaining power to get more. Like a vicious circle, this weakening of the centre due to the strengthening of enterprises was directed against the centre itself: the weaker the centre, the stronger enterprises became. The state budget deficit grew, market disequilibrium deepened, and as a result, supply constraints intensified. Growing demand strengthened the economic security of enterprises. Because this way of functioning had lasted so long, enterprises and the centre had created an economic structure convenient merely to themselves. Therefore although only a few genuine monopolies exist, most enterprises, whether big or small, behaved like monopolies, and the whole economy is controlled by industry lobbies.

The degree of monopolization is determined by the degree to which the market is controlled by individual enterprises and not by the *number* of such enterprises. In reality, the degree of monopolization is considerably higher than indicated by the organizational structure of the

Polish economy. By the end of 1989, 950 out of 4,500 enterprises were monopolies. The degree of monopolization in Poland is high because these enterprises are the largest ones. Previously in the Polish economy where excess demand existed, a particular type of monopoly, one functioning under conditions of economic security occurred. This might be called a 'comfort monopoly', which describes the situation in which a monopolist exploits his privileged situation in the market to ensure his own security rather than to increase profits. Such types of monopoly have existed for many years in Poland. They are characterized by low efficiency, an aversion to technological progress, and excessive costs. The fact of comfort monopolies showing unjustified costs was specific in the Polish situation, and included, for example, the costs of unwarranted and unrealized investment projects. Excessive costs also resulted from expenditures on social projects, such as building luxurious rest houses or organizing expensive trips abroad for workers and their families.

4 Obstacles to demonopolization

It is not unexpected, therefore, that monopolies and oligopolies brought economic losses. Changing this pathological organizational structure of the economy is the essential element of the Balcerowicz plan and economic reform itself; it is a struggle against special interests which also has political meaning. The first attempts to destroy monopolies and introduce an anti-monopoly policy aroused the resistance of these special groups. This is why to achieve the desired end, democracy and legislative action is important, but the introduction of new legislation itself takes time; democracy does bring about some additional costs as a result of the initial 'trial-and-error' learning process. The dissolution of local monopolies, those intermediaries in the purchasing and processing of agricultural products, the federations of agricultural cooperatives is an example. Although agriculture in Poland is very dispersed, these food purchasing and processing units created big organizations and were local monopolies. The dealers fought for their priority and enjoyed the privileged position of comfort monopolies in local markets such as dairies, bakeries and enterprises processing fruits and vegetables. Destruction of these comfort monopolies was preceded by a fierce political struggle. At present, peasant parties representing the interests of peasant organizations constitute a very strong lobby in parliament.[2] When compared with others, these parties are enormously powerful, for two reasons. First, in the new political situation, the interests of private farmers are for the first time considered equal to those of other sectors of the economy. Second, farmers have a strategic product, food, at their disposal. (In 1991, 47 per cent of household income is spent on food.)

Eventually, federations of cooperatives, those dealers who had siphoned off a considerable part of profits, were eliminated. However, purchase and food processing are still boycotted by the previous beneficiaries. Although the federations, which previously dictated the terms on which they would buy to thousands of scattered farms and the terms of sale to retail buyers, have disappeared, suppliers and buyers are still paying a high price for that success, namely the resulting chaos in the food processing and distribution industries. New forms of ownership such as companies are anxious to take over the job of dealers. Will they too become monopolies? This danger is still present, as the old managers were quick to become part of the new firms. Now it is necessary that food prices should come under anti-monopoly controls, but it is likely that the Agency of Agricultural Markets may not be adequate for this task.

5 Demonopolization in the Polish economy

There are many examples where monopolies created obstacles to reform. In 1989, the food market in Poland was flooded with excessive supplies, especially of butter, coming mainly from Western European countries. This meant that there was in particular a lack of demand for Polish butter, and therefore an inability to make good on commitments for milk delivered by farmers for processing. The problem was solved by the dairy cooperatives which delivered butter instead of money to the farmers. This butter was more expensive than that in the rural shops; it was not fresh as it was coming from an unsold reserve; and it was in quantities exceeding the needs of farmers' households. The farmers' protests evoked an interesting response by cooperative managers, who stated that the farmers who sold milk to the cooperatives were in fact members of these cooperatives. Under such difficult conditions, they had to share the risk faced by cooperatives. In this way they were to protect the cooperatives--which were necessary for local markets--from bankruptcy.

Another example occurred in the autumn of 1990, when a lack of dealers produced a monopolistic situation in which local sugar processors could impose their own terms on sugar beet farmers. This brought them into conflict with farmers, and an attempt by the Ministry of

Agriculture to mediate the dispute was unsuccessful as farmers wanted higher prices. A new governmental office, the Agency of Agricultural Markets, could have seized this opportunity to initiate new regulatory activities, but it did not do so.

Previously, the Anti-Monopoly Department of the Ministry of Finance, which functioned up until 1990, had been successful in destroying the egg monopoly in 1989. This action resulted in lower egg prices and the elimination of excessive costs of the intermediaries and of monopoly profits.

Lately, the Polish agricultural sector has faced competition from large imports of food from Western Europe. While protective tariffs could be imposed, if they are too low, the agricultural sector may not be able to survive. Western countries protect their farmers; Polish farmers will find it hard to compete with international competition, as they are not competitive at home. The Agency for Agricultural Markets was expected to buy up excess supplies, but unexpectedly large state budget deficits in 1991 prevented funds being released for this purpose. The problem of agriculture is compounded because the farmers' lobby in parliament is divided and thus weak, which raises the question: who will defend the interests of food producers? It is important that state policy for agriculture be strengthened as soon as possible to protect the farm sector.

In 1990, the Anti-Monopoly Department of the Ministry of Finance was transformed into the Anti-Monopoly Board in recognition of its increased importance in the government's anti-monopoly policy. The three most important case studies of 1990 involve the automobile, textile and housing markets.

(a) The automobile market
The first important decision faced by the Anti-Monopoly Board was to control the price of medium litre capacity automobiles produced by the only producer of this type of car, the Zeran Automobile Factory in Warsaw. The Board believed the June 1990 increase in automobile prices to be unjustified, and ordered the factory to lower prices to the previous level, effective immediately. The Factory refused to comply, putting forward the following arguments: that it was not a monopoly, and therefore should not come within the Board's jurisdiction; that lower prices would result in bankruptcy; that about 20,000 workers would lose their jobs; and that the government does not protect domestic industry with tariffs.

This enterprise is, however, a monopoly because it is the only manu-facturer producing medium-sized automobiles. While there is another factory producing passenger automobiles in Poland, it makes only small litre capacity cars. As of the end of 1990, the state budget partially subsidizes automobile prices, but in general, buyers have been discrimi-nated against for years. Despite high prices, the Factory faces financial crisis, and does not meet the state bank's requirements for obtaining credit. Thus it faces the danger of bankruptcy in the near future. For many years, it had been functioning as a comfort monopoly, which re-sulted in inefficient production, its main cause of financial problems now that its comfort monopoly has definitely ended. Nevertheless, its power with respect to the centre (its manager was in the nomenklatura of the Central Committee of the Polish United Workers' Party) has de-clined, although protective tariffs of 14 per cent are still in effect ('Privatization Plans' 1990).

Demand was regulated by rising prices and a growing share of taxes in the higher price of automobiles going to the state rather than being met by an increase in output. The tax going to the state was equal to 100 per cent of the factory price (prime cost and producer's profit), and in this way, high prices limited real demand. The limited supply of au-tomobiles was justified by the inadequate supply of fuel in the country, with the argument being made that an increase in the number of auto-mobiles would bring about a need to import additional fuel, which had to be paid for in hard currency. This would in turn intensify the hard currency shortage.

Under the new conditions, the Factory claims that high import duties are needed, as imports of cheaper and better foreign automobiles would ruin the Polish automobile industry. Because technological change takes time and involves certain learning processes, creation of an indus-trial policy is needed in which it must be required that profits be used exclusively for modernization in order to obtain import protection and subsidies.[3] If this condition is not met, protection and subsidies should be eliminated, allowing the enterprise to go into bankruptcy. It would be better to permit imports of foreign cars, if forcing the Polish industry to meet world competition makes it modernize, increase output and lower prices. If it cannot do this, then protective tariffs and controlling the prices of old, environment-polluting automobiles is worthless. The industrial policy of the government should be integrated with others in order to be effective. Strategic aims, not only short run and partial ones, must be formulated clearly and consistently.

It seemed as though the decision made by the Anti-Monopoly Board would accelerate the Factory's closing. The automobile lobby began to defend its interests, however, and the case was presented in the Anti-Monopoly Court. The Court demanded that the Board present a way to protect the Automobile Factory from irrecoverable losses caused by adherence to its decisions. Perhaps thanks to the skills of its lawyer, the Factory defended the higher prices of its cars, and administrative tools in the case proved to be unsatisfactory. But soon the Factory faced a real danger: a sudden unexpected flood of second-hand Western cars, as Western car dealers discovered the potential of the Polish car market. These inexpensive, high quality cars satisfied the demand from the newly enriched entrepreneurs from the new private sector, and automobile imports overwhelmed the Polish car market for a time. Cars confer prestige in Poland, and even lower-income buyers prefer older but cheaper Western cars to new Polish ones. In this way, before higher protective tariffs on imported cars were imposed, the home market 'lost' about $1 billion. Does the Automobile Factory now understand its perilous situation? To protect itself, it entered into negotiations with foreign companies about assembling their cars in Poland; the question now is whether it can make this change in time or go bankrupt.

Furthermore, the $1 billion spent on car purchases summarizes the situation well. First, it confirms the new wealth of the new group of owners in the new private sector. This sector is enjoying a special tax holiday, and pays very little tax (it is estimated that it pays less than 3 per cent of its profits as tax) while the state budget goes further into severe deficit. Second, the process of impoverishing the majority of the population is accompanied by a lack of a government income redistribution policy, and it is questionable whether even the Solidarity government will be forgiven for this. Third, the large amount of the new wealth from the initial stages of transition did not strengthen the birth of the capital market, being spent on consumption instead. This effect of privatization was unexpected, and creates many doubts about the prospects for privatization. (Only about 8 per cent of Poles surveyed intend to buy shares of privatized companies.) It does, however, underscore the problems faced in the transition to a market economy.

(b) The textile industry
The problem of demonopolizing the textile industry is not significantly different. Accustomed to the position of a comfort monopoly for years,

this industry produces expensive clothes in outdated designs and unattractive fabrics. As the economy opened up and because of a comparative price advantage, demand shifted to imports, mainly from low-cost producers in Greece, Turkey and Germany, which are sold by many small retailers. While this clothing was highly successful initially, the quality of fabrics and fashions, durability and style, was lower than in Poland. Considerable information is required to compare the quality of products and hence understand the true nature of comparative advantage. Because the market is overwhelmed by disoriented customers, however, the Polish textile industry may also collapse.

Just as in the automobile industry, an industrial policy should be implemented in the textile industry. This policy should consist of subsidizing those enterprises which adjust production to changes in demand. In other words, subsidies should be used selectively to support enterprises applying new technologies. Other incentives might be applied to domestic clothing producers. This might be done by reducing some taxes, especially the tax on excessive wage increases, making cheaper credit available or giving government orders on condition that producers undertake the production of some particular type of clothing, such as unprofitable items for children or protective clothing.

The textile industry may be on the edge of collapse, as is confirmed by pessimism in Lodz, its largest centre. In spite of radically deteriorating wages and growing unemployment, these workers do not protest, and it seems that awareness of poor prospects for the industry results in acceptance of these worsening conditions. The majority of workers employed in this industry are women, and female industries have never enjoyed high wages in Poland. The average level of wages for women is 30 per cent lower than the average male wage. Female participation in social funds[4] has always been lower in the textile industry than in other, privileged industries. Women's low bargaining power results in their disadvantageous position. When compared with another lobby, the auto industry for example, women in textiles do not effectively fight for the interests of their own industry because of a lack of bargaining power. As a result, there is no one to pressure the government for the correct industrial policy for light industry. An important question that must be answered is this: will Lodz, a centre of industry for women, be neglected by government policy? If the industry does collapse, will thousands of new jobs for women be created soon?

(c) The housing industry

The anti-monopoly policy in housing is intended to revitalize a housing recovery in Poland where about 1,400,000 families have no living quarters of their own. One thousand people share 284 living quarters in Poland, as compared with 370 in Hungary and 429 in Austria. Consequently, there is a large housing shortage even after shifting to a demand-constrained economy. Subsidies granted to the housing industry are large; therefore another governmental aim is to get rid of the monopoly of the housing cooperatives. The aim is to control and unify rents for flats under all kinds of ownership while simultaneously subsidizing only poorer tenants.

As in the previous system, the amount of rent charged for a flat depended on the type of ownership. Differences in rents for identical flats depended on different costs and the amount of subsidy granted by the state budget. Rents in tenants' cooperatives are many times higher than those in municipal flats, and the differences in the proportions of household incomes going to housing can be as large as 1:10 (Dryll 1990; Kulesza 1991).

Cheap municipal flats, occupied for many years by their tenants, have resulted in huge potential savings to them. This form of ownership was common after the War, but very few municipal flats are available now. Tenants benefit from special rental allowances only because they obtained a municipal, and not a cooperative, flat. As there is no difference in average income level between residents of cooperative and municipal housing, there is no reason to subsidize affluent residents of municipal flats. Both groups include poorer as well as richer people, but tenants in cooperatives pay considerably higher rents. However, even these high charges cover only a minor part of costs of operating them, and subsidies are received from the state budget towards running the buildings (Dryll 1990; Kulesza 1991). Poor and rich tenants are equally subsidized, and this irrationality causes distortions in the housing industry as well as social dissatisfaction.

For many years, the housing industry has required reorganization. Several attempts to introduce changes proved ineffective, and in spite of huge subsidies and a severe housing shortage, the problem has not been adequately addressed. As with the case of the clothing industry, a housing lobby does not exist, and the Federation of Homeless People has no bargaining power. The budget of the paternalistic socialist state covered all the costs of housing. Paradoxically, the entire housing industry was increasingly subsidized out of the state budget even while the deficit was growing. Ultimately, the final consumer bears the cost of mismanagement.

The creation of demand restrictions in housing and the availability of subsidies to the poorest tenants will force the housing industry to lower the costs of building and managing multiple-dwelling units. If there were a capital market in operation in Poland, new investors could enter the industry and introduce new technologies. The supply of flats could then increase as the effects of economies of scale are combined with new technologies, and the decision-making time frame becomes a long-run one. Inefficient, uneconomical monopolies and oligopolies which have been functioning for years as comfort monopolies will be forced to leave the industry. Administrative removal of monopolies via a new housing policy, entry of new investors and the introduction of subsidies for only a few of the poorest will at last promote the creation of a housing market with horizontal competition. Now there is not even a trace of such competition because of the paternalism of the socialist state, which forgives mismanagement and finances all expenditures. First, creation of a demand restriction makes competition possible; second, the destruction of the housing monopoly is a condition indispensable for improvement in the housing industry. The first step has already been taken, as a new plan for housing has been proposed by the government. This would increase rents for all tenants and simultaneously introduce subsidies for some tenants whose rent payments exceed a certain proportion of income. Perhaps this will be the first of further successful actions in this area, although it also creates problems for social policy. That is, if tenant independence is to be encouraged, this proposal may simply end up continuing the old paternalism which excessively burdened the state budget with expenditures on uneconomical housing. In addition, it is one-sided because it emphasizes demand and does not consider the impact on supply, that is, on the number of available flats and the costs of construction and operation, which is why it is important to encourage demonopolization and the entry of new investors in the industry.

6 Defences in the face of bankruptcy

Monopolies in an industry characterized by shortage exhibit the behaviour of comfort monopolies. For example, when facing bankruptcy, they sell fixed assets; there is a specific division of commitments in the process of administrative disposition of the enterprise; and they create commercial credit.

Selling property is connected with the need to meet their most urgent financial commitments, mainly the continued payment of wages. Selling unnecessary fixed assets is generally a good thing to do. This creates two problems: (1) evaluation and selection of the fixed assets to be sold to meet short-run needs; and (2) their proper pricing. Strong local protests against selling real properties of state enterprises cheaply are well known.

Another method of protecting monopolies facing bankruptcy is a specific reorganization of a plant occurring simultaneously with reneging on commitments. This means that a large enterprise splits into many smaller ones, but only one of these 'new' enterprises takes over all the commitments of the former single enterprise. This enterprise then plays the role of scapegoat, as it is known in advance that it is not able to make good on these commitments. Subsequently, the remaining enterprises buy the functioning fixed assets from the bankrupt firm at a very low price. As in the former system, group interests are realized with the losses being borne by the final consumer.

The most common method used by an enterprise in order to survive is to create some kind of commercial credit. Commercial credit is established when suppliers extend credit to their buyers, who in turn extend credit to their buyers and so on. Thus this creates a system of mutual obligations and dues, unlike the previous automatic credit extension of state banks. Previously, only banks granted credit, and this was how the government could control state enterprises. Now the appearance of this new type of credit is an immediate result of the budget constraints imposed on enterprises by the Balcerowicz plan. These credit restrictions were intended to force the bankruptcy of inefficient enterprises, and would be controlled by banks. However, the unexpected development of this new kind of mutual credit by enterprises suggest that this credit-granting process is beyond the control of banks and the government, i.e. money is endogenous. Consequently, the whole economy suffers from payment bottlenecks. Enterprises gave each other 2.5 times more credit than the total amount granted by banks. A huge number of debtors appeared, but none are forced into bankruptcy since enterprise-creditors are unable to force this onto an enterprise-debtor. This effectively means that the state bank has lost control of the finances of state enterprises. Intensity of payment congestion is confirmed by a lengthening period of capital turnover, for example to 70 days, but an extension to 120 days is also occurring. Therefore effectively weak, economically inefficient units are protected by commercial credit. The price for paralysing the economy and making it possible for inefficient enterprises to continue to exist, just as before, will once more be paid by the final consumer.

The threat of inducing inflation also occurs, and a corrective solution has been introduced. State banks have been obliged by the National Bank of Poland to acquire all the obligations of debtors from creditors. This was aimed at regaining the control of banks over the credit lines and bankruptcies of state enterprises, but has not worked because creditors have not consented to sell their debts to the state banks. The additional operating costs that they would have to meet is not at issue, but good relationships with their contracting partners is: it is likely that they do not want to risk upsetting a long-term relationship. The unwillingness of creditors to sell their obligations to state banks results from the awareness that they too are indebted themselves, which evokes a special kind of solidarity between creditors and debtors, a loyalty of a buyer to a supplier (who has nevertheless credited the transaction).

This is how enterprises adapt to the difficult conditions of functioning under the introduction of demand constraints. The state loses control of enterprises which it no longer owns; weak firms find many ways to protect themselves from bankruptcy; and the stronger the enterprise, the easier that task is, so destruction of monopolistic structures becomes more difficult.

7 Privatization and its problems

The government is justifying its programme of privatization by pointing out the low efficiency of state-owned enterprises. It is also hoping that the combination of privatization, demand restrictions and its anti-monopoly efforts will create conditions promoting competition. Many inefficiencies exist, including an excessive development of the capital goods sector; lack of development of services; outdated, polluting technologies; low productivity and poor work discipline; and lack of proprietors' management skills and initiative, among others. The scope of privatization is different from that carried out in the past. It is intended to be a transition from an inefficient and ineffective monopoly of state ownership to an efficiently functioning, private ownership system, with the state having only a control function. Consequently, the transformation process may take a long time.

Legislation in 1990 created the basis for large-scale privatization which will be accomplished by transferring state enterprises to private owners. It was preceded by a political struggle between proponents of two different methods of privatization: enterprise self-management and citizen ownership. The first favours 'workers' shareholding' in which the shares in an enterprise are shared out among its employees. The objective is to tie the workers closely to the company and encourage genuine concern for its operations and the result of workers' efforts. Such shares would be offered to workers at extremely preferential prices (which would also lower the treasury's income). The second approach favours issuing privatization coupons to citizens, each coupon representing a share of national property. They will serve to determine the sale of rights to shares issued as a result of the transformation of state-owned enterprises; the purchase of rights to participate in financial institutions which hold shares resulting from the transformation of state-owned enterprises; and the purchase of enterprises or parts of them which are privatized directly.

Several questions have been raised, especially about the sale of shares to workers. Will enough workers buy shares? Can they afford to buy them, given low incomes? What is to prevent the new owners from buying shares and immediately reselling them? There is also a problem with behaviour. Ignorance about how a stock market market works and the inheritance of uncertainty about the future of one's own property, however small, caused an unwillingness to accumulate in many socialist countries which limits willingness to buy shares. There is also some risk connected with share ownership, and there is a danger that the stock will be sold off to provide immediate income. This is especially likely as the initial period of the Balcerowicz plan successfully ended inflation by draining the savings of enterprises and households. As there was already a low standard of living caused by the long-lasting economic crisis, the danger of a further decline in national output and fear of a subsequent fall in the standard of living makes it likely that if households do gain extra income, they are likely to consume it rather than invest it.

In any event, in a country where for nearly half a century, owner characteristics were being eliminated, it is doubtful if the fact of gaining shares is identical with the restoration of the entrepreneurial spirit. In the beginning, there is the possibility of speculation in shares; later there will be doubts about the reasonableness of the long-run decisions made by enterprises (which depend on who owns shares and how many each possesses).

The privatization process includes three different methods. The first is for the capital of a state-owned company to be put into a form such that its shares can subsequently be allocated outright or traded in a capital market. This is intended mainly for large- and medium-sized companies which would be difficult to sell in their entirety because of their size. The second route involves liquidating an enterprise, usually an unprofitable one, in order that all or part of it may be bought by private individuals or leased. Any enterprise may apply for commercialization, the first stage of privatization, and there are advantages in doing so. Newly privatized enterprises can pay higher wages because they face reduced taxes on excessive wage increases. This is intended to encourage privatization by giving private enterprises an advantage as compared to the remaining state-owned enterprises which do not get a similar tax break.

Finally, encouraging more small private enterprises, mainly in trade and services, will be accomplished by giving unlimited licences to private persons. This involves registration of the company and payment of a token licence fee. It enables small private businesses to be established, parallel to the already existing state and cooperative forms of ownership.

This type accomplishes a great deal, although affecting mainly trade: in 1990, four times as many private firms in trade were created as were liquidated, but only 30 per cent more in industry. This is probably due to its less risky nature due to the short time horizon and turnover of capital, which is rational for those used to the uncertainty and risk connected with any private activity.

However, this in turn, although encouraging competition in trade, often accelerates the bankruptcy of the larger competition, as the new enterprises often sell on the streets just outside existing retail establishments.

8 Conclusion

Although the Balcerowicz plan is intended to improve the functioning of the Polish economy, so far it has produced social problems, the potential for political unrest and few concrete economic improvements. The shock therapy treatment for preparing the preconditions for the eventual operation of a fully privatized market economy has, it seems, not been as successful as the more gradual approach adopted in Hungary, for example. The three aspects of the Balcerowicz plan—privatization, marketization and demonopolization—are supposed to turn Poland into a modernized economy comparable to those in the West. So far, the transition has encountered resistance and a desire to see more benefits for the majority.

Those who benefited from the old monopolistic system are trying to protect their privileges, so they presented the first obstacles to change. The agricultural lobby protested the liquidation of local monopolies, but were not successful in preventing it. However, agriculture faced a real danger, as a lack of protective tariffs made possible a flood of food imports into Poland. Polish farmers are not competitive, and unless they have access to outside financing and can get significant assistance from the government so that they can modernize and improve productivity, will not be able to expand output and compete with imports. They also suffer from lack of a strong organization to represent the interests of dispersed farmers.

The textile industry was in a monopolistic position for years and its needs for modern equipment were ignored by the central planners. Now it suffers from demand constraints and is losing sales to imports. Again, lack of access to financing prevents textile firms from meeting changes in demand, and there is the possibility that the absence of effective government policy will harm the industry. Furthermore, even though it employs a large number of women, there is no women's lobby to fight for the industry. If the industry fails, how much would it cost to create jobs for the thousands of newly unemployed women in Lodz? No study has yet been done to answer this question.

Protection of special interests was partly successful in the automobile industry, where the industry lobby successfully protected the Zeran Automobile Factory against monopoly charges. But this success was negated by the flood of cheap, high quality second-hand cars from the West. What it is now considering is the possibility of assembling cars for foreign companies; the alternative is bankruptcy.

The most sensitive area, because of its social implications, is the housing industry, which will not improve without access to outside financing, structural changes and government assistance. There is no lobby here representing those waiting for housing; construction firms are inefficient; and because they are local monopolies, existing housing cooperatives have no incentive to change. Government policy here should be oriented to helping the industry revitalize, especially by encouraging the development of institutions able to inject needed financing into the industry for new construction.

In general, it is possible to identify problems with each of the plan's aspects, problems which can also have implications for other countries attempting a transition. First, three unwelcome results occur with marketization. Rising unemployment due to firms failing is already a reality. Rising income inequality is a result of two forces: first, the wealth created by the initial freeing of the economy was concentrated in only a few hands; second, policies to control inflation and sop up excess demand (taxes, elimination of subsidies, rising prices) had an adverse effect on a large part of the population. Both these produce a potential for political unrest which so far has been contained by widespread support for the Solidarity government. The third result emerges from the process of marketization and worsens the existing problem of excess demand. This occurs, as noted previously, because as the centre weakens and enterprises get more power, they have been able to obtain more investment funding. Ironically, the result has been a larger-than-expected state budget deficit, partly due to the losses of the large state-owned enterprises, while tax concessions (or holidays) have reduced state tax revenues.

Although demonopolization is a worthy goal, domestic monopolies have managed to find a variety of devices to protect themselves. This means that inefficient, high-cost production persists and also that special interest groups can successfully defend their privileged positions. Neither result does much to improve the economy's functioning or reduce the social problems associated with the transition.

Finally, three problems have emerged with the privatization schemes. Most important, what Poland needs is the development of an innovative or entrepreneurial spirit, which is not the same as privatization. That this has not been encouraged is shown by the behaviour of the new entrepreneurs: instead of using their new-found profits constructively in the capital market or in new investment, they bought consumption goods, especially imported ones. This is related to a second problem. There is a fear that the privatization schemes will encourage speculation rather than real production activity. And third, those who have lost income as a result of the transition process are likely to sell any shares they are allocated as quickly as possible in order to maintain their living standard. Those who are wealthier will be able to buy them at low prices now and have the potential for making large gains in the future, thus worsening income inequality and adding to social problems.

Even though the ends may be desirable, the success of the transition will be determined by whether these problems can be mitigated so that political support can be maintained. The Balcerowicz programme will only be successful if these negative aspects can be managed so that the benefit of economic transformation can be gained without wrenching changes. This is why it is so important to include an industrial policy as part of the transition. Because the system is being changed from a supply-constrained to a demand-constrained economy, the most important new tools should be fiscal and monetary policy tools. However, there will be difficulties in introducing effective ones, as Poland, unlike market economies, has no experience with them.

One particular need is for appropriate policies to deal with the problems of high unemployment and inequality of income distribution. Although inflation has been controlled, recession should not be seen as the only way to end it. Also, the tax increase on excessive wage increases has been seen to have an unequal impact, for several reasons. It does not take account of the different initial situation of different enterprises, but makes the poor units poorer while the rich ones gain. Second, even in an improving economy, workers cannot be paid more because the tax is highly progressive, thus an equal tax rate does not reward improvements in efficiency which was its goal. Third, the tax does not prevent flourishing enterprises from paying higher wages (as it was supposed to do) since they can afford to pay five times more in tax than for excessive labour.

Any policy proposal must help make Polish firms competitive with foreign ones, and help start up new small businesses. Possible policies might include protective tariffs (at least temporarily), access to low-cost credit on favourable terms, subsidies (but granted only on condition of modernization), and selective government purchases. Such policies might also be selective by sector, including, for example, lower rates of interest for the agricultural sector and a subsidization policy for the residential construction industry and for low income tenants.

Monetary and fiscal policies need coordination with an anti-monopoly policy which itself needs to be improved. This might include setting up an anti-monopoly project and strengthening the Anti-Monopoly Board's staff. The project should identify structurally competitive industries (a concept unknown in the previous system) and force competition in them. Monopolistic industries might be subject to such anti-monopoly controls as price control. In all cases, decisions should be based on economic arguments, not on legal ones.

Industrial policy should also include political considerations. So far, the Polish government has been able to count on public support for its proposals, but to retain this support, it is necessary that positive results emerge.

Notes

1. For example, in the 1980s a campaign for removing the taxation of excessive wage increases was carried out (See 'Risk and Courage').
2. During the period in which the new cabinet was established, this lobby was the only one to oppose both the introduction of the Balcerowicz plan and the appointment of Balcerowicz as Deputy Prime Minister. This reflected the lack of priority given to the agriculture sector in 1990.
3. In Japan the Ministry of International Trade and Industry (MITI) imposes import quotas and the Japan Development Bank gives subsidies in the form of low interest loans to the automobile industry strictly for modernization. In the United States, the government co-signed a loan to Chrysler Corporation under the strict condition that it restructured and modernized.
4. Editors' note: The social fund is a concept specific to socialist countries, and derives from their system of national income accounting. The total value of aggregate consumption is composed of two parts. One part is equivalent to wage payments for labour. The second part is the social fund, which in effect finances the provision of education, health care, recreation and other state-provided services which are free or partially free (such as cultural activities) to users. Thus to say that women's participation in social funds is low means that they do not take as much advantage of these state-provided services as men. There are many reasons for this, including holding full-time jobs, being responsible for raising children, and running households and farms, all of which impose tremendous demands on their time.

References

Chandler, A. D., Jr. (1980). *The Visible Hand: The Managerial Revolution in American Business*, Cambridge: Harvard.

Czarniawski, R. (1990). *Privatisation: The Statutes with Comments*, Warsaw: Poltex.

Dryll, I. (1990). 'Rents Now Held in Leash', *Economic Life*, No. 40.

Kolodko, G. (1991). 'Inflation Stabilization in Poland: A Year After', in *Polish Economy in Transition*, part II, Warsaw: Zycie Gospodarcze.

Kornai, J. (1986). *Growth, Shortage and Efficiency*, Warsaw: State Scientific Publishers.

Kornai, J. (1990). *The Road to a Free Economy, Shifting from a Socialist System: The Example of Hungary*, New York: Norton.

Kowalik, T. (1991). 'Marketization and Privatization: The Polish Case', *The Socialist Register 1991*, London: Merlin.

Kulesza, H. (1991). 'Which Way to Housing Regularity', *Zycie Gospodarcze*, No. 5.

Lipton, D. and Sachs, J. (1990). 'The Case of Poland', *Brookings Papers on Economic Activity*.

'Risk and Courage', *Zycie Gospodarcze*, No. 4, 1991.

'Privatisation Plans', *Gazet Wyborcza*, No. 23, 1990.

Sachs, J. (1990). 'Eastern Europe's Economies', *Economist*, No. 23.

Zamagni, S. (1987). *Microeconomics*, Oxford: Basil Blackwell.

10 Whatever Happened to the East German Economy?

*Heinz D. Kurz**

> The Germans make everything difficult,
> both for themselves and for everyone else.
> *Johann Wolfgang Goethe*

1 Introduction

On July 1, 1990, a monetary, economic and social union became effective between the Federal Republic of Germany (FRG) and the German Democratic Republic (GDR). The Deutsche Mark (DM) replaced the Eastmark. Children under 15 years, adults under 60 years, and pensioners were allowed to exchange 2000, 4000, and 6000 Eastmarks, respectively, on a 1:1 basis. The exchange or conversion rate applied to most other stocks of money and financial claims, including household savings and company debt, was 1:2. Wage and price contracts and pension claims were converted at a rate of 1:1. The average rate of exchange of DM for stocks of Eastmarks was approximately 1:1.8.[1] Trade barriers and barriers to capital and labour movements between the two Germanies were abolished. Anticipating complete German unification, the legal, tax and social insurance system of West Germany was extended to East Germany. On October 3, 1990, in line with article 23 of the West German constitution, East Germany declared itself part of the Federal Republic of Germany.

While some of the socialist economies in transition followed the prescriptions of one variant or another of the so-called 'shock therapy', the east German economy was exposed to a shock without at first hardly any therapy at all. The results of the east German case are now visible with greater clarity. The currency union has triggered one of the deepest economic crises affecting an economy in world history. According to Karl-Otto Pöhl, then president of the Bundesbank, the DM was introduced 'without preparation and at the wrong exchange rate'; the 'too-hasty changeover' resulted in a 'catastrophe'.[2] The decay of the east German economy, which was slow before the currency union, became precipitant thereafter: the economy jumped

191

from the frying pan right into the open fire. In view of whatever has happened to the east German economy, the grounds on which some commentators have expressed concern with or outright opposition to German unification appear to be the wrong ones: it is not the alleged growth in economic power beyond limits which renders the new Germany a potential threat to its neighbours, it is rather the spectre of socio-economic and eventually political destabilization in Germany as a whole which should be of concern. The order of magnitude of economic and social distress in east Germany is such that if no quick and effective remedy to solve the problems, in particular the problem of unemployment, is found, political stability in Germany is in jeopardy, with unforeseeable consequences for Europe as a whole.

This chapter investigates the free fall of the east German economy and possible remedies for a recovery. Section 2 compares the situation in the two German economies prior to monetary union in terms of a few economic indicators. Section 3 summarizes briefly some views, which were widely shared when German unification was within reach and shortly thereafter, and which portrayed the problem of the integration of east Germany with the western part as an easy task that could be accomplished within a few years. The emergence of the sharp recession in the east German economy consequent upon the economic union is dealt with in section 4. A discussion of the main factors responsible for the decline in economic activity and employment will follow in section 5. Section 6 is dedicated to a brief analysis of the long-term perspectives of the east German economy. The concluding section contains a few remarks on economic policy strategies to overcome the current difficulties.

2   The situation in the two Germanies prior to monetary union

In order to be clear about the order of magnitude of the economic and social problems to be solved in the wake of German unification, and to put the new Germany in an international perspective, it is useful to recall a few indicators characterizing the two Germanies.[3] Table 10.1 gives the population and size of the former FRG, the GDR, and unified Germany, respectively. The population of east Germany accounts for 21.4 per cent of the population of unified Germany, and its territory for 30.3 per cent. While the population of the new FRG is the largest in western Europe, it is only slightly more than one half of that of the Russian Republic and less than one third of that of the United States.

Table 10.1: Population and size of Germany.

	Population (in millions)	Area (km^2)
United Germany	78.5	357,050
FRG (West Germany)	61.7	248,713
GDR (East Germany)	16.8	108,337

The workforce in 1989 was 8.9 million in East Germany and 29.7 million in West Germany, which implies participation rates of 54 and 48 per cent, respectively. While almost half of the workforce was female in East Germany, the female participation rate in West Germany was 38 per cent. Unemployment in West Germany has been 8.7 per cent in 1988 and 7.9 per cent in 1989, whereas no unemployment was reported in East Germany.

In terms of their respective employment structures the two economies exhibit remarkable differences (see table 10.2). Thus the employment shares of the primary sector and manufacturing are substantially larger in East Germany, whereas the shares of services and trade are considerably smaller. These differences reflect a couple of factors the most important of which appear to be: (i) the original integration of the two economies in different systems of the international division of labour, i.e., the Eastern and Western trading blocs, respectively; (ii) different levels of economic development; and (iii) different ideological attitudes towards the trade and service sectors which were considered 'unproductive' and therefore given little attention by the East German planning authorities.

Table 10.2: Employment by sector, 1987-1988 (per cent of total).

	West Germany	East Germany
Agriculture, forestry and fishing	4.2	9.9
Energy and mining	1.4	3.2
Manufacturing	29.7	33.8
Construction	6.6	6.1
Trade	14.5	7.8
Transport	5.6	6.8
Services, government	38.0	32.4

Sources: FRG, Statistisches Bundesamt, Arbeitszählung, May 24, 1987, Fachserie 2, Heft 4; Statistisches Bundesamt, Bevölkerung und Erwerbstätigkeit. GDR, Deutsches Institut für Wirtschaftsforschung, Wochenbericht 17/90, p. 243.

Up to 1986 the former GDR reported relatively high and stable rates of growth of net material product (NMP) produced. As shown in table 10.3, this was followed by a gradual decline, and in the last quarter of 1989 output performance deteriorated dramatically: NMP produced fell by 3 per cent compared with the corresponding period of 1988 (UN 1990, p. 90). This was mainly due to considerable losses in the labour force from emigration[4] and growing tensions in the domestic economic and political system and uncertainties about its future. While the East German economy showed signs of an accelerating decline, economic activity in West Germany in the years preceding monetary union was brisk.

Table 10.3: National income and industrial output, 1986-1990 (annual percentage change).

	East Germany		West Germany	
	Net material product	Industrial output	Gross domestic product	Industrial output
1986	4.3	3.7	2.3	2.0
1987	3.3	3.1	1.7	0.4
1988	2.8	3.2	3.7	3.6
1989	2.1	2.3	3.3	4.9
1990	-19.5	-28.1	4.7	5.5

Source: UN 1990, p. 208 and p. 221.

This was the economic situation in the two Germanies prior to July 1, 1990. Thereafter the economic decline in east Germany turned rapidly into a disaster as net material product and industrial output declined 19.5 and 28.1 per cent respectively. Compared to their 1989 values, by contrast, the projected net material output for 1990 was an increase of 4 per cent (UN 1990, p. 57). It is expected that net material product will decline another 19.5 per cent in 1991 (UN 1991, p. 41). The trend in west Germany was neatly amplified by a boom that was fuelled by additional demand coming from east Germans. Was this development to be foreseen?

3 Expecting a new *Wirtschaftswunder*

As soon as the option of German unification was within reach, many West German politicians nourished the expectation among the population of East Germany that unification would bring them quick economic prosperity. The Chancellor of the FRG, Helmut Kohl, went as far as to maintain that after unification many east Germans would immediately be economically better off and none would be worse off. In agreement with the parties backing his coalition government, the Christian Democrats and the Free Democrats, he also stood for the view that the cost of German unification would be of an order of magnitude which would not necessitate an increase of taxes.[5] It was argued that the extension of the market economy to east Germany would quickly activate entrepreneurial spirits hitherto dormant in the east German population, and attract western investors seeking production locations with low input costs and rapidly growing new markets. These two factors would have to be complemented with only relatively small amounts of resources, financial and other, provided by the western government in order to straighten out a variety of difficulties of an essentially short-run nature: whereas other central and east European countries would have to go through a time-consuming and costly process of trial and error in their attempt to replace the old order with a new one, the integration of the former GDR into a unified Germany required little else than the adoption of the ready-made, success-proven West German blueprint. The coming of a new economic miracle— *Wirtschaftswunder* mark II—was counted upon.

This notoriously optimistic outlook taken by ruling politicians was partly supported by several economists, who, despite their greater sobriety and realism, advocated the view that the rich FRG could without major difficulties shoulder the not quite so rich GDR and carry its population within a few years to the same level of private and public opulence. In an analysis of the east-west economic development in the coming decade, Wilhelm Krelle (1990) engaged in the following intellectual experiment. Assume that income per head in west Germany will grow at a rate of 2.5 per cent per year (which approximates its long-term average rate of growth); assume in addition that in the year of German unification, income per head in east Germany was one half of the west German value (an assumption which turned out to overestimate the east German level). Which rates of growth of income per capita must be realized in east Germany in order to catch up with the west German level within 10, 15 or 20 years, respectively? The answer is to be found by solving the following equation for g, the required growth rate:

$$y_0 \, e^{0.025t} = \frac{y_0}{2} \, e^{gt},$$

where y_0 is the west German income per head in the initial period, and t is the number of years required to catch up to the west German level. Hence, if $t = 10$, 15 or 20, then the required growth rates g must be 9.4, 7.1 or 6.0 respectively. Krelle commented: 'These are all not impossibly high rates of growth' (1990, p. 8).

McDonald and Thumann (1990) suggested two scenarios for east Germany, both of which imply rapid growth: in the more optimistic scenario A, the average rates of growth of output and labour productivity per annum are 10.5 and 11.5 per cent, respectively, while the corresponding rates in scenario B are 6.5 and 9 per cent. Interestingly, these authors pointed out that the scenarios should not be looked at as 'projections' but rather as providing 'a consistent framework' within which issues related to German unification can be explicitly examined, and they added: 'The challenge over the next ten years is clearly formidable' (McDonald and Thumann 1990, pp. 79-80). Yet if the authors did have doubts that the two scenarios can be reasonably taken as the two extremes defining the corridor in which the actual course of events will presumably take place, doubts which surface throughout the study, then they could perhaps have corrected (at least) their less optimistic scenario downward. As it stands, their study, which was done for the IMF, conveys with its simulations the impression that the process of east Germany's recovery and catch-up will either be very quick or at least quick.

This optimism was considerably curtailed in view of the actual economic and social development in east Germany. The optimistic outlook has given way to mostly gloomy perspectives. The *Sachverständigenrat*, the west German equivalent to the American Council of Economic Advisers, decided to refrain altogether from presenting a quantitative short-term forecast for the east German economy (see *Jahresgutachten* 1990/91). What has happened, and why?

4 The short-run economic effects of monetary union

The speed at which the east German economy plummeted into a deep depression is unparalleled in modern history. As table 10.4 shows, in the month following the currency union, in July 1990, manufacturing output fell more than 30 per cent compared to its June level, and more than 35 per cent compared to the 1989 average. By December 1990 output had fallen 54.5 per cent relative to the 1989 value, a decline that continued unabated in the first half of 1991. In some sectors, such as building materials, metallurgy, textiles, light industry and electronics, the decline in economic activity was even more severe; a subgroup of industries lost over 75 per cent of its 1989 value. In other sectors, such as water supply, energy and machinery, and transport equipment, the decline was less pronounced. In a third group, including chemicals and food, the drop in economic activity was close to the average of manufacturing as a whole. Substantial declines in output occurred also in the non-manufacturing sectors of the economy, i.e. in agriculture, construction, transport and communication, and trade.

Table 10.4: Output and employment in east Germany.

Period	Industrial output (1989 = 100)	Unemployment in 1000s			
		Industry	Construction	Transport & comm.	Trade
1989	100	3193	460	619	784
1990		3086I	439	613	760
Jan.	94.4				
Feb.	96.6				
Mar.	97.8				
II		2961	371	580	722
Apr.	97.0				
May	92.1				
June	86.0				
III		2690	359	554	654
July	56.0	2777	361	553	671
Aug.	47.9	2710	367	558	661
Sept.	48.9	2584	350	552	634
IV					
Oct.	49.5	2452	343	525	582
Nov.	50.9	2388	337	512	554
Dec.	45.5				

Source: Gemeinsames Statistisches Amt, Monatszahlen, November and December 1990. The employment figures refer to the number of wage and salary workers.

The massive decline in economic activity is also, albeit until now to a lesser extent, reflected in the employment figures. Consequently, output per worker employed in manufacturing, i.e. labour productivity, in the second half of 1990 was considerably below its 1989 level. By February 1991, the unemployment rate measured in per cent of the civilian workforce was at 8.9 per cent (see table 10.5). On top of that 21.8 per cent of the workforce was reported to be on involuntary part- or short-time work. In July unemployment had reached more than 1 million or 12.1 per cent of the civilian workforce. It is estimated that those working short-time on average are employed for less than half of ordinary working hours, and that most of them will eventually become unemployed. The emergence of mass unemployment affected every major sector of the economy and, with a few exceptions, every type of worker and profession. The sectors hit most severely by unemployment and short-time employment are trade, construction and industry. Unemployment is expected to continue to rise throughout the near future. However, this rise will not be adequately reflected in registered unemployment. The figures of registered unemployment do not take into account: (i) the large number of early retirements; (ii) civil servants in a 'waiting position' (*Wartestand*), i.e. in a kind of intermediate status, which in the medium run will, however, result in redundancy for most of the civil servants involved; and (iii) the growing number of people engaged in reskilling programmes. The total number of people belonging to these three groups may well get close to 1 million. In this context it is also worth mentioning that the population and the workforce in east Germany are gradually declining due to migration and commuting to west Germany.

Table 10.5: Unemployment and short-time work.

Month	Unemployment		Short-time employment	
	in 1000s	Per cent of civilian workforce	in 1000s	Per cent of civilian workforce
1990	141.1	1.6 June		
July	272.0	3.1	656.3	7.4
August	361.3	4.1	1,450.0	16.9
Sept.	444.9	5.0	1,728.7	19.3
Oct.	536.9	6.1	1,703.8	19.1
Nov.	589.2	6.7	1,709.9	20.1
Dec.	642.2	7.3	1,794.0	20.5
1991	757.2	8.6 Jan.	1,840.6	21.1
Feb.	787.0	8.9	1,947.1	21.8
March	808.3	9.1	1,989.8	22.0
April	836.9		2,005.4	
May	842.3		1,968.5	
June	842.5		1,898.9	
July	1,068.6		1,610.8	
August	1,063.2		1,451.7	
Sept.	1,028.8		1,333.4	
Oct.	1,048.5		1,299.5	
Nov.	1,030.7		1,103.0	

Sources: Wirtschaft und Statistk, various issues.

The removal of the belt protecting the east German economy from international competition on the day of the currency union also had important implications for the level and structure of prices. Before economic, union prices in the GDR were essentially administered prices, reflecting, *inter alia*, a variety of political goals and motives. After economic union, prices of tradeables had to adjust to the going prices in world markets. The change from prices in terms of Eastmarks to prices in terms of DM entailed remarkable changes in absolute and relative prices. While consumer prices, expressed in terms of the east German consumer price index, remained basically unchanged until the beginning of 1991 when subsidies on basic consumer goods such as energy and transportation were eliminated or reduced, producer prices, expressed in terms of the price index of manufactured goods, fell by almost 50 per cent in a single month. The relative constancy of the consumer price index and the dramatic decline of the producer price index are, of course, again the outcomes of rather divergent developments on the more disaggregated levels. As regards the cost of living, clothing and footwear, durable consumer goods (furniture, electrical and electronic appliances) and transportation and communication became substantially cheaper, while health care products, food, drink and tobacco rose in price. The index of the cost of living does not, however, adequately reflect the fact that with economic union the east German population got access to a much wider variety of products of generally higher quality. As regards producer prices, those sectors whose decline in output was above average generally also experienced the more drastic decline in price. Due to the combined effect of falling quantities and prices, by December 1990 sales proceeds (in DM) of the manufacturing sector as a whole had fallen less than 30 per cent of its average 1989 level (in Eastmarks).

As mentioned in the introduction, the state treaty on monetary union required that pre-existing wage and salary contracts be carried over, with payments in Eastmarks converted to DM at par. Both immediately before and after monetary union nominal wages and salaries rose substantially. From 1988 to 1989 average monthly wages showed a 3 per cent increase from 1041 to 1072 Eastmarks. After settling at 1205 Eastmarks in the first half of 1990, average monthly wages rose to 1545 DM in October, which implied a growth of more than 40 per cent, compared with the 1989 level. As more recent developments show, this trend will continue into the foreseeable future; the 50 per cent mark appears to have been passed already.

In order to form an opinion on what these substantial increases in nominal wages imply in terms of real disposable income of east German households, a few additional aspects should, however, be taken into consideration. First, a growing number of workers became either unemployed or underemployed. Social union extended the west German labour law and the comparatively favourable unemployment benefits scheme with some modifications to east Germany. Unemployment benefits amount to 65 per cent of former net wages if persons engage in reskilling programmes; if they have children they may get an extra 8 per cent. Short-time workers get 68 per cent of their previous net wages if they have children, and 63 per cent if they don't. These amounts are paid by the state. In many cases the wage contracts in east Germany require that the firm pays an additional 22 per cent. Yet it is to be expected that most short-time workers will become fully unemployed. Second, economic union meant that, in principle, wages and other incomes of east Germans became subject to the west German tax and social security system with its higher marginal tax rates on income and substantial social security payments out of wages and salaries.[6] Third, due to the slackening of the labour market and partly also due to the shift in the institutional regime, east German workers lost most of the fringe benefits and additions to their basic wage, such as overtime and shift premiums, they could count on in the past. This being said, the massive increase in nominal wages in east Germany still represents one of the most startling effects of economic and political union and a major obstacle to quick recovery and restructuring of the east German economy. How can this increase in wages be explained?

An explanation can be sought in the following reasons (see also Akerlof et al. 1991, pp. 45-50). First, it was argued, particularly by IG Metall, the strong western union of metal workers, that unity requires equal wages. This argument was seconded by the further argument that high wage increases in the east would be an effective means to stop the migration to the west, which was envisaged to increase the competitive pressure on western wages. Western unions therefore supported eastern unions in their pressure for wage parity and assisted them in wage negotiations. Second, there was no real counterpart to the trade unions on the employers' side which could effectively withstand the unions' demands. The managers of firms were still to a large extent those installed by the previous regime: politically discredited, inexperienced in collective bargaining, and, perhaps most important, aware of the fact that most of them would be displaced anyway, irrespective of the wage agreements reached. Third, since many workers and managers in east Germany expected to become unemployed soon, their interest in higher wages and salaries was predominantly motivated by rendering more favourable the main circumstance on which unemployment benefits would depend, i.e. the terminal level of earned income.

What were the proximate causes of this dramatic decline in output and rise in unemployment?

5 Proximate causes of the economic depression in east Germany

(a) Shift in effective demand. The first cause of the sharp decline in output in east Germany immediately after currency union was of course

the swift and massive diversion of spending away from eastern toward western goods. Consumers, and to a lesser extent investors, were keen to buy previously unaccessible western products, in particular cars, both new and used ones, and electrical appliances. This shift in demand was reflected in a pronounced boom in west Germany and in a reduction in the German foreign trade surplus in August 1990; in January 1991 the German trade balance, known to be notoriously in surplus, showed a deficit. At the same time east Germany's imports from its trading partners in the East declined dramatically: from July to October 1990 imports fell more than 70 per cent. This decline sharply aggravated the economic situation in the former Comecon countries and contributed to the acceleration of the dissolution of the Eastern trading bloc. East Germany's exports to the East increased in the second half of 1990; this development is, however, exclusively due to additional exports of previously not-traded products such as agricultural goods and shoes to the crisis-ridden Soviet Union.[7] East German firms will in all probability soon experience substantial reductions in demand for their products from Comecon countries. Whereas in the past exports and imports among socialist countries were essentially politically decided, the East European trading partners of east German firms now have to pay for their imports in hard currency, of which they are notoriously short. Hence it is to be expected that once existing barter trade contracts expire, they will reduce their imports from east Germany and instead buy higher quality products, particularly investment goods, on the world markets. There exist clear indications that a major decline in east Germany's trade with Eastern Europe and the Soviet Union is already taking place.

There is also some evidence that total investment spending in east Germany declined. This is hardly surprising, given the uncertain future east German firms are facing and the extremely unfavourable cost-price terms they are confronted with, which gives them hardly any incentive and little opportunity to restructure and modernize their plant and equipment. This leads to the second major reason for the deep depression into which the east German economy plunged, which is of much greater importance and will be felt for a long time to come: the lack of competitiveness of most east German firms, or, in other words, the obsolescence of large parts of the physical capital stock and, correspondingly, of the stock of human capital, given post-currency union prices and wages.

(b) Capital stock obsolescence. In July 1990 the east German econ-

omy was not simply opened to the world market: it was rather exposed to international competition on terms defined by the German monetary union, which were equivalent to a huge revaluation of its currency. As to the size of this revaluation, the following consideration is useful. Prior to monetary union the East German Ministry of Trade, for internal purposes, calculated the so-called 'currency yield coefficient' (*Devisenertragskoeffizient*), which gives the amount of DM received per unit of Eastmark employed in the production of export goods. In 1989 this coefficient was 0.23, i.e. the GDR got 0.23 DM in exchange for goods exported worth one Eastmark. Hence monetary union implied a revaluation of 4:1 to the previously used internal exchange rate. Since wage contracts were converted at a rate of 1:1, this involved an increase of the wage rate in terms of export goods of approximately 400 per cent. It should come as no surprise that east German export industries were sent into a tailspin. No economy which exhibits some degree of openness could absorb such a shock without serious damage, and even with some prior preparation, adjustment to the new circumstances would be difficult enough. The east German economy however was entirely unprepared for the new situation. In a few weeks it became clear that the overwhelming majority of east German firms producing tradeables are not competitive and will have to go out of business. An entire economy is on the brink of bankruptcy.

Many firms lack competitiveness because of the low quality or outmoded character of the products they produce. In so far as these products are produced by means of capital goods which are specific to their production, and thus cannot be utilized elsewhere, these capital goods can be wholly jettisoned. Others may in principle be used in different lines of production provided it is profitable to do so. Yet many of these lines, although competitive in terms of product quality, will not survive, because due to inferior technology, and hence low labour productivity, the costs of production per unit of output exceed product prices. The nonpositive profitability of these firms is reflected in a nonpositive capital value. Notwithstanding this, parts of an otherwise obsolete capital stock may still be used. For example, while a firm's plant and equipment may by and large have to be scrapped, structures and other fixed capital items are perhaps still worth employing for what they can get if combined with more advanced machinery. Finally, there are those firms, which although they are able to cover production costs, will founder because of the absence of adequate marketing and product distribution.

The removal of previously existing trade barriers caused the prices of tradeables to adjust to world market levels. The dramatic decline in producer prices referred to above reflects this adjustment. At the exogenously given new prices and the wage rates and salaries in east Germany, the vast majority of firms would be unable to cover production costs, even if they could produce at levels of output that minimize unit costs. Many firms are not even able to cover short-run variable costs. The few firms that are profitable are very often barely so, which means that they generate insufficient internal funds for accumulation and innovation purposes to keep up with their competitors. Hence, while some of them may survive in the medium run, they will not be able do so in the long run. If, up to now, many firms have not yet gone bankrupt it is because the Treuhandanstalt, the resolution trust which is responsible for the privatization of the east German industry (see below subsection c), has provided subsidies and loans which allow them to sell their products at prices below actual average costs of production. Hence, a further decline in output is to be expected once the Treuhandanstalt terminates bailing out unprofitable firms.

A fairly sophisticated approach to assess the competitiveness, or lack thereof, of east German firms and Kombinate in industry in the environment after unification has been presented by Akerlof et al. (1991). According to these authors '[a] firm is 'viable' now ... if its *average short-run variable cost* per DM earned is less than unity' (p. 15; emphasis in the original). To adjust for differences between total cost and short-run variable cost they remove all interest and depreciation, exclusive of repairs that are indispensable for the continuation of operation of plant and equipment. In addition, by using the east German input-output table they try to estimate the effects of changes in the tax system, in the cost of imported intermediate inputs, and in wages on the cost structure. The main results of their investigation can be summarized as follows:

1. The difference between producer prices in the GDR prior to currency union and short-run variable cost thereafter amounts to just over 50 per cent in industry. This reduction in costs corresponds almost exactly to the reduction in east German producer prices.
2. After currency union the proportion of wage costs to total costs in east Germany is substantially higher than prior to it.
3. After currency union the short-run variable cost per DM earned (cost-proceeds ratio) on average in industry is 1.84. Only the energy sector as a whole is able to cover its short-run costs: its cost-proceeds ratio is 0.85.
4. There is substantial variance both across sectors and across firms within

sectors in costs. However, in sectors other than energy only a few firms and Kombinate are viable, i.e. exhibit cost-proceeds ratios below unity.

5. Only 8.2 per cent of the workforce in industry is employed in viable Kombinate; hence 92.8 per cent of industrial workers are employed in firms that cannot even cover short-run variable costs.

The alarming conclusion of Akerlof et al. (1991, p. 20) reads: 'At the time of currency union, it was widely rumoured that one third of east German firms would go out of business. The micro data presented ... offer a far more pessimistic view of the likely viability of the east German economy. In the absence of massive productivity improvements or substantial subsidization most eastern industry will have to close down'.

Since early 1991, when the Akerlof et al. study was completed, the difficulties encountered by east German firms have been considerably aggravated by the dramatic increases in hourly wages and the soaring levels of the rate of interest. As is well known, the capital value of a firm equals the discounted stream of expected net returns. Higher wages increase costs and tend to reduce expected net proceeds; and a higher real rate of interest increases the discount factor. Hence, both developments reinforce one another in rendering an ever-larger portion of the east German capital stock and the jobs associated with it economically obsolete.

Figure 10.1 illustrates schematically the lack of competitiveness and thus viability of (large parts of) the east German economy (leaving out of consideration the impact of a rising level of the interest rate). Both the output-labour ratio or labour productivity y_i and the output-capital ratio x_i, both estimated at some normal degree of capacity utilization, are significantly lower in east Germany compared to west Germany ($i = e(ast), w(est)$). According to some sources (average) labour productivity in east Germany is not more than 30 per cent of labour productivity in west Germany. The socio-technological characteristics of the two economies can be summarized in terms of the inverse relationship between the (average) level of the 'real' wage rate and the (average) rate of return on capital or profitability associated with the two systems of production.[8] The west German economy is represented by the line W, while the east German economy is represented by the line E. Before unification, with wages in west and east Germany at levels of ω_w and ω_e, respectively, the corresponding rates of return were r_w and r_e. The effect of the substantial rise in wages in east Germany and the shift of demand away from eastern toward western products which took place after unification on the rates of return in the two economies can now be illustrated as follows. Taken separately, the increase in east German wages to about 45 per cent of west German levels, i.e. from ω_e to ω'_e, implied a reduction in the rate of return from r_e to r'_e. With y_i denoting labour productivity in country i, we have:

$$y_e = 0.3y_w \text{ and } \omega_e = 0.45\omega_w.$$

The value of the share of wages in west Germany, ω_w/y_w, will here be taken to be 0.6. Hence, the increase in the level of wages implied, *ceteris paribus*, an increase in the share of wages in east Germany, ω_e/y_e, to 90 per cent of national income, with the consequence of a rate of return that is barely positive on average. For example, if wages should have risen already to a level of more than 50 per cent of the west German level as some sources maintain, then this factor alone would have reduced the average rate of return to a level below zero.

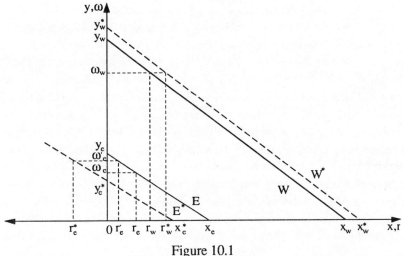

Figure 10.1

We now have to take into account that the shift in demand created a boom in the west and a depression in the east, reflected in a higher average rate of capacity utilization in the former and a considerably lower one in the latter. An increase (decrease) in overall capacity utilization can be represented in the diagram in an outward (inward) shift of the respective wage frontier: thus W is replaced by W* and E by E*.[9] The higher (lower) degree of utilization of plant and equipment in existence entailed an increase (decrease) in the rate of return in the west (east) to an average level of r_w^* (r_e^*). As figure 10.1 shows, in the post-unification conditions the average rate of return of east German firms is negative. It goes without saying that a negative average rate of return is compatible with positive rates yielded by some firms or even whole industries. However, in the present case the number of profitable firms or industries appears to be extremely small.

(c) Privatization. A major problem of any transition from a socialist to a capitalist system is the privatization of industry and land. The unification treaty makes a clear distinction between the pre- and the post- 1949 expropriations. While the former have been declared to be exempt from privatization and compensation, the latter are considered nullified. Hence everything expropriated since the foundation of the former GDR is, in principle, to be given back to its legitimate owner(s). It is estimated that approximately one third of the total property that can be privatized belongs to this category. The number of applications for the return of or compensation for expropriated property that have been filed exceeds one million:[10] golden years ahead for lawyers!

The agreed-on route to reprivatization and compensation became a major obstacle to east German economic recovery. As long as property rights are unclear and costly disputes over these rights persist, potential investors will not risk engaging in business in east Germany.[11] Only recently have steps been taken to speed up the privatization process and render capital investment more simple and less risky despite competing and unresolved property claims: on March 15, 1991, the German parliament passed a law substantiating article 41 of the unification treaty which under certain circumstances allows exceptions to the reprivatization of expropriated property in order to render possible investment which is beneficial to the economy as a whole. The new law, which in principle reaffirms the maxim: 'return of property rather than compensation', until the end of 1992 allows several exceptions to this rule. On behalf of employment, the provision of housing and the rebuilding of infrastructure, expropriated plots of land or firms may be sold or let on a long-term basis, even if previous owners are opposed to it.

The privatization of the remaining two thirds of industry and other property in east Germany has been put into the hands of the Treuhandanstalt, a gigantic resolution trust which is part of the Finance Ministry. Treuhandanstalt managers are responsible for the liquidation of about 8,000 companies in east Germany. Some 20 per cent of these companies are public utility companies which, as a rule, will become communal property, whereas the remaining 80 per cent will be privatized following a two-step procedure. First companies will be transformed into joint stock companies or into other legal forms of enterprise; then they will be sold on the international capital market. Before the end of March 1991 the Treuhandanstalt shut about 300 of the companies and sold about 1,000 others, mostly small enterprises.[12] The agency has become a major target of fierce criticism and, sadly enough, also a target of deadly terrorism.

What is at issue is the gigantic problem of selling two thirds of the productive apparatus of an entire economy. This route to privatization exhibits serious shortcomings (cf. also since 1990). First, it starts from the premise that the east German capital stock can be bought with current savings. This might be a valid assumption if the savings actually activated for this purpose would be international rather than essentially national savings. However, since for a variety of reasons so far some 90 per cent of the demand for east German firms has come from west Germans, there is the problem of a mismatch between effect demand and offer: west German savings fall short of the value of the capital stock in supply. The implication of this is that the prices of the objects sold by the Treuhandanstalt are driven down and because of the additional finance needed by investors the rate of interest is driven up. It should come as no surprise that actual proceeds fell vastly short of the Treuhandanstalt's expected proceeds. Secondly, the decided route to privatization is much too time-consuming. Third, it is not only inefficient but also highly problematic from the point of view of the distribution of property and wealth: what we in fact witness is that the 'property of the people' of the population of the former GDR is redistributed away from the east Germans. Hence both in terms of economic efficiency and in terms of distributive justice the current policy of privatization (of those parts of property that are not subject to restitution) is a failure. It should quickly be replaced by a new scheme guaranteeing that at least the remaining property is given to the people in the new *Länder,* e.g. in terms of shares of firms or the entire east German capital stock, the details of which could be worked out against the background of the experience with such schemes in Eastern European countries.

6 On the long-term prospects of the east German economy

The long-term prospects of east Germany will depend to a large extent on the policy measures taken by the Federal government. The recent political developments in the former GDR, as in the majority of socialist countries, can indeed be envisaged as just another historical lesson demonstrating that each new phase in the process of human emancipation bears not only opportunities but also risks. The main question therefore is whether the efforts necessary to ward off destructive tendencies will be undertaken to grant the realization of the emancipatory potential of our age.[13]

As mentioned in section 3, prior to German unification, leading representatives of the political parties forming the west German government, most notably Chancellor Kohl, expressed extremely optimistic views as to the duration and costs of the catch-up process of the east German economy. Chancellor Kohl went as far as to maintain that eastern living conditions would match those of the west within three to five years after unification. He thus implicitly contended that growth rates of income per head in east Germany of almost 20 per cent per year were feasible. Since it cannot be assumed that the required growth in income per head in east Germany will essentially be brought about by income transfers from west Germany—current transfers and pending tax increases have already met with resistance from the west German population—this growth will sooner rather than later have to find its source in an above-normal growth of east German output per head. Given that in 1990 and early 1991 real output growth in east Germany was negative and will presumably remain negative for some time, the growth rates to be achieved in the years thereafter must not only make up the initial difference in income per head, but also the actual increase in this difference since economic union. In order for Chancellor Kohl's forecast to come true, the required growth of income per head in east Germany in the years 1992-95 would have to assume annual levels of 30-50 per cent. There are no historical precedents that render any credibility that such growth is possible.

It cannot be presumed, therefore, that the process of catching up with the western part of Germany will be accomplished in a few years. It is even doubtful that the gap will be closed at all. It is indeed to be expected that while the east German economy will recover from the current depression, the level of economic activity will be persistently lower than in its western counterpart. It cannot even be excluded that in the long run the absolute and even relative gap may widen rather than narrow. It goes without saying that such a development of the east German economy as a whole is compatible with rapid growth in some of its regions and industries.

Whereas in a centrally planned economy a high degree of uniformity in providing people with material goods across regions can, in principle, be realized in terms of a system of transfers, in a market economy such an equalization in living conditions is generally not observed. Various regions rather exhibit substantial and lasting differences in terms of major economic and social indicators, such as per capita income, labour productivity etc. How can the persistence of these differences be explained? A major cause is to be sought in the phenomena of cumulative causation and positive or negative feedbacks (e.g. Arthur 1990).

As has become clear since the opening of the former GDR to the west, relatively large parts of its economy are still *resource-based* (agriculture, mining, bulk-goods production) and others are highly resource-intensive. These parts, however, are largely subject to diminishing or at best constant returns. Those parts of the economy that are *knowledge-based*, on the other hand, are relatively small compared with the west German economy. Yet they appear to be predominantly subject to increasing returns. Products such as computers, software, aircraft, automobiles, and telecommunications equipment are characterized by a high systemic complexity. While they require large initial investments in research and development, and tooling and marketing, once the product is designed, production costs are relatively small and unit costs fall with the level of output. The production of these commodities offers substantial sources of learning by doing and learning by using.

The economy of east Germany is relatively weak in this field of productive activities which for the most part are characterized by increasing returns. This fact will generate negative feedbacks that hamper the future development of the economy in the five new *Länder*. A firm that lags behind its competitors will, in all probability, remain lagging behind, with a growing distance between it and the most advanced firms. Since the firm lacks competitiveness it will sooner or later be driven out of the respective market(s). For the east German economy as a whole this implies that it will largely specialize in fields where it has a comparative advantage. These fields, however, are those which offer little scope for technological dynamism and may, therefore, in the long run turn out to be a dead end. Thus, because of negative and positive feedbacks the established pattern of regional concentration of industry becomes self-reinforcing. This implies that east Germany will lose many of its firms and branches operating in high-tech and even medium-tech fields: most of these firms will go bankrupt and new firms will settle at more attractive locations, attempting to reap the benefits gained by locating near firms operating in the same input and output markets. In general, these latter firms will tend to move to west Germany. If the attractiveness exerted by the presence of other firms always rises as more firms are added, some region will always dominate and shut out all others. It is to be expected that large parts of the five new *Länder* will belong to the second kind. It seems that the east German economy, for obvious historical reasons, is locked into an inferior path of economic development. It may well become the equivalent of Italy's *Mezzogiorno*: Germany's *Mezzanotte*.

Whether this possibility will or will not materialize depends of course, *inter alia*, on the economic (and social) policy carried out in the years to come. In the concluding section we shall briefly turn to some of the issues involved. A few remarks must suffice.

7 The role of economic policy
So far private investment of west German and other firms in east Germany is small. In many cases firms were concerned with establishing a distribution network for goods produced in the west rather than with building factories: east Germany is considered a welcome new market to be supplied with commodities produced elsewhere, but it is not yet perceived as an attractive place to locate production and to invest. There are several reasons for this 'absenteeism' of private investment, the most important of which seem to be the following:

1. Due to unclear property rights, investment in east Germany is often regarded as too risky and postponed until the property issue is solved in a satisfactory way.[14]
2. East German infrastructure is in a shambles. Without a well-functioning system of telecommunications, a proper system of public transport facilities (roads, railway etc.) and a restructuring of other parts of infrastructure such as schools, hospitals etc. private investment will not be forthcoming.
3. The lack of an efficient administration in the new *Länder* is detrimental to economic recovery. There are many cases reported of firms willing to invest which, however, were frustrated by a stubborn state bureaucracy not attuned to the requirements defined by the new situation.
4. Due to a ruthless attitude toward the environment, air, land and water in east Germany are heavily polluted. Before private investors are willing to install factories on production sites whose general quality is dubious, an environmental check and clean-up is necessary.
5. The people in the GDR over more than four decades have been taught that private property and the profit motive are disdainful. Private, self-interested initiatives and activities were discounted and discouraged and all answers to social problems were sought in an 'étatist' way. Given this social climate,

people understandably enough have difficulty in adjusting to the new circumstances, which are characterized by the 'revaluation of all values': the east German population is caught, as one author succinctly remarked, in a position of 'learned helplessness' (*erlernte Hilflosigkeit*). There is a lack of entrepreneurial spirit and an overabundance of an 'entitlement mentality' (*Anspruchsdenken*). As Rainer Kunze, the poet, put it, it is the wall in the minds of the people which is even higher and more difficult to abolish than the wall which separated the two Germanies. What is at stake is the re-education of a whole population. Compared to it the necessary retraining of large portions of the east German labour force appears to be a minor task.[15]

Clearly, while some of these factors impeding economic recovery of east Germany can be removed in a fairly short time, others are more obstinate and long-lived and can be overcome, if at all, only over a longer period.

Ever since Adam Smith, the provision of a well-functioning infrastructure has been considered an indispensable precondition of the growth of the wealth of a nation. Presently, infrastructural investment in east Germany financed by the Federal government can safely be considered to be one of the most important tasks. Moreover, given idle productive resources in east Germany such investment can be undertaken without running the risk of severe inflationary tendencies. In order to achieve a maximum employment effect in east Germany, local firms predominantly using local productive resources should be given preference whenever possible. The cost of this investment, though substantial, would be comparatively low to west German taxpayers, since otherwise unemployed workers become employed. Employed workers, of course, pay income taxes and contribute to social insurance rather than receive employment benefits. Hence the Federal budget as a whole would be affected to a smaller extent than otherwise: wage payments, tax revenue and contributions to social insurance would be substituted for unemployment compensation. Moreover, such a policy would be beneficial in the long run: it would improve the attractiveness of the new *Länder* as locations for private investment and it would prevent the deterioration of the capacity to work and decay of self-esteem of workers which is a necessary by product of prolonged periods of unemployment.

The Federal government has also tried to enhance the attractiveness of the new *Länder* via tax incentives (e.g., generous depreciation allowances) and direct subsidies (investment grants for equipment, low interest loans, etc.) to entrepreneurs willing to invest in east Germany.

However, so far these measures have had little effect on the volume of private investment in east Germany. It would also be false to expect that private investment could bear the brunt of a rapid economic recovery in east Germany. Since as a consequence of monetary union and the increases in wages (and the rate of interest) the east German capital stock was to a large extent rendered obsolete, it will require the investment, a *flow*, of many years to replace the existing *stock* with new plant and equipment and thus to create new employment opportunities. It follows, somewhat ironically, that any policy that aims at a quick mitigation of unemployment in east Germany has to neutralize in one way or another the negative impact of monetary union and of wage increases on the competitiveness of east German firms, i.e. it has to render the use of at least parts of the *existing* east German capital stock profitable. On the assumption that the agreed upon wage increases cannot be recontracted or temporarily frozen in, the only way to do this is to heavily subsidize production and employment in east Germany. A proposal to this effect was originally put forward by west German trade unions which, however, later dropped the proposal on the grounds that it would indiscriminately favour both unprofitable and profitable firms. Yet a scheme of wage subsidies and employment bonuses has been suggested (see, in particular, Akerlof et al. 1991) which is said to provide the appropriate incentives for firms to hire workers who would otherwise be unemployed, and which at the same time would prevent the subsidies from becoming permanent thanks to a built-in mechanism which would gradually abolish them as they accomplish their task. The implementation of such a scheme, by raising the capital value of some firms above zero, would at the same time make it easier for the Treuhandanstalt to privatize former state-owned property by selling firms which otherwise, because of their negative capital value, could not be sold. Moreover, by providing jobs in the five new *Länder* the scheme would reduce the massive migration from east to west and would thereby also help to curb the political and social tensions currently building up in both parts of Germany.

Clearly, such a scheme of wage subsidies and employment bonuses can only be considered a second-best policy solution, since the main problem is not tackled, which consists of the fact that east German wages exceed east German labour productivity. Also, the second serious problem is not dealt with: the problem of high unemployment benefits. Since the latter are closely tied to the level of wages, huge transfer payments will put an additional strain on the west German taxpayer. Moreover, the higher the level of unemployment benefits, the lower is the incentive to east German workers to seek a job. It follows that a major problem hampering the recovery and restructuring of the east German economy is to be seen in the rapid adjustment of east German hourly wages to west German levels. This development is detrimental both to the survival of the east German capital stock and thus to the survival of jobs associated with it, and to the accumulation of new capital and thus to the creation of new jobs. The higher are east German wages, the higher are unemployment benefits, the larger is what in the terminology of the classical economists may be called 'unproductive consumption', and consequently the smaller are the funds available for fresh accumulation.

There is a growing concern in Germany about the costs of German unification and more particularly about the rising deficits of the Federal and the *Länder* budgets. Some politicians suggest that these deficits should be reduced via massive spending cuts. Such a policy, were it to be adopted, would most certainly lead to even higher deficits rather than lower ones. For it would further reduce output levels and thus employment, thereby increasing transfer payments and reducing tax income. Curtailing public spending and the judicious subsidization of east German enterprises would aggravate the situation rather than improve it. It would be an enormous waste not to use the productive powers of people, who will have to be supported anyway, to contribute to the restructuring of their economy. Moreover, a policy of austerity would not only be economically ineffective, it would also run the risk of politically destabilizing the new Germany. With the lessons of history in mind, Germans should seek to make everything easier, both for themselves and for everyone else.

Notes

* Professor of Economics, University of Graz, Austria. This chapter was written in Spring 1991 while I was Theodor Heuss Professor of Economics, in the academic year 1990-91, in The Graduate Faculty, The New School for Social Research, New York, U.S.A. While the main text remained essentially in its original form, some of the data were updated. I should like to thank Eva Kigyossy-Schmidt and Mark Knell for valuable discussions of some of the issues involved.

1. See *Monatsberichte der Deutschen Bundesbank*, 42, No. 7, July 1990.
2. Speech delivered in the Economics and Currency Committee of the European Parliament on March 19th, 1990; see *The Week in Germany*, The German Information Center, New York, March 22, 1991.
3. The sources used include *Statistisches Jahrbuch der Bundesrepublik Deutschland*, edited by Statistisches Bundesamt, *Statistisches Jahrbuch der DDR*, edited by Staatliche Zentralverwaltung für Statistik der DDR, and *Monatsberichte der Deutschen Bundesbank*; various issues.
4. A major event in this context was the decision of the Hungarian government in

September 1989 to open its border with Austria to citizens of the GDR. This led to a massive migration of East Germans, who spent their holidays in Hungary, to West Germany.

5. The implication of this ill-founded view, and the political decisions based on it, are soaring budget deficits of the central state and the Länder and a real rate of interest (nominal rate minus rate of inflation) in mid 1991 of more than 6 per cent.

6. New tax allowances were granted in east Germany in February 1991 which slightly reduced the tax burden, and the income tax is being phased in only gradually. The major problem as pointed out in a UN (1991, p. 150) document, 'is the establishment of a functioning internal revenue system'.

7. For a discussion of the problems associated with the losses of markets in the east in the aftermath of the currency union, see Deutsches Institut für Wirtschaftsforschung, *Wochenbericht 12/91*, March 1991, pp. 126-8.

8. The reader familiar with the concept of the 'wage' or 'factor price frontier' is aware of the context within which the latter is used. (For a discussion of the concept, see, for example, Kurz (1988).) He or she should thus also be aware of the purely impressionistic character of the above thought experiment which sets aside numerous important differences between the two economies, e.g., differences in the respective wage baskets, different modes of operation of plant and equipment and thus different notions of 'normal' capacity utilization, etc. It should also be clear that the concept of the rate of return means different things in capitalist and socialist economies. In the latter it may be seen to be closely related to the rate of growth of net material product.

9. For a discussion of the relationship between the degree of capacity utilization and profitability, see Kurz (1990, chapters 9 and 10).

10. See *The Week in Germany*, March 22nd, 1991. See also the statement by A. Grosser reported in Whitney (1991): 'They got the issue of compensation all wrong, so now there are a million claims on property, factories and enterprises, no civil service to process them, and not enough new investment yet to rebuild the economy'.

11. According to Sinn the privatization decision 'may have been the biggest mistake in the ... unification policy of the West German government' (1990, p. 31).

12. See *The New York Times*, April 5, 1991.

13. This problem, in general terms, is the main concern of A. Lowe (1988).

14. According to Siebert (1991) the property rights issue is the most important problem which has to be solved before the restructuring of the east German economy can effectively take place.

15. For a discussion of some of the issues involved in the retraining of the workforce, see Hoene (1991).

References

Akerlof, G.A., Rose, A. K., Yellen, J. L., and Hessenius, H. (1991). 'East Germany in from the Cold: The Economic Aftermath of Currency Union', *Brookings Papers on Economic Activity*, 1.

Arthur, W.B. (1990). 'Positive Feedbacks in the Economy', *Scientific American*, February 1990, 92-9.

'Gesamtwirtschaftliche und unternehmerische Anpassungsprozesse in Ostdeutschland' (1991). First joint report of the German Institute of Economic Research (Berlin) and the Institute of World Economics (Kiel). Deutsches Institut für Wirtschaftsforschung, *Wochenbericht* 12/91, Berlin, 123-43.

Hoene, B. (1991). 'Labor Market Realities in Eastern Germany', *Challenge*, July-August 1991, 17-22.

Krelle, W. (1990). 'Ost-West Wirtschaftsentwicklung im nächsten Jahrzehnt', Paper presented to Nationalökonomische Gesellschaft in Vienna, 7 June 1990.

Kurz, H.D. (1988). 'Factor price frontier', *The New Palgrave. A Dictionary of Economics*, edited by Eatwell, J., Milgate, M., and Newman, P.,vol. 2, London:

Macmillan, 271-73.

Kurz, H.D. (1990). *Capital, Distribution and Effective Demand,* Oxford: Polity Press and Basil Blackwell.

Lipschitz, L. and McDonald, D. eds. (1990). *German Unification - Economic Issues,* Occasional Paper No. 75, International Monetary Fund, Washington, D.C.

Lowe, A. (1988). *Has Freedom a Future?* New York: Praeger.

McDonald, D. and Thumann, G. (1990). 'East Germany: The New Wirtschaftswunder?', in Lipschitz, L. and McDonald, D.

Sachverständigenrat zur Begutachtung der gesamtwirtschaftlichen Entwicklung (1990). *Jahresgutachten* 1990/91. Stuttgart: Metzler-Poeschel.

Siebert, H. (1991). 'The Integration of Germany: Real Economic Adjustment', *European Economic Review,* vol. 35, 591-602.

Sinn, H.W. (1990). 'Macroeconomic Aspects of German Unification', *Münchener Wirtschaftswissenschaftliche Beiträge,* Discussion Paper No. 90-31.

The Week in Germany, German Information Center, New York, various issues.

United Nations (1990). *Economic Survey of Europe in 1989-1990,* Geneva.

United Nations (1991). *Economic Survey of Europe in 1990-1991,* Geneva.

Westphal, U. (1991). 'Economic Outlook for the Federal Republic of Germany', Paper presented at the LINK meeting, New York, March 1991.

Whitney, C.R. (1991). 'Europe Discovers the German Colossus Isn't so Big after all', *The New York Times,* April 21, 1991, E3.

11 Lessons from China on a Strategy for the Socialist Economies in Transition

*Mark Knell and Wenyan Yang**

1 Introduction

China has introduced a wide range of economic reforms since 1978. The decision to introduce these reforms was prompted by relatively low rates of productivity growth compounded by chronic shortages of both consumer and producer goods. As a consequence, a centralized socialist organization of the market where money and prices are passive and over 90 per cent of total output was distributed through a network of supply and marketing cooperatives (Robinson 1964) is being transformed into a socialist planned commodity economy where prices and money are active and up to 80 per cent of total output will be allocated through state-regulated markets (Zhao 1987). The intended results are sustainable rates of economic and productivity growth that will lift China into the ranks of the industrialized countries by 2050.

Prior to these reforms, China was a typical 'classic' shortage economy in which sellers' markets predominated. Shortages of basic consumer goods such as sugar, soap, bicycles, sewing machines and coal (for household use) persisted and bottlenecks in energy, materials and transport constrained production. Economic reforms have transformed China into a 'mixed' economy where buyers' markets appeared in many sectors while sellers' markets continue to exist in certain basic good sectors including raw materials, energy and some consumer goods.

What is even more remarkable is that this transformation occurred amid sustained relatively high growth rates. The Chinese experience contrasts with that in Eastern Europe and the former Soviet Union, where the attempt at economic reforms has been met with disastrous economic decline and social and political instability. Even as China embarked on an economic austerity programme in late 1988, net material product still grew by nearly 5 per cent in 1990, while declining by more than 10 per cent in Bulgaria, Poland and Romania, and around 4 per cent in Czechoslovakia, Hungary and the Soviet Union (UN 1991). Industrial output depicts an even more striking pattern.

A quick examination of the reform experiences in these countries brings one's attention to the different approaches taken to transform the economy, namely the 'shock therapy' approach adopted by countries experiencing the deepest downturn and a more cautious, gradualist path to reform followed by China. While draconian measures such as privatization and overnight price liberalization characterize the 'shock therapy' approach, gradual price reforms and the emergence of a non-state sector that is highly dynamic and growing steadily are the trademarks of the Chinese approach. Short-term economic performance in these countries is dramatically different enough to bring up interesting questions such as: 'Are there alternatives to the 'shock therapy' in the transformation of socialist economies?' and 'What useful lessons can be learned from the Chinese reform experience?'.

This chapter will approach these questions by first examining industrial reforms introduced in China after 1978. Attention then shifts to the results of the reform, that is, the rapidly growing non-state sector and the persistence of problems in the state sector. Sections five through seven provide a theoretical foundation for analysing the Chinese transition and discuss the implications for a transition strategy. Finally, a conclusion summarizes the most important lessons learned for restructuring the industrial sector in the socialist economies in transition.

2 Industrial reform in China during the 1980s
China, like Eastern Europe after the Second World War, followed the Soviet central planning model. Pre-reform China was caught up in a shortage-investment-shortage spiral with recuring periods of growth and stagnation. The primary objective of economic reforms was to break this vicious cycle and maintain economic growth while improving living standards. Industrial reform was implemented as a component of this national project with its particular goal being to increase industrial output and efficiency. In China, the turning point was the Third Plenary Session of the Thirteenth Congress of the Communist Party which took place in 1978.

One of the most important features of the Chinese reform is the decentralization of power. In the economic realm, the individual production unit and its managers are allowed more autonomy in decision-making. Underlining the reform movement was also the realization that in a rigid central planning environment, there is a lack of incentives for better economic performance. It is hoped that decentralization will encourage more initiatives on the parts of managers and workers alike.

Profit-sharing was first tried to reform the sluggish industrial sector of China, being initially introduced in 1978 and again in 1981 to create incentives for better economic performance. Under this scheme, a fixed percentage of a firm's profit was added to the workers' welfare fund for housing, child-care, cafeteria facilities and other benefits for employees. On average, retained profit accounted for less than 10 per cent of total profits. In 1981 profit-sharing took the form of a profit contract under which participating firms contracted to send a fixed amount of profits to the state plus a percentage of any profits above this quota, usually under 60 per cent.

Starting with small state firms, managers were allowed to sign a profit contract with the state promising to achieve a set of specified goals in return for their salary and bonuses. In effect these managers lease assets and workers from the state and take the accompanying responsibilities. The system grants a high degree of managerial autonomy; by early 1991, 85 per cent of state enterprises were operating under such contracts.[1]

Price reform is another component of the reform programme in China. The basis of planned prices was relative prices prior to 1949 and rigidity in the Chinese planning system kept that structure virtually intact during the years prior to the economic reforms. Concurrent with the reforms in state enterprises, prices were gradually freed from administrative central control.

Early on, China raised the administered prices of various goods and services in order to stimulate production, but this was not always successful. Enterprise reform in conjunction with higher prices led to expanded supply, but some commodity prices assumed a two-tier price structure. In a two-tier price system, firms sell a planned amount of their output at a set price and fetch a higher market price for any above-plan production. The intention was to use market forces to encourage the production of goods and services that are in short supply and eventually eliminate administrative price-setting.

There were yet other commodities whose price was completely freed from state control. These were commodities whose supply satisfied demand sufficiently, therefore the disparity between government-set and free market prices was small. This group was small in number and expanded over time. By 1991, the prices of approximately 65 per cent of agricultural commodities and 55 per cent of consumer goods were determined by the market.[2]

Since 1985, no major industrial reforms have been legislated, but, on an experimental basis, real reform continued (e.g. Wood 1990). The creation of joint stock companies was attempted on a small scale, and the financial sector has seen changes such as setting up exchanges for security trading. These reforms all aim at changing the behaviour of enterprises.

In one of the latest industrial reform experiments, 50 state enterprises in the northern province of Jilin were given complete autonomy in decision-making. The management of these firms are allowed to set the market price for their products, and to assume full responsibility for production planning and management, as well as labour hiring and promotion. No indication, however, was given as to how soon the practice will be extended to other firms or how long the experimental period will last.

Another important step in the Chinese reform programme is the establishment of new property rights to allow private ownership of the means of production, albeit on a relatively small scale. Urban and rural collectives were encouraged both as a means to tap into the pool of financial resources outside state control and as an outlet for surplus labour.

3 The emergence of a non-state sector

A combination of the appearance of surplus labour created by the almost-complete transformation of agricultural collectives into family farms between 1980 and 1983, and the newly established property rights led to an explosive growth of rural industrial enterprises. Some of these enterprises are privately owned while the majority are collectively owned. Decentralization also encouraged local government and private ventures to invest in production. A breakdown of investment in fixed assets by source of finance shows the increasing importance of non-state ownership. As table 11.1 indicates, the fastest growing sources of investment are foreign capital and self-raised funds.

The composition of total industrial output according to ownership shows a clearer pattern of the rising role of non-state enterprises in the Chinese economy. Table 11.2 shows that the share of industrial output produced by state enterprises declined steadily from nearly 76 per cent in 1980 to approximately 55 per cent in 1990. Preliminary data indicate that the share of state enterprises has dropped below 50 per cent in

1991.[3] The share of private enterprises, on the other hand, grew from less than 0.5 per cent to close to 10 per cent in the same period.

Table 11.1: Investment in fixed assets by source of finance (annual percentage change).

	1985	1986	1987	1988	1989
TOTAL	38.8	18.7	20.6	22.1	-6.9
State budget	-3.5	4.9	7.9	-15.3	-15.2
Domestic loans	94.4	25.1	40.0	9.4	-21.7
Foreign investment[a]	89.9	102.4	32.7	45.1	7.7
Self-raised funds & others	41.6	17.9	19.1	33.5	-2.4

Source: Statistical Yearbook of China, various years.
[a]Including foreign borrowing administered in state budget.

The growth of the non-state industrial sector can also be seen in the number of firms with different forms of ownership. Without considering the size of firms, table 11.3 shows that the private sector was the fastest growing component of the industrial economy. Although the private sector's share in total industrial output is still quite small, less than 10 per cent in 1990, its near doubling in numbers in a 5 year period demonstrates the high spirits of private entrepreneurs in China. It also deserves mentioning that these are industrial ventures, i.e., *production* firms that had been set up in response to profit opportunities in the economy.

Table 11.2: Percentage share of industrial output by ownership.

	State	Collective	Private & other
1980	76.0	23.5	0.5
1981	74.8	24.6	0.6
1982	74.4	24.8	0.7
1983	73.4	25.7	0.9
1984	69.1	29.7	1.2
1985	64.9	32.1	3.1
1986	62.3	33.5	4.2
1987	59.7	34.6	5.7
1988	56.8	36.2	7.1
1989	56.1	35.7	8.3
1990	54.5	35.7	9.8

Sources: 1980-1989: *Statistical Yearbook of China, 1990.* 1990: *Beijing Review,* October 7-13, 1991.

These newly created enterprises played an important role in eradicating shortages in certain sectors of the Chinese economy. In the consumer good sector, aggregate supply meets demand in most areas. While excess supply appeared in the market for a few consumer items, a shortage of well-known brand consumer goods continued. The Chinese economy appears to be a mixture of a mostly demand-constrained consumer good market and a resource-constrained producer good market as a result of economic reforms.

Table 11.3: Number of industrial enterprises by ownership.

	1985	1990
State-owned	93,000	104,000
Collective	1,742,000	1,685,000
Private and other	3,350,000	6,182,000

Source: Beijing Review, October 7-13, 1991.

4 Reaction of the state sector to economic reforms

Despite efforts to reform, Chinese state enterprises continued to negotiate loans and taxes with the government. The government, on the other hand, would like to turn these enterprises into efficient operations but is fearful of the possible social consequences of closing down large state-owned enterprises. As a result, intentions to reform the state sector have rarely been matched with concrete measures. At the end of 1991, about one third of all state enterprises were in the red, despite ten years of economic reform. All indications show that the competition from collective and private firms in an emerging buyers' market is making the task of reforming the state-owned enterprises more urgent.

It should be pointed out that the poor performance of state enterprises does not imply the lack of reforms in this sector. What is lacking are effective measures that will change the behaviour of enterprises. Industrial reforms have largely failed to result in a fundamental mod-ification of behaviour on the part of large-sized state enterprises.

As discussed earlier, profit-sharing was introduced in China's industrial sector in two forms in 1978 and in 1981. Although additional incentives were added, these and similar reforms did not fundamentally change the management of enterprises, nor did they change the relationship between state authorities and enterprises. On the contrary, Granick (1990) points out that authority was still dictated from above; output and prices were set more by plans than by market forces; management was responsible to the state authority rather than to its workers or others. The profit standards (sharing ratio, profit quota and ratio of above-quota profits retained by the enterprise, etc.) were targets of bargaining. Firms tried to negotiate for a higher retaining ratio and a lower contract quota. This meant that not many changes in the basic structure of the economy took place. Consequently, reform measures did not address the central cause of the shortage problem. While the incentives provided by these profit-sharing schemes may be necessary for the reform of the Chinese economy, they were not sufficient to cause significant changes in behaviour, especially in constraining investment. Moreover, excess demand for credit and industrial inputs was not sufficiently curbed.

Inertia within the old structure created obstacles which also caused slowness in behavioural adjustment. First, reforms cannot be expected to eliminate persistent shortages overnight, and uncertainties created by shortage of required inputs will prevent a firm from fulfilling its production quota as planned. Secondly, the existing prices of industrial inputs in China are still artificially maintained. Gradual price liberalization created the new problem of a two-tier price structure for the same good. Under these circumstances, the difference between two types of losses, one caused by system-generated external difficulties and the other by firm-specific internal mismanagement, is blurred. Even if managers reached an agreement with the state on the profit standard, they could still break the rules by appealing to higher authorities should they find themselves unable to meet their performance standards. Shortage of required inputs, artificially high input prices and low product prices were often cited as objective conditions over which managers had no control. Although there was a degree of truth to these claims, they, together with negotiations, allowed mismanaged firms to get away with poor performance. Consequently, rules were not enforced and firms' behaviour remained unchanged.

It can be argued that the profit-sharing scheme itself allowed negotiations between state and firm to continue. Persisting shortages and an unfair price structure strengthened the bargaining power of firms. Consequently, enterprises could retain their profits but escaped any punishment for losses. Financial accountability was not established through these reform measures, therefore failing to eliminate the microfoundation of shortage.

In the second stage of economic reform starting in 1984, more prices were allowed to fluctuate in response to market demand and supply conditions, with the government still controlling the prices of a few vital commodities such as basic foodstuffs and primary inputs. At the firm level, large- and medium-sized state-owned enterprises paid taxes on profits and kept the rest (a practice called substituting taxes for profits). Smaller state-owned firms were contracted to individuals or collectives. A user fee was charged on state budget-allocated investment fund.

As in previous attempts to decentralize the market, these measures resulted in overinvestment and an intensification of shortage. As table 11.4 illustrates, investment in fixed assets by the state sector increased at a rate of over 15 per cent for three consecutive years, and declined only during the course of an austerity programme, in 1989. The distribution of total investment by source of finance reveals an interesting pattern: while state budgetary allocation to investment declined, enterprises became more dependent on bank credit and other financial sources to support their investment drive. In other words, reform plans aimed at cooling down the investment hunger through the introduction of decentralization and market forces simply shifted the source of finance, rather than curbing investment demand. Unless financial accountability is also established, the desire to invest will not be modified.

Table 11.4: Investment in fixed assets by state-owned units (annual percentage change).

	1986	1987	1988	1989
Total	17.7	16.1	18.1	-6.5
By source of finance:				
State budget	5.5	7.7	-15.7	-14.9
Domestic loans	16.2	25.4	16.3	-19.5
Foreign investment	106.7	31.2	44.4	5.9
Self-raised funds	11.9	15.5	25.1	-1.2
Other	64.5	6.8	47.2	2.7

Source: Statistical Yearbook of China, various years.

To see that behavioural change takes more than the announcement of a reform plan, one only need observe the cyclical changes in the rate of growth, inflation and the corresponding policy swings in China. When decentralization unleashes the enthusiasm of local governments and enterprises, both growth and inflation increase, fuelled by investment waves and bank credit expansion. However, as output grows, profits do not necessarily rise because inventories may rise in buyers' markets. This will be followed by contractionary policies to cool off the economy, and during these stabilization periods, economic reform slows down. Then, just as the authority feels comfortable enough to experiment with further reforms, the cycle repeats itself. These cycles clearly indicate that enterprises react to policy measures following the old pattern of behaviour instead of changing it. The emerging banking system and the availability of foreign investment merely facilitated the expansion and contraction.

State enterprises face many problems, including large inventories of finished product (200 billion yuan or $37 billion at the end of 1991, approximately 8 per cent of total industrial output in 1991); mounting bad debts (nearly 40 per cent of all state enterprises were in debt in 1991), and consistent losses accompanying output expansion (about one third of all enterprises are losing money), and these problems are the mirror images of the lack of financial accountability.

The most important factor that caused the investment boom and wage/bonus increase was the observation that managers of firms did not update their expectations. When autonomy was given to them, their response was to expand rapidly under the expectation that they would be able to sell everything they produced, and would not be accountable for bad decisions. Local governments' also joined the heated investment boom hoping expansion of productive capacity might broaden their revenue base because the second stage reform plan called for the replacement of centralized budget allocation by a decentralized procedure. Under the new rule, local governments budgets are determined by the profits of firms under their administration. It is also possible that the rush for enterprises and local governments to invest when they get more autonomy may be fuelled by uncertainty concerning the continuation of the reform. They might have thought that they had to hurry so as not to miss the opportunity. Financial reform provided the convenience of credits for the expansion-hungry firms and local governments. The result was rapid growth in investment spending and consequent intensified shortage and price inflation.

Problems surrounding the enforcement of rules naturally follow the previous discussion. To succeed in reducing shortage and increasing efficiency in the second stage of reform, rules must be consistently enforced without exceptions. Much has to be done to harden the financial constraint through enforcement of the rules. The contrast between state and non-state enterprises in their performance further proves this point.

5 Toward a post Keynesian theory of transition
The success of the Chinese reform in the non-state sector and the lack of behavioural change in the state sector call for an explanation. The most systematic study of the problems of socialist economies is presented by Kornai. His theory provides a starting point toward a post Keynesian theory of transition. According to Kornai it is the relative softness of the budget constraint which determines the extent of excess demand (or shortage) in a socialist economy. The softness or hard-

ness of the budget constraint refers to the external tolerance limits to losses independent of the objectives of the decision-maker in the firm. Kornai (1980, pp. 302-3) argues that five conditions must hold to have a perfectly hard budget constraint: (1) prices must be exogenous; (2) tax system must be hard; (3) there are no free state grants; (4) there is no credit; and (5) there is no external financial investment. A softening of the budget constraint arises, therefore, when the strict relationship between expenditure and earnings has been relaxed, as for example when there is the expectation that external finance is available, and can occur *inter alia* by soft subsidies (negotiable state grants), soft taxation (negotiable rules), soft credit (negotiable terms) and soft administrative prices (prices adjust to costs). Since an essential feature of a soft budget constraint is the negotiability of rules, contracts and grants, Kornai concludes that the soft budget constraint is a manifestation of the paternalistic role of the socialist state. Hence, a soft budget constraint is a characteristic feature of the socialist firm sanctioned by the socialist state, while a hard budget constraint is characteristic of the capitalist firms since rules, contracts and grants are non-negotiable and enforced by the state through the legal code.

The softness of the budget constraint has three consequences. First, demand and relative prices are independently determined; that is, as the softness of the budget constraint increases, the own-price elasticity of demand approaches zero. Second, the choice of input combinations will be insensitive to price change, so that resources tend to be allocated inefficiently. Third, the goals of decision-makers tend to be over-ambitious, generating excess or unconstrained demand for inputs. These consequences ultimately lead to unconstrained demand on the part of enterprises. Shortage of producer goods will appear. Since there is no absolute insulation between this sector and the consumer goods sector, resources will be siphoned away from the latter into the former and shortage will appear in both sectors. Widespread product deterioration as well as delays and inefficiencies in services will occur in such a shortage economy. To overcome these problems, Kornai argues, the budget constraint ought to be hardened by reducing state paternalism and increasing the effect of price signals in the market. The objective is to create incentives to improve quality, cut costs, introduce new products or new processes—in short, to get the firm to behave in an entrepreneurial manner.

The key to understanding Kornai's argument rests on the proposition that receipts must equal expenditures for the budget constraint to be hard. When the budget constraint is hard Say's (and Walras's) Law asserting supply creates its own demand is said to exist and when it is soft, Keynes' notion that demand creates its own supply is said to exist. Any degree of softness implies disequilibrium or a non-Walrasian equilibrium which is often described by the non-Walrasians as a Keynesian equilibrium. Extending this approach, Kornai (1990b) describes both socialist and capitalist economies as having a persistent long-run tendency to remain in a disequilibrium (or non-Walrasian equilibrium). Policy prescriptions are based on a notion of disequilibrium where there is a systematic tendency toward a Walrasian equilibrium. But, as Keynes points out, since the budget constraint is an ex ante concept and based on expectations, there is no necessary systematic tendency toward the ideal Walrasian equilibrium, given that the demand for investment (and other inputs) is determined independently of the supply of investment (and other inputs).

In fact, it might be said that a hard budget constraint in Kornai's sense is too hard for entrepreneurial activities. As pointed out by Chandler (1977), administered pricing practices, i.e. mark-up pricing, developed out of historical necessity to support mass production and research and development. Similarly, the inclusion of credit money or organized credit spreads risk throughout the economy and over time to improve efficiency. In general, receipts and expenditures are not equal because entrepreneurs and enterprises need to and can obtain capital and credit through the financial markets of a capitalist economy. The key difference, therefore, is not whether there is a hard budget constraint in Kornai's sense, but whether clear financial responsibility can be traced. A more general formulation of Kornai's budget constraint, based on Keynes' principle of effective demand and an institutional view of the enterprise, may be better suited to explain why shortages have been reduced in the Chinese economy. Within such a framework, goods are distinguished from money and the institutional structure is accounted for. Hence, both credit money and mark-up pricing are allowed, as well as the idea of non-negotiability in loans, taxes and subsidies. By distinguishing between goods and money, risk and uncertainty are accounted for, and the growth of the firm is no longer limited by the amount of profits available for investment. Being more general, the financial constraint better explains shortage in socialist economies and is more useful in analysing a transition strategy to a market-based economy.

A hard financial constraint requires the equality between total financial outlays and total financial resources available to an enterprise, including all forms of credit at pre-specified terms. Financial accountability refers to the fact that enterprises are responsible for all financial consequences of their actions, because of the binding nature of contracts and agreements. When there are soft grants, negotiable soft loans and flexible rules, a soft financial constraint exists, and the lack of financial accountability implies the maximization of output *at all costs*. Because of this there is an insatiable desire for growth and a tendency to regard the investment goods sector as more important than the consumer goods sector. Resources will be channelled into the investment goods sector, where expansion is limited only by the availability of material resources. Excess demand persists, lengthening the construction period of new plant and equipment and creating a sellers' market in the economy.

The Keynesian financial constraint also implies that the generation of excess effective demand and therefore shortage at the macroeconomic level is endogenous rather than being determined by behavioural assumptions. Since decisions to save and invest are determined independently of one another, shortage persists through overinvestment, which has a softening effect on the budget constraint but not necessarily on the financial constraint. This also implies that certain other endogenous factors, such as the pricing behaviour of firms, contributing to the softness of the budget constraint are independent of effective demand and therefore of shortage. Hence, the basic cause of overinvestment and excess effective demand is not the softness of the budget constraint *per se*, but the institutional (including legal) structure underlying the socialist economy which determines pricing behaviour, the role of financial institutions as well as financial accountability.

Since financial institutions are governed by laws, there is a limit on the ability of the state to change policies. Changes in laws and rules, including taxes, subsidies etc., will have an impact on the hardness of the financial constraint. Thus, negotiable state grants, negotiable rules or taxes and negotiable terms for credit can also affect the hardness of the financial constraint, depending on the effect these laws and rules have on the microeconomic behaviour of the firm or decision-maker. One objective of economic policy in a resource-constrained economy is to achieve a hard financial constraint. However, unlike the hard budget constraint, a hard financial constraint enables a firm to spend more than it earns by borrowing at terms specified in a legally binding contract. Uncertainty and risk are reflected in the terms of the contract. If a firm is unable to pay back a loan, either a new loan is granted or the existing loan must be restructured at strict terms, otherwise bankruptcy will follow. A certain amount of flexibility is therefore allowed in the credit constraint so long as both parties agree to the new terms. Hence, it is clearly possible to have a soft budget constraint *à la* Kornai enveloped by a hard financial constraint, since corporate debt can be rolled over indefinitely. Moreover, recognizing that money is a means of deferring decisions concerning the use of claims on resources amounts to an explicit rejection of Say's Law.

6   Implications of the Chinese reform experience for a transition strategy

There are two broadly defined strategies for the transition from a centrally planned economy to a market-oriented one and advocates of both 'shock therapy' and 'gradualism' consider the elimination of shortage one of the primary objectives of a transition strategy. Indeed, one virtue the 'shock therapy' strategy can claim is the speed with which shortages are eliminated. Both Poland and eastern Germany converted from a resource-constrained economy to a demand-constrained economy almost overnight. An undesired side effect of the transition, however, was a rapid contraction of these economies as output, employment and labour productivity plummeted.

A reason why Lipton and Sachs (1990) argued for such a rapid conversion to a demand-constrained private economy is the elimination of both legal and illegal 'second economies'. According to Lipton and Sachs (1990, p. 90), second economies are created in a shortage economy by 'arbitrageurs who buy output at the official price and sell it at a 'grey' (legal) or 'black' (illegal) market price'. Moreover, they believe that the queue of buyers in a shortage economy is made up of these arbitrageurs. Evidence from China indicates, however, that second economies are made up primarily of entrepreneurs, namely, individuals or villages and township collectives creating new enterprises *producing* goods that individuals queue for. Even if there are no queues or price-distorting subsidies, these entrepreneurs often enter a market because they have lower costs or better products. Although there are arbitrage activities, especially among new private urban enterprises, the majority engage in production.

The key to understanding the nature of the second economy, irrespective of whether enterprises are legal or not, is to distinguish between two types of second economies. On the one hand, a second economy can be created to engage primarily in arbitraging activities, through which certain demands can be satisfied by reallocating existing resources. On the other hand, it can also be created to engage in production that takes up the slack in a shortage economy. In other words, it becomes a question of whether price or quantity is the primary adjustment mechanism in a shortage economy. For Lipton and Sachs (1990, p. 92) 'excess demand is dissipated by waiting in lines, and overall utility is reduced accordingly'. This amounts to saying that people are able and willing to purchase goods in the second economy at higher prices because it reduces the time spent in queues, *provided* this time has a monetary value.

The nature of the quantity adjustment mechanism was well understood by Adam Smith (1776, pp. 74-75):

> The quantity of every commodity brought to market naturally suits itself to the effectual demand. . . .[if] the quantity brought to market should at any time fall short of the effectual demand, some of the component parts of its price must rise above their natural rate. . . .If it is wages or profit, the interest of all other labourers and dealers will soon prompt them to employ more labour and stock in preparing and bring it to market. The quantity brought thither will soon be sufficient to supply the effectual demand.

While Smith was not concerned with the problem of arbitrage, he did see that when the market price is above the natural price (a market clearing price reflecting a uniform rate of profit across all industries), there is an incentive to expand production and/or enter the industry— given the level of effectual demand at the market clearing price. Instead of increasing supply, the 'shock therapy' programme essentially reduced demand before allowing the quantities brought to market to increase. What is missing in this story is an investment function which ties together Keynes' principle of effective demand with Smith's notion of effectual demand.

Accepting Smith's adjustment mechanism, then clear property rights which guarantee free entry and exit would be sufficient to increase the 'quantity brought to market', assuming the private sector adopts a superior technology or unutilized resources exist. The Chinese case illustrates that a legal 'second economy' does reduce shortages by providing a vent for excess demand in the private consumer good sector. Indeed, as table 11.5 shows, the gap between market prices and state prices has narrowed. Via this route, China did not completely eliminate shortages, but then again, it did not experience a contraction of effective demand and output.

Table 11.5: Ratio of free market prices to state prices.

1962	1965	1970	1975	1980	1985	1988	1989
270	140	142	184	148	128	117	112

Source: Statistical Yearbook of China, 1989 and 1990.

Smith's adjustment mechanism works in a shortage economy even when there are subsidies. So long as the market price is above the natural or market clearing price, state subsidies do not present important barriers to entry. However, because the market price does not converge to the subsidized price, shortages will not be eliminated, unless subsidies are extended to the private sector as well. In other words, if subsidies are viewed as important, as they have been for certain key basic goods, consumer necessities and services, then they should be applied across the board to all enterprises, whether state or private.[4] This will then encourage the private sector to expand and therefore eliminate shortages.

Unlike the 'shock therapy' proponents, Kornai's non-Walrasian approach to the transformation process is based on a Keynesian quantity adjustment mechanism. To increase supply, and hence reduce shortages, Kornai focuses on international trade in the short run and on the *creation* of a private sector in the long run. Recognizing both the importance of the spontaneity of the private sector as well as the difficulties inherent in privatizing state enterprises, Kornai (1990a) acknowledges that a dual economy will continue to exist 'for the next two decades'. Nevertheless, total liberalization of prices in the state sector should be attempted as soon as shortages are reduced to a level which will not lead to rapid inflation. Because the profit motive is not important for state enterprises according to Kornai, he proposes that investment spending in these enterprises be limited from above so that resources from the newly emerging private sector are not siphoned off.

In the dual economy of post-reform China, the siphoning-off effect of state enterprises on the private consumer goods sector is minimal because it is now essentially a buyers' market. In terms of financial resources, however, there is a tendency for an austerity programme to have a greater effect on private industry, because private enterprises often have fewer opportunities to obtain credit through the state banking system or informal markets. Nevertheless, the *creation* of a private consumer good sector can act as a vent for shortage in these markets without the adverse effects of 'shock therapy' or the severe siphoning-effect observed by Kornai. Eventually this will encroach on inefficient state enterprises as Chinese entrepreneurs learn how to produce and market goods.

The central point is that China is going through a gradual transition in which a rather large private sector has emerged. What is most important is that this sector was *created* by Chinese entrepreneurs, most of whom were peasants just ten years ago, and not simply transformed from existing state enterprises.[5] Indeed, as the official rhetoric points out, the objective of the Chinese government is not to privatize existing state enterprises, but to *create* a socialist commodity market economy with a variety of ownership forms. In reality there are state enterprises which have responsibilities to local governments and the central planning office, and a private sector made up of individual, village, township and urban private enterprises. What appears to be most important is that the Chinese economy is a 'mixed economy' in which sellers' markets and buyers' markets coexist.

7 From sellers' market to buyers' market

The introduction of a second market economy in China made up of non-state rural, village, township and urban enterprises eliminated shortages in most consumer good sectors. Persistent shortages are limited to certain producer good sectors which tend to be dominated by state enterprises that are large in size and inefficient in operation.

To eliminate shortage, property rights which allow for the entry and exit of private and collective enterprises must be established. Because sellers' markets prevailed in the past, opportunities existed for a private and collective sector to enter markets and sell products at prices usually above the administratively determined one. Eventually prices fell in the private sector and the government reduced subsidies in many sectors, creating a tendency for prices in the 'dual economy' to converge toward a single price. As the private and cooperative sector expanded, buyers' markets were created for an increasing number of products.

The creation and expansion of the private and cooperative sector led to the transition from a sellers' market to a buyers' market in most consumer goods sectors. Because some industries remained a sellers' market, the Chinese economy became a 'mixed' economy in the sense that some industries were demand-constrained and others were resource-constrained. In terms of ownership, the Chinese economy has become mixed as well (see tables 11.2 and 11.3). Moreover, because ownership of the rural village, township and urban private and cooperative enterprises was known, financial responsibility could be assigned, implying that these enterprises have hard financial constraints in the

Keynesian sense. However, because state enterprises continue to negotiate credit, subsidies and taxes, they appear to have soft budget
constraints.

It should be emphasized, however, that the objective of creating a
second economy is the creation of a buyers' market, not the hardening
of the budget constraint. Because markets are institutions, it is the
macroeconomic environment within which enterprises operate that explains the persistence of disequilibrium and shortage. In buyers' markets, enterprises tend to operate with reserve capacity for flexibility in
adapting to changes in market conditions and effective demand. In sellers' markets, enterprises tend to produce at full capacity and increase
productive capacity as fast as possible since all output can be sold, and
there is an insatiable desire for growth at all levels of the economy. This
then tends to encourage planners to set overly ambitious targets. To
achieve a high rate of growth, a large portion of national income has to
be invested. In such an environment, effective demand will continuously outstrip capacity, and enterprises, fearing shortages, will stockpile
raw materials, inputs, equipment and other supplies. These near-universal shortages strengthen the inducement to invest, further intensifying
the pressure of demand on capacity. Moreover, because there is little
competition in a sellers' market, there is little incentive to innovate. In a
sellers' market, there is very little motivation for quality control and
cost reduction. If it is combined with a centrally planned fixed price
system, a sellers' market leads to slow productivity growth, widespread
cost over-runs and quality deterioration.

The creation of collective and private enterprises has introduced
competition into the Chinese economy and generated enough supply
to convert most consumer goods markets into buyers' markets. These
non-state firms obviously face a hard financial constraint, at times
maybe too hard. But their contribution toward the elimination of shortage is that they supply goods, rather than having a hard financial constraint. This assessment is also supported by the observation that shortages at the macro-level are being gradually eradicated in China, a country where the dominant economic force is still the state sector, which
continues to have a soft financial constraint. But this too may change
as the state sector becomes subject to a buyers' market and is forced to
act in an entrepreneurial manner.

Alternatively, excess demand can be reduced by imposing an austerity programme at the same time that all prices are liberalized. The sudden fall in real income will render most goods unaffordable to most of

the population, which creates a perverse buyers' market where supply exceeds the relatively low level of effective demand. Higher prices and privatization do not necessarily lead to increased supply when existing capacity is already up against a resource constraint. More likely, the confusion caused by such draconian measures will delay the supply response further. It is probable that the rapid decline of the Eastern European and Soviet economies is not a strictly temporary phenomenon, and it is imperative that the social and economic cost of such a 'shock therapy' should be questioned.

The entry of collective and private enterprises which adhere to a hard financial constraint is helping China eliminate shortages by increasing the total supply of goods and services. 'Shock therapy', on the other hand, tries to eliminate shortages through choking off demand while hoping the supply side will eventually respond. Available evidence suggests that the Chinese approach may be an alternative 'therapy' without the 'shock'.

8 Conclusion

Over a decade of economic reform in China has brought profound changes in the economy. High rates of growth have been maintained while inflation has been under control for most of the time. Economic growth has improved the general standard of living in the worlds most populous country. Reforms have transformed a centrally planned shortage economy into one of mixed ownership and increased reliance on the market mechanism. There are valuable lessons to be learned from the Chinese reform experience.

The most important lesson is that there is more than one path between a centrally planned economy and a more market-oriented one. Despite its shortcomings, the gradualist approach taken by China avoids the high economic and social costs of 'shock therapy'. Moreover, the disappointing economic performance of Eastern European countries and the former Soviet Union may not be a short-term phenomenon. In the long run, it is still debatable whether the benefits of the 'shock therapy' are greater than that of a more gradual approach.

Another lesson is that the elimination of shortage is crucial in a transition strategy. While price adjustment is effective in reducing demand in the short run, output adjustment is the solution that is most desirable in the long run.

Finally, while the creation of a dual economy in China avoided the high economic and social costs of a 'shock therapy', it also created new problems for sustainable future growth. Economic reforms have succeeded in eliminating shortages through the creation of a dynamic non-state sector, but the state sector is becoming a burden on the economy. As discussed in section 4, output growth of state enterprises is accompanied by stagnating productivity and large losses. Growing inventories of unsold finished goods and mounting bad debt among state enterprises threaten future growth if not resolved.

The dichotomy of the Chinese economy demonstrates that a demand-constrained economy does not automatically lead to competitive behaviour, which will only be induced by the presence of the 'correct' economic and social institutions. As long as enterprises are not financially accountable for their actions, they will stay in business even if they are producing unwanted or uncompetitive goods. This is often the case among Chinese state enterprises (as it was in the previously centrally planned East European economies).

Is privatization the only way to establish financial accountability? Theoretically, financial accountability can be established when clear property rights are defined. Even an owner as vague as 'the state' does not have to be paternalistic in Kornai's sense; it can instead be entrepreneurial in Schumpeter's sense. The reform movement in China may provide a realistic example of an alternative to privatization, the selling off of existing state properties. If the current momentum in the expansion of the collective and private sector continues, then over time two possibilities occur: (1) the inefficient state enterprises *will* go bankrupt if bankruptcy laws are enforced; and (2) competitive pressures from the non-state sector will lead to institutional changes that induce behavioural change in the state sector. Of course there is also the possibility that the growth of the non-state sector is sacrificed in order to maintain the state sector, causing the Chinese economy to stagnate. Only time will tell which scenario will materialize.

Notes

* The views expressed in this chapter are the authors' and do not necessarily reflect those of the United Nations Secretariat in New York.
1. *Economic Daily*, February 14, 1991.
2. *US News and World Report*, May 27, 1991.
3. The *Financial Times* reported on January 7, 1992 that the share of industrial output provided by the state sector in 1991 was 45.6 per cent.
4. There remains, however, a budgetary problem which forces the government to *select* those industries they wish to subsidize.
5. It should be noted that there is a similarity between the development of rural industry in China and proto-industrialization in Europe just before the appearance of capitalism.

References

Bauer, T. (1978). 'Investment Cycles in Planned Economies', *Acta Oeconomica*, 243-260.

Byrd, W. A. (1987). 'The Impact of the Two-Tier Plan/Market System in Chinese Industry', *Journal of Comparative Economics*, 11, 295-308.

Byrd, W. A. (1991). *The Market Mechanism and Economic Reforms in China*, Armonk: M. E. Sharpe.

Byrd, W. A. and Qingsong, L., eds. (1990). *China's Rural Industry*, New York: Oxford University Press.

Chandler, A. (1977). *The Visible Hand: The Managerial Revolution in American Business*, Cambridge: Harvard University Press.

Granick, D. (1990). *Chinese State Enterprises*, Chicago: Chicago University Press.

Kornai, J. (1980). *The Economics of Shortage*, Amsterdam: North Holland.

Kornai, J. (1990a). *The Road to a Free Economy*, New York: Norton.

Kornai, J. (1990b). *Vision and Reality, Market and State: Contradictions and Dilemmas Revisited*, Budapest: Corvina.

Lipton, D. and Sachs, J. (1990). 'Creating a Market Economy in Eastern Europe: The Case of Poland', *Brookings Papers on Economic Activity*.

Riskin, C. (1987). *China's Political Economy: The Quest for Development since 1949*, New York: Oxford University Press.

Robinson, J. (1964). *Notes from China*, London, Basil Blackwell.

Smith, A. (1776). *An Inquiry into the Nature and Causes of the Wealth of Nations*, Oxford: Oxford University Press [1976].

State Statistical Bureau of China, *Statistical Yearbook of China*, various years.

United Nations (1991). *The World Economic Survey 1991*, New York.

Wong, C. (1986). 'The Economics of Shortage and the Problem of Reform in Chinese Industry', *Journal of Comparative Economics*, 363-387.

Wood, A. (1990). 'Nominal Pause, but a Degree of Real Progress', *Financial Times*, October 4.

Zhao, Z. (1987). 'Advance Along the Road to Socialism with Chinese Characteristics', Report delivered at the 13 National Congress of the Communist Party, Oct. 25, *Beijing Review*, Nov. 9-15.

12 Conclusion: Implications for Socialist Economies in Transition

Mark Knell and Christine Rider

1 Introduction

It was argued in the first chapter that the collapse of the centrally planned socialist economies can be traced to the institutions which support these economies. Indeed, as Kalecki (1970) argued: ' The institutional framework of a social system is a basic element of its economic dynamics and thus of the theory of growth relevant to that system'. Yet when blueprints for reform are suggested, the self-regulating aspect of the market mechanism is emphasized and the necessary institutional arrangements are down-played.

What is clear from the variety of blueprints suggested and the papers contained in this book is that there is no single blueprint for success. It would be easy if there were, and sometimes reading the economics literature, it seems as though there is. But reality indicates otherwise. Several different issues are linked together in the discussions about the transition process, and it may be helpful to separate them and place them in the context of this book; this is done in the next section. This makes it easier to identify their characteristics—and then it can be seen that the 'solution' to one may have an adverse impact on another. This is an important insight because the 'restructuring' of the socialist economies in transition is not always made up of a set of complementary elements.

Two important observations are made in this chapter. First, most of the blueprints regard marketization and privatization as the answer to all economic problems. We prefer to view markets and private property as complementary (but not identical) institutions that together engender certain kinds of motivations and behaviours, some of which *may* lead to a higher standard of living. Second, there is strong preference for 'shock therapy' over a 'gradualist' path. 'Shock therapy' has been applied in Poland (1990), eastern Germany (1990), Czechoslovakia (1991) and the former Soviet Union (1992), while the latter route was followed by Hungary and China. We believe that controlling speed and sequencing is crucial to the transformation process, and that rapid marketization and privatization may not lead to a higher standard of living, or if it does, only at very high social and economic costs.

From this, it should be seen that an over-riding concern of this book is critical of the narrow focus of most blueprints for the transition process. These blueprints often neglect different approaches to economic theory and policy, and they also neglect the existence of other economic activities and institutions necessary for economic life. As has been made amply clear in the papers contained in this book, an approach which explicitly takes into account structural, behavioural and institutional arrangements is necessary to develop a strategy combining the best, rather than the failings, of all economic systems.

2 The objective of marketization and privatization

Attempts at marketization and privatization took place in Eastern Europe before the final collapse in the late 1980s. One such attempt was made by Poland in 1956 which was aborted because of political pressures. In this case there was a real attempt at 'crucial reform'.

Current attempts at restructuring the centrally planned economies go beyond 'crucial reform' and are based on an almost blind faith in the self-regulating market mechanism. Because of this, blueprints for marketization and privatization often overlook six important points. First, that economic relationships between people are more than just exchange relationships (as between buyer and seller), they are also production relationships. They also involve power (e.g. employer-employee), socialization (e.g. work-place relationships), competition (e.g. between firms), and learning (e.g. new technologies and apprenticeships). Hence, even if the exchange relationships are 'rationalized', the final outcome may not be the best economically if no account is taken of improving the other aspects.

Second, firms are not market institutions: firms produce things, while markets (buyers and sellers) exchange things. Hence a 'firm' is meaningless unless exchange takes place, because there is no point in just producing, but firms necessarily precede markets: only things that have been produced can be exchanged. In fact, markets and firms should not be seen as substitutes, for they are complements, and the prerequisite for a successful transition process is the ability to identify the roles that each 'actor' plays. In addition, the very existence of firms introduces relationships that are not based on voluntary market transactions between equally empowered individuals. Coercion is involved— the development of management hierarchies and the 'science' of management is a response to the need to prettify what is essentially coercive: solving the principal-agent problem. This issue is important because of the property rights questions raised by the privatization of state property, and because of the ever-present concern with incentives.

Third, the price mechanism is not simply a device that answers the basic allocation question of economics, it also has other functions, and the more successful it is in fulfilling these functions, the less successful it is in efficiently allocating resources. These other functions associated with prices are intimately connected with the ability of firms to successfully compete in the marketplace. For example, prices have a financial role: a price can be set to generate earnings over and above current costs so as to finance expansion plans. They have a strategic role: a well-positioned firm could deliberately underprice so as to gain a foothold in a new market or to bankrupt a weaker competitor. They have a conductive role, enabling costs to be passed on to buyers, and again, a more powerful, well-established firm has an advantage here. These roles exist because there is no Walrasian auctioneer in most economic activities, and firms, especially in manufacturing and services, have influence over the prices they sell at. None of these are likely to coincide with what might be called an 'efficiency' price, where long-run costs are minimized. It is even possible to question such a position as a sensible approach to managing the firm, because it implies the absence of any slack with which to react to unforeseen events. For example, an electrical utility could never operate at such a level because this implies that it would never have the personnel available to meet emergencies such as downed power lines. For a real life firm, operating effectively is not necessarily the same as operating at the point of lowest long-run average costs.

Four, competition primarily takes place on the basis of technology. To reduce uncertainty, manufacturing and service firms prefer stable prices and allow inventories and capacity utilization to vary. They compete through process and product innovations. To increase the profit rate, firms introduce new technologies and new ways to organize production. To increase profits, new products are introduced to attract customers away from other firms. Hence, to be competitive, firms must learn to innovate.

Five, privatization does not necessarily lead to higher efficiency. Lessons from Great Britain indicate that privatized firms often do not respond to the market and that state-owned firms often respond to the market if the state acts in an entrepreneurial way. Indeed, it was found that successful privatizations necessitated the state to act in such a way (Yarrow 1986). In other words, the issue is not whether there is a necessary connection between privatization and increased efficiency, rather the connection is made in the context of particular behaviours and motivations.

Finally, the sixth point concerns money as opposed to financial institutions. Economists remain divided over the question of endogeneity, especially regarding causality and control. If these are contentious issues in a developed market economy, how much more contentious will they be in Eastern Europe and the former Soviet Union? Mistakes with policy-making are quite likely because expertise with macroeconomic policy is extremely limited, and a policy vacuum, or misguided policy, could have disastrous results that would be difficult to remedy or rectify.

Although the image of a well-functioning market economy running itself is appealing, it is a false image. Perhaps the appeal exists because any one influence or 'agency' is only a small part of the total influence, unlike the case in a centrally planned economy where it is easy to identify the location of decision-making and power because it is concentrated. But obviously, smooth operations are not accidental. They are the result of both the correct structure and the correct behaviour patterns for the particular functions being performed. It is even possible to question the perfectly competitive market model as desirable. Moving even part way towards competitiveness in the economic sense would be costly to maintain, involve the loss of economies of scale, and like liberty, would require constant vigilance. There need to be more institutions and mechanisms guarding against the abuse of power. Probably most telling is that 'perfectly' competitive markets are not viable, and viability is more important than efficiency.

What also seems to have been ignored in the entire marketization and privatization process is that there are different types of markets which operate in different ways. This then implies that different devices will be required to assist the effective operation of each. For example, product markets in core mass production manufacturing industries are predominantly oligopolistic, using administrative pricing. At issue here is how to maintain the advantages of economies of scale and innovativeness associated with some of these industries, while guarding against abuses. Other peripheral manufacturing industries and most service industries are more competitive and require a supportive environment (including adequate infrastructure provisions and support services) for the maintenance of competitive conditions.

In labour markets, negotiations between participants are more important than in product markets. There are also other factors to consider here, predominantly the fact that the 'price' of labour can never fall below some socially acceptable level. Because of the importance of the functioning of labour markets in non-economic areas, it is necessary to adopt an effective strategy. This in particular is an area where principles of economic democracy become important: to improve productivity, provide incentives and encourage the sense of responsibility necessary for effective (and productive) work.

Financial markets appear to be competitive but actually are very volatile. What is important here is to retain their necessary aspects—providing liquidity and financing—without the harmful aspects—speculation and instability. Particularly vital is the need to prevent the ability to amass paper wealth from unbalancing the social approval necessary for restructuring. A valuable legacy of the Eastern European economies is their greater egalitarianism, and the resentment towards a few who have already made fortunes as a result of the imperfections existing at the beginning of the transition could threaten the continuing consensus.

Any economic system functions well when people know what to do and how to behave. If the intention is to turn from a centrally planned economy to a market-oriented one, it will be difficult to get a well-functioning system in those places where there is little or no history as a market economy. Behaviour patterns take a long time to learn, and if the 'role models' are lacking, the learning process has to take longer. Although some in Eastern Europe maintain that they do have a historical experience as market economies, the environment today is so different that their past experience will provide few useful clues for suitable behaviour.

The sense of accountability that economic actors in all their roles must have is more important than privatization. There are some ways of encouraging this, which can be combined with other mechanisms intended to promote economic stability and other desirable aims of a socialist society. For example, planning can provide a basis for an industrial policy which focuses on certain key economic variables, and workers' councils can provide the basis for true economic democracy while also having an effect on incentives similar to that of employee stock ownership. These institutions are complementary to the market mechanism—but are contradictory to so-called 'free markets'. However, the extension of democratic institutions is important: for so long as democracy is only identified with political voting rights and elections, it will be impossible to develop truly free societies. After all, democracy is a process, not a thing which can be simply introduced and then left alone; it must be continually nurtured and reinforced.

3 The speed and sequencing of marketization and privatization

The speed and sequencing of marketization and privatization of the socialist economies in transition are crucial for the success of the transformation process. There are two broadly defined approaches to the transition to a market-oriented economy: 'shock therapy' and 'gradualist'. 'Shock therapy' basically asserts that (almost) instant price liberalization and rapid privatization will unleash the innate qualities of entrepreneurship and industriousness without necessarily having to rebuild the entire institutional structure. The 'gradualist' approach asserts that a new institutional structure is required to ensure proper motivations and behaviours. How do we know what the proper sequence is or how long or short the right time is?

Evidence from Eastern Europe and the former Soviet Union suggests that these countries are entering a depression that will be at least as deep as the Great Depression of the 1930s. Austerity programmes associated with 'shock therapy' are the main reasons for the rapid declines in output and activity in Poland and eastern Germany. An almost simplistic reliance on the market mechanism has also sent Czechoslovakia into economic decline, and the collapse of the central planning mechanism in the former Soviet Union has created chaos in that economy. At the same time, evidence from China suggests that gradual price liberalization and the creation of a private sector leads to rapid economic growth and higher living standards.

Rapid marketization and privatization combined with an austerity programme is the main cause of economic decline in Eastern Europe and the former Soviet Union for two reasons: (1) uncertainty caused by an unstable macroeconomic environment discourages entrepreneurial activities; and (2) even if entrepreneurial activities are encouraged, behaviour does not respond quickly to the new institutional environment. The irony of the shock therapy approach is that an austerity programme is needed because of instabilities caused by a rapid transition process. In an attempt to stabilize the macroeconomic environment, investment falls because prospective entrepreneurs are either unsure what to do or are afraid to enter a market because of large uncertainties. This problem is compounded by a rapid decline in effective demand caused by the austerity programme. And without adequate effective demand, the economy cannot be restructured.

Rapid price liberalization causes other problems too. An important consideration for the socialist economies in transition is that the transition process is one moving between autarky and the open economy. When they were a separate trading bloc independent of the world economy, relative prices in the East differed greatly from those in the West. Hence, while liberalizing prices reduces barriers to entry, it also subjects the domestic industries to competitive world prices. Because many industries in Eastern Europe and the former Soviet Union have negative value added at world prices, the potential for massive bankruptcy exists. As the threat of bankruptcy becomes real, there will be calls for protectionism and nationalism. The best way to get around this problem is to introduce industrial and strategic trade policies which focus on restructuring and strengthening potentially viable enterprises before privatization is attempted.

Industrial policies become all the more important when the industrial structure is taken into account. Eastern Europe and the former Soviet Union created a highly centralized monopolistic industrial structure in the years prior to the collapse. Because of this, certain barriers to entry will remain in many manufacturing industries as prices are liberalized. Foreign competition will ease the problem, but will also increase the threat of bankruptcy. However, this threat may strengthen the monopoly power of these firms if protectionism and nationalism grows.

Economic growth of Eastern Europe and the former Soviet Union will also be constrained because of bottlenecks in the infrastructure. Because of a lack of attention to services, especially transportation, communications and distribution, development of the private sector will be limited. One positive sign which appears in eastern Germany is the massive rebuilding of the infrastructure which has both an income effect and a debottlenecking effect. But this requires a large infusion of public funds similar in scope to the Marshall Plan fund which were used to rebuild Western Europe after the Second World War.

The rapid decline of these economies also adds another problem: Most individuals in these economies are currently at a low standard of living, yet are being told that their sacrifices now will be necessary to achieve higher standards later. This sounds suspiciously like the same promise made earlier in the century at the start of the planning stage of their development efforts. The task facing the reformers is difficult:

how to get some positive short-run results without damaging the long run prospects. Granted that any transition process as massive as this one will generate structural and technological unemployment; however, evidence suggests that most of the unemployment is created because of policies which neglect the principle of effective demand. Even in eastern Germany, where wages were pushed up to an unreasonably high level, effective demand problems exist. Adolph Lowe (1955) once remarked that the principle of effective demand is overemphasized when dealing with the problem of unemployment. Unfortunately, in the socialist economies in transition, both Keynesian and industrial policies are being neglected in favour of relying on the self-regulating aspects of the market mechanism.

References

Kalecki, M. (1970). 'Theories of Growth in Different Social Systems', *Scienta*, June.

Lowe, A. (1955). 'Technological Unemployment Reexamined', in G. Eisermann, ed., *Wirtschaft Und Kultursystem*, Stuttgart: Eugen Rentsch Verlag.

Yarrow, G. (1986). 'Privatization in Theory and Practice', *Economic Policy*, 2.

Index

Bottlenecks, economic, 48-50 *See* also
    shortage
Budget constraints
    hard, 224-227
    soft, 165, 225
Bukharin, N., 4
Buyers' market, 57, 100, 103, 216, 221,
    223, 230, 231, 232

Capacity, reserve, 92
China
    economic reform, 215-223
    excess demand, 222-224
    industrial output, 220
    price liberalization, 217
    role of second economy, 228-229, 231-
    232
Corporations
    managerial, 144-146
    social, 146-148
    social, comparison, 149-152

Economic decentralization, 13-19, 27, 29,
    170-172, 227-230
Economic systems
    mode of operation, 85-88
Economic transition, 52-58, 227-231
    evaluation, 235-239
Embargo, League of Nations, 6

Foreign trade, socialist countries, 135

General equilibrium theory, criticism of, 32-
    39
Germany
    effects of monetary union, 196-200
    unemployment, 198
    unification, 191-192, 206-207
Germany, East 192-194, 196-200, 207-209
    economic policy, 210-213
    obsolesence of capital stock, 201-202
    price liberalization, 198-199
    prospects for recovery, 207-210
Gomulka, W., 68
Gosplan, 3

Harrod-Domar (Kalecki), 8-12, 84-85
Hungary
    monetary policy, 161-164

Industrial innovation (increasing returns),
    11, 18, 34-36, 209
Inflation, 102-105
Informal sector, 104-107
International Monetary Fund, 54, 61, 117,
    122-123, 137, 196

Kaldor, N., 11-12, 34-36, 87
Kalecki, M., 9-11, 69-71, 79-81, 236
Keynes, J. M., 58
Keynesian economics, 43, 49, 61, 113, 154-
    159, 164, 167, 230, 232, 224-227
    effective demand, 10, 12, 46, 49, 84,
    103, 122, 126-127, 131, 200, 226-229,
    232-233
    excess demand 1, 9-12, 19, 43, 49-50,
    54, 84, 88, 94-99, 97, 106-110, 126,
    132, 227-232
    monetary theory, 155-158
Kornai, J., 11, 43, 87-88, 223-228, 230, 234

Lange, O., 8-9, 70-71, 78-79, 83
Lowe, A., 44-48, 50, 52, 57, 62, 243

Market economy
    characteristics of, 84
    efficiency, 143-144
Marx, K., 2
Money
    endogenous, theory of, 155-157, 164-
    167, 225-227
    Keynesian theory of, 155-158
    Monetarist theory of, 156
    transmission mechanism, 155-156

Nationalization, 5-6, 12-13
New Economic Policy, 3-4
Nuti, M., 78

Pareto optimum, 28, 42
    criticism of, 32-38, 43-44
Planning
    adoption in Eastern Europe, 12-13, 26
    organization of, 173-174
    Soviet centralized, 2-8, 26
    theory of, 24-26
Poland
    agriculture, 176
    automobile industry, 177-179
    bankruptcy strategies, 182-183
    Economic Council 68, 71-77
    economic reform, 65-80, 116-136
    excess demand 126, 170-171, 174-175,
    188
    housing, 180-182
    income inequality, 172
    industrial policy, 134-136
    inflation, 121-122, 126
    monopolization, 172-175
    price liberalization, 120
    real wages, 131-133
    stabilization, 119-122, 171-172, 123-
    126

textile industry, 179-180
workers' councils, 67-70
Preobrazhensky, E. A., 4
Prices
liberalization of, 120, 198-199, 217
role of, 88-89
Privatization, 141-142, 151-152, 184-188, 207
Profit, 31
incentives, 38

Reform, market-oriented, 29-30

Sellers' market, 1, 9, 11, 14, 48, 57, 100, 103, 216, 227, 231-232
Shock therapy, 52-58, 120-126, 132, 171-173, 192, 218, 228-234, 237, 242

Shortage, 4, 26-28, 43, 45, 48-49, 54-55, 57, 84, 87, 88-89, 91-95, 98-112, 119, 121, 124, 171, 178, 181-182, 216-217, 220-234 *See also* bottlenecks
Smith, A. 94, 211, 229
Socialism, characteristics of, 85
Solidarity government, 57
Soviet industrialization debate, 4
Sraffa, P., 24, 49
Sraffian theory of production, 89-91, 100-102, 204-206
Stalin, J., 4
Structure analysis, 45-47

War communism, 3

Yugoslavia, monetary policy, 158-159